Markets, rules and institutions of exchange

MANCHESTER
1824

Manchester University Press

New Dynamics of Innovation and Competition

This series, published in association with the ESRC Centre for Research in Innovation and Competition at the University of Manchester, emanates from an engagement of the Centre's research agenda with a wide range of internationally renowned scholars in the field. The series casts new light on the significance of demand and consumption, markets and competition, and the complex inter-organisational basis for innovation processes. The volumes are multidisciplinary and comparative in perspective.

Series editor:
Mark Harvey, Senior Research Fellow at CRIC 1997–2007

Markets, rules and institutions of exchange

edited by
Mark Harvey

Manchester University Press
Manchester and New York

distributed in the United States exclusively by Palgrave Macmillan

Published by Manchester University Press
Oxford Road, Manchester M13 9NR, UK
and Room 400, 175 Fifth Avenue, New York, NY 10010, USA
www.manchesteruniversitypress.co.uk

Distributed in the United States exclusively by
Palgrave Macmillan, 175 Fifth Avenue, New York,
NY 10010, USA

Distributed in Canada exclusively by
UBC Press, University of British Columbia, 2029 West Mall,
Vancouver, BC, Canada V6T 1Z2

British Library Cataloguing-in-Publication Data
A catalogue record for this book is available from the British Library

Library of Congress Cataloging-in-Publication Data applied for

ISBN 978 0 7190 7670 1 hardback

First published 2010

Typeset
by Toppan Best-set Premedia Limited
Printed in Great Britain
by TJ International Ltd, Padstow

Series foreword

The CRIC–MUP series New Dynamics of Innovation and Competition is designed to make an important contribution to this continually expanding field of research and scholarship. As a series of edited volumes, it combines approaches and perspectives developed by CRIC's own research agenda with those of a wide range of internationally renowned scholars. A distinctive emphasis on processes of economic and social transformation frames the CRIC research programme. Research on the significance of demand and consumption, on the empirical and theoretical understanding of competition and markets, and on the complex inter-organisational basis of innovation processes, provides the thematic linkage between the successive volumes of the series. At the interface between the different disciplines of economics, sociology, management studies and geography, the development of economic sociology lends a unifying methodological approach. A strong comparative and historical dimension to the variety of innovation processes in different capitalist economies and societies is supported by the international character of the contributions.

The series is based on international workshops hosted by CRIC which have encouraged debate and diversity at the leading edge of innovation studies.

CRIC was an ESRC-funded research centre based at the University of Manchester.

Contents

List of tables, figures and boxes

Tables

Figures

Boxes

1

Introduction: putting markets in their place

Mark Harvey

Markets are going through turbulent times. Even prior to the credit crunch and the global crises in financial markets of 2008–09, commodity markets for food and fuel had witnessed huge price spikes, unparalleled since the 1970s. Speculative housing bubbles were widespread. Alan Greenspan's admission that light-touch regulation had failed, and that belief in markets as self-correcting mechanisms was mistaken, was one striking instance of the re-emergence of the understanding that the state and regulation are critical for market operations (*Financial Times*, 24 October 2008).[1] Further than that, Paul Krugman, recently awarded the Nobel Prize for Economics, heralded the 'return of depression economics' (Krugman, 2008) and the need for political lessons to be learnt for the macro-management of financial markets. A swath of banking collapses and massive bank recapitalisations (or nationalisations) signalled the fact that only state political action was capable of restoring and re-instituting markets on a more solid footing. States, and states acting in consort, have had to come to the rescue of financial markets so key to capitalism. The moments of grave crisis made manifest how states underwrite and underpin markets at all times, whether turbulent and or in relative equilibrium. Gone are state-free, non- or a-political economies of markets.

Several aspects of governments' management of the rescue from depression resonate with an already occurring shift in relations between state and market, evidenced by the politically led creation of a new 'green' technology platform to replace the petrochemical one, dominant from the post-war Golden Years. Global climate change and its economic consequences present a major challenge to sustained economic growth to which markets – left to their own devices, and extreme price volatility – were not adequately responding (Stern, 2007). Indeed, if the oil price of nearly $150 per barrel had not been overtaken by the credit crunch, its depressive effects could have only been much greater and more sustained than the oil shocks of the 1970s. In Europe and the USA, in China, India and Brazil, targets for renewable fuels, some mandatory, have effectively given state guarantees to firms to create new markets for renewable fuels, and other renewable energy platforms. The shift back to nuclear power for electricity-generation markets has been led politically, creating a range of intermediate markets and supporting a range of provisioning firms, within a complex regulatory environment and state subsidy. Since 2005, an entirely new range of markets emerged: the trading in carbon offsets, based on notional credits from carbon reduction schemes purchased by companies whose emissions exceed a carbon 'cap' or agreed target. Along with the new markets, a new type of firm emerged, intermediating between the carbon creditors and debtors, such as the Carbon Neutral Company and Climate Care (*Financial Times*, 26 April 2007, p. 8). This new array of markets and firms provide a paradigm case of 'politically instituted' economic organisation. As such, they pose some unsettling questions to many assumptions about capitalism as a 'market society'.

Do these 'politically instituted' markets signify the dominance of markets, when they emerge only through political actions undertaken by states? How can one understand such markets under the paradigm of 'states *versus* markets'? How does one consider the role of the state, when states are regulators, certainly, but also the architects and builders of markets? Above all, the examples of renewables, nuclear and carbon-offset markets serve to illustrate both innovation in, and variety of, market forms within contemporary capitalisms. There is no singular or universal order or 'law of the market', let alone one that emerges spontaneously through the interaction between those two supposedly lead actors in the market theatre: 'The Buyer' and 'The Seller'.

This book emerged out of a dialogue between a number of approaches to develop a new understanding of the role and forms of markets in society today: economic sociology, evolutionary economics and a renewed (but not the 'new') institutional economics. Although some critiques of a variety of economists' views of markets are contained within individual chapters, our main purpose was to advance alternative understanding, rather than repeat sterile confrontations with mainstream economics. The book is also a product of a dialogue between two groups of scholars, resulting from a series of workshops held by the Centre for Research in Innovation and Competition (CRIC) at the University of Manchester, and Centre d'Economie de l'Université Paris Nord (CEPN). Coming from different disciplinary and theoretical perspectives, we shared a belief in developing analytical approaches firmly grounded in empirical research of 'actually existing markets', bounded by space and time.

Paradoxically for a book whose main focus is on markets, the different approaches represented here share an objective: to dethrone 'self-regulating' markets, both theoretically and empirically, from the pedestal on which they are commonly located. There are many ways that markets are commonly attributed a mis-placed centrality:

- As a primary mode of allocating scarce resources within capitalist societies, hence playing a dominant coordinating or integrating role in the
economy and society.
- As a spontaneous order that emerges as a consequence of universal laws
of supply and demand under conditions of competition, the most extreme
versions of which suggest a tendency towards perfect equilibrium.
- As the primary arena for calculation of opportunity and risk in the
pursuit of economic ends or interests by economic agents.
- As the economic embodiment of individual freedom and choice
that forms the natural counterpart to political institutions of electoral
democracy.
- As a socially constructed space for the performance of economic theories,
beliefs and techniques.

For these and indeed many other reasons, capitalism has been described as
a market society, and markets have been deemed to be '*the* central institution in capitalism . . . on condition that most of the production passes
through the market' (Swedberg, 2005: 12).

Re-positioning markets

The approaches represented here re-position markets and their significance
in capitalist economies in a number of ways to be raised here, an exercise
aimed both at a more balanced analysis and at emphasising the empirical
richness and variety of market forms and dynamics. From a theoretical
standpoint, we share the view that markets cannot be considered as 'self-
regulating' or as endowed with their own autonomous laws. Markets are
fundamentally institutionalised economic processes, conditioned in space
and time. In several ways we attempt to explore more deeply what we
mean by institutionalisation. Variation in market form and scale is both
historical and comparative, and there are also important sources of variation within and between the classical categories of markets: labour, product
and service, and capital markets.

The repositioning of markets involves a recognition that they are but one
phase in a process that stretches from production, through distribution to
consumption. Often markets are treated as if they were only spaces for
transactions and exchanges of property rights. The fascination (and now
frisson) of financial markets has accentuated this analytical detachment of
markets from the broader economic context (Knorr Cetina and Preda,
2005; McKenzie et al., 2007). The division between financial markets and
the 'real' economy, Wall Street and Main Street, has encouraged a conceptual treatment of them as almost autonomous spheres. Although the impacts
on the 'real' economy of the financial market crisis have become only too
rapidly and easily visible, the reverse impact of crises in economic growth
on the financial meltdown has received less attention (Urry, 2009). Yet the

squeeze on consumer spending with high energy and food costs undoubtedly contributed to the collapse of consumer confidence leading up to the credit crunch, and the bursting of the housing bubble. Putting markets in their place, therefore, requires recognition not only of the interdependence between financial and other markets, but of markets (including financial ones) as a coordinating phase between production and consumption.

Much neo-institutional analysis treats markets as autonomous spaces for exchanges of property rights, in terms of transaction costs. However, the way the exchange of goods or services is articulated with their distribution is critical to any understanding of markets, as the contrast between a market stall and internet shopping reveals. There is always an articulation of some kind, and how that articulation between exchange and distribution is instituted is critical to the spatial and temporal fix of markets, in ways recognised by economic geographers.[2] Over and above the narrower issues of whether to make or buy, and the Coasian problematic of firms versus markets, the repositioning requires recognition of the importance of developing divisions of labour and specialisation for the emergence and destruction of markets (North, 1990, 2005a, 2005b). Both horizontal and vertical divisions of labour entail proliferation of, and interdependence between, markets. A great deal of focus of theorisation and even empirical cases of markets is on the *internal* dynamics of a putative market: these internal dynamics are generally speaking what are falsely elevated to a central feature of capitalism. The recent turn to performativity has exaggerated this tendency by focusing on the role of economic ideas, theoretical algorithms, and the calculative tools of agents' behaviour within markets. Shifting the concern to the relation between division of labour, and vertical and horizontal interdependence between markets requires a radical change of perspective, as well as a rebalancing of the emphasis on internal dynamics. This shift in perspective also involves the broadest conception of division of labour, one that incorporates all those activities occurring after the final exchange of an end consumer market, activities necessary to consumption, properly speaking (Glucksmann, 2009).

Although clearly linked to evolving divisions of labour, from a Schumpeterian tradition innovation processes are central to market creation and destruction, taking us away from any market-internal dynamics of equilibrium, in order to include changes in production and consumption. Extending this perspective beyond its locus classicus in product or process innovation to consideration of innovation in the activity of exchange and market forms, the 'social technologies' (Nelson, 2005, 2008; Nelson and Sampat, 2001) of the organisation of markets can also be the object of intense innovation, including innovation in the articulation of exchange and distribution. Contemporary examples of how retailing outlets combine and coordinate novel bundles of goods and services, or internet with face-to-face shopping and home delivery, demonstrate market variety. The innovation is as much in how goods are bought and sold as in what is bought and sold. Competition between different modes of exchange and between different market organisations, in turn, result in the continuing creation and destruction of markets. This only highlights the need to broaden the theoretical frames by which markets are understood.

Finally, the dethroning of markets as the central institution of capitalism involves a recognition of the secular expansion of non-market provision of goods and services. Most advanced capitalist economies are characterised by between 30–40% of their GDP sustained by different forms of exchange from those of the typical market organisation, through taxation and compulsory insurance. Growth of education and health care, most notably, so central to the growth of the economy as we are constantly told, rest on rights to goods and services acquired through citizenship and residence, underpinned by obligations of taxation. Yet between these manifest forms of non-market provision of goods and services there are also many intermediate forms that depart significantly from markets as characterised by discretionary exchanges. Closest to market forms, incentives imposed by taxation significantly affect the functioning and pricing of markets, as with punitive taxation on tobacco or restrictions on tobacco consumption behaviour. Markets for tobacco or cars, for example, may be open or closed when defined by age restrictions or medical conditions. Closer to taxation or compulsory insurance are various forms of supposedly private or commercial medical care and especially pension provision. These acquisitions may become non-discretionary conditions of employment, in the one case, or be conditional on restrictions of discretionary choices over assets in the other, whether for pension stakeholders or pension fund holders. Even the most marketised forms of pension, such as the 410 ks in the USA (Wolff, 2004), impose constraints over disposal of assets that make these property forms significantly different from equity ownership.[3] As with the non-discretionary conditions of carbon emission capping, it may be a legal requirement to purchase a private pension on opting out of a public or state pension. A distinction can be drawn between discretionary choice made under (and affected by) regulatory conditions for market transactions, and limitations or removal of discretionary choice through conditional obligations or legal compulsion, a difference between regulated markets and hybrid organisations of exchange. Although varying greatly from country to country, there is a plethora of such hybrid market/non-market forms in many contemporary economies. Given the widespread presence of regulated, tax-incentivised, restricted, and hybrid forms of exchange, in addition to the many varieties of non-market provision and organised exchanges of goods and services, the centrality of market coordination to capitalist political economies becomes distinctly questionable.

The re-positioning of markets for their role and significance within contemporary capitalist economies thus involves several dimensions. Theoretically, markets are no longer the expression of ahistorical, universal, or timeless laws: they cease to be 'self-explanatory' on the back of being deemed 'self-regulating'. Empirically and analytically, they are now situated in a broader framework encompassing multiple phases, and new divisions of labour in the broadest and societal sense. Their creation and destruction, far from emanating from endogenous dynamics, are analysed in the more integrative and encompassing terms of industrial transformation and innovation, including innovation in consumption and by consumers. Their own organisational form is itself an object of innovation and competition. Finally, there is not only huge variation within the broadly market form of institutionalised exchange, but 'markets' themselves are placed within a wide spectrum of intermediate and hybrid forms of exchange, and situated alongside – indeed articulated with – non-market forms of exchange for goods and services. Capitalist political economies are much more than market economies, and from various standpoints we argue that markets are better understood when 'put in their place'.

Analysing markets as institutions

The approaches to understanding markets advocated in this book distinguish themselves from several of the dominant current approaches in other ways: economic sociology (Granovetter, Greif, Fligstein, Bourdieu, Callon) or neo-institutional economics (North, Coase and Williamson). This section aims to critically survey these alternatives by way of context to our contribution to the debate. Markets are pre-eminently economic institutions, even though legal, political and cultural institutions quite clearly condition them, and hence must be included in any integrated, holistic account of societal variation. It is impossible to understand the varied place of markets in different socio-economies, notably between continental Europe and the Anglo-Saxon countries, without this wider analytical framework. Nonetheless, it is all the more important to understand and specify what it is that we mean by economic when speaking of markets as economic institutions, and to insist that there are sources of economic variation distinct from, but in interplay with, legal, political and cultural sources of variation.

As a bridge between this and the preceding discussion, it is useful to start with a discussion of Karl Polanyi and the concept of embeddedness. Preferring to use the term 'market economy' to 'capitalism' to describe industrial economies that emerged from the end of the eighteenth century in Europe (Polanyi, 1944), Polanyi regarded distribution and exchange as the primary economic processes for integrating society (Polanyi, 1957, 1968). For him, the main dynamic driving markets that emerged and dominated society in the nineteenth century was the 'double movement' between self-regulation and regulation. It was a dynamic between a tendency to convert everything into market commodities, and a counter-tendency to protect and safeguard society from the otherwise inevitable crippling of human life, destruction of the environment, and chaos of monetary volatility. For him, labour, land, and money were 'fictitious commodities', and if they were subjected (politically and economically) to self-regulated markets like any other commodity, society would destroy itself and its environment.

Regulation and self-regulation of economic processes of exchange and distribution provided a dynamic tension that cannot be confused with the opposition between embeddedness and disembeddedness. Polanyi used the term 'embedded' infrequently and 'disembedded' even less so, but the dominant sense of the terms was of economic activity relatively differentiated or undifferentiated from political, social and cultural contexts (Harvey, 2007; Harvey et al., 2007; Hopkins, 1957).[4] Thus, it is quite consistent to have an institution, such as an exchange rate, as both highly regulated *and* disembedded, strongly differentiated as economic. Markets, from the nineteenth century onwards at least, were relatively disembedded or differentiated economic institutions, whether strongly or weakly regulated. Although not according markets the centrality attributed to them by Polanyi, we wish to retain this notion of markets as primarily and specifically *economic* institutions, and treat them as such – even when, at some extremes, their architect is the state.

New economic sociology approaches to markets

This insistence on treating markets as primarily economic institutions distinguishes the approaches advocated here from several of the main directions taken by the 'new economic sociology', and especially the notion of embeddedness as it has been developed by Granovetter and others. As against more trenchant concepts of embeddedness that suggest a dissolution of the economic into the social or political, effectively denying any specifically or societally differentiated economic processes or institutions (Block, 2003; Krippner, 2001; Lie, 1991, 1992), there is a persistent ambiguity in Granovetter's seminal paper and his subsequent development of the concept (Granovetter 1985, 1992a, 1992b; Granovetter and McGuire, 1998; Yakubovich et al., 2005). Although presenting a powerful critique of neoclassical assumptions of 'undersocialised' economic actors, many of the central aspects of economy are left untouched by 'embeddedness' (Nee and Ingram, 1998; Zukin and DiMaggio, 1990):[5] the division between wage labour and capital; the institution of property; the functioning of exchange mediated by money; the historical differentiation between capital, labour and product markets . . . the list could go on. It is not so much a sociological theory of the economic,[6] as a theory of social behaviour in a taken-for-granted economic space, which markets, be they for labour or electricity, inhabit. Social networky people in an economic world.

Failure to address the issue of the specificity or differentiation of economic processes and causalities underpins this ambiguity. On the one hand, the networks are social and, on the other, the activities they are engaged in are presented as unproblematically economic. Are they just friendships, weak ties (Granovetter, 1973), or power blocks that could equally well occupy and shape any field of activity, or is there something about the economic activities engaged in that affects the nature and explanatory force of networks' social dynamics? The development of the social network concept of embeddedness in relation to labour markets (Granovetter, 1992a) already highlights its limitations. The explanation has the restricted scope of job-seeking within 'the market', an explanation that certainly powerfully undermines neo-classical representations of economic agency, but takes for granted the institution of wage labour itself, so central to an understanding of capitalism (Swedberg, 1994, 2005). Yet the wage as an economic institution of exchange and price is fundamentally variable, both historically and comparatively, in ways that also condition entrance, engagement and exit at a different level.

The ambiguity is demonstrated even in a case that apparently addresses the conditioning or construction of a prototypically economic aspect of markets, the price institution of electrical supply in the USA (Yakubovich et al., 2005). In effect, two competing and alternative pricing systems were promoted by different power blocs within the supply industry, one eventually dominating through mobilisation by key players of trade associations and customers.[7] The argument is made that the dominant pricing institution prevailed irrespective of, even despite, its merits from a specifically economic standpoint. In addressing the issue of which of two alternative pricing institutions endured (two alternative modes of instituting exchanges and resource flows), success is attributed to the social-networky, non-economic explanation. Yet the fact remains that one of possibly two viable institutions formed a basis for subsequent expansion, growth of revenues, and monopolisation through a price institution securing repeated exchanges. The social network explanation may indeed have something to say about which of the two alternatives prevailed, little with respect to the economic viability of pricing institutions. It takes that aspect of the economy as given, falling beyond its frame. As a type of explanation it passes the economy by. Beyond a certain point, it lives with the dominant disciplinary divide: sociological explanation for one type of activity, economic explanation for another. Yet tantalisingly it invites an analysis of the institutionalised character of economic flows of resources through price mechanisms, and signals by default the need to address that issue.

A similar issue arises with a variant of social-network conceptualisations of markets, Actor Network Theory (ANT) (Callon, 1998), particularly as now developed in conjunction with performativity theory (McKenzie, 2006; McKenzie et al., 2007). In its strongest form, performativity theory proposes that when an economic idea (model, algorithm, technique, mathematisation) is used in practice by agents, it can 'make economic processes more like their depiction by economics' (McKenzie, 2007: 56). Like a performative utterance (for example, 'I arrest you in the name of the law'), an economic theory produces the reality expressed in the statement. McKenzie's accounts of the Black–Scholes–Merton algorithm in options markets made prices perform in the way that was predicted by the model, when many agents adopted the model and used them in practice. The model was performative – at least for a time, and in a certain geographic scale and space. Callon suggestively connected performativity with the social arrangements (*agencements*: Callon, 2007) – the mechanics, techniques, material technologies, social networks – in which models, techniques or procedures could become expressive and, in particular, a relative closure of the economic world from 'outside' influences. Economic models, calculative economic agents, become performative within these constructed contexts.[8]

When Greenspan admitted that the economist's whole intellectual edifice collapsed with the financial crisis, however, it was clear that something much greater had happened than that this edifice ceased to perform. The dynamics of the crisis are not limited to a crisis of economic ideas and their performative effects, whether in McKenzie's terms of counter-performativities when economic ideas produce realities contrary to their description (McKenzie, 2007), or in Callon's terms of the de-containment of the constructed world in which the ideas worked, and an 'overflowing' of the environment that surrounded it. Callon indeed recognises the Achilles heel of performativity theory in accounting for non-performativity, and it is striking to compare his analysis with the much more developed analysis of evolutionary economics (Callon, 2007: 332–4). For the latter, an ontology of sources of variation, on the one hand, and a selection environment, on the other, are the starting point for evolutionary theories of economic change. But this analysis necessarily pushes the analysis to consider the wider contexts of markets, beyond considering them narrowly in terms of arenas of economic ideas for context-bounded calculating economic agents and their relatively closed networks.

Banks collapsed, homeowners had their houses repossessed, the state suddenly reappeared, now on centre stage. The role of regulation – such as the repeal of the Glass–Steagall Act of the previous Great Depression – came to the fore. Deregulated activity sliding into outright fraud exposed the critical importance of law for the functioning of markets. In short, performativity theories – by restricting their analysis to market-internal dynamics, and by failing to examine the space–time conditions under which the performativity of ideas, algorithms, tools, devices are effective, ineffective or dislocative – demonstrate their limited value for an integrative institutional economic analysis of markets. Illuminating though the account of the effective performativity of the Black–Scholes–Merton algorithm certainly is for a space–time-bounded, market-internal analysis, the scale and nature of the current crisis makes one wonder whether performativity analysis will be as transient an instituted mode of 'thinking the economic' as the economic institutions of Collateralised Debt Obligations and Structured Investment Vehicles.

Another major economic sociology approach to markets, the conceptualisation of markets as 'fields', is critical of the limitations of network

approaches from several standpoints (Swedberg, 2003): the lack of appreciation of the significance of states, especially in setting relevant legal
frameworks; the failure to address established institutions at a structural
level; and the lack of recognition of the significance of power relations
between actors, whether economic or political. The two main exponents of
market as field, Fligstein (1996, 2001, 2005) and Bourdieu (2005), articu-
late the concept, or rather metaphor, of field in different ways, which in
turn affects their analysis of markets. Fligstein employs a more fluid notion
of a space within which power-plays – the politics – of markets occur, and
occasionally substitutes terms such as 'arena' almost synonymously with
field.[9] The use of the term 'arena', for example, suggests almost an empty
stage, which actors enter and exit, with the field properties limited to being
that of shared space, the real traction engendered by the actors. As we shall
see, this raises questions for the scope of the explanation, especially for
effects produced exogenously to a field, coming in from 'out of field'. For
Bourdieu the field is much more a forcefield, a structure within and by
which actors' relative power (symbolic, social, economic) is defined.[10] As a
consequence, Fligstein's analysis appears to define fields as temporarily and
contingently stabilised structures, emphasising periods of emergence and
crisis, as well as endurance. Bourdieu's fields, at least when applied to
markets,[11] are much more characterised by the static dynamics of the field
itself, the synchronous distinction and positioning of the major market
players.

For both authors, the state plays a dual role of some significance, firstly
as the source of legislation by which the 'field settings' are established, the
legal parameters of action within which market transactions occur, but
secondly, at least as importantly, as a major in-field player. Fligstein especially emphasises the fact that states build themselves by building market
infrastructures, extending the scope and nature of their political and legal
powers in so doing, as opposed to being neutral arbiter or disinterested
purveyor of rules, above the fray. The case is forcefully made with respect
to the construction of the European Union and the Single Market (Fligstein
and Mara-Drita, 1996; Fligstein and Sweet, 2002). Equally important, the
state as procurer or investor, tax incentiviser or credit regulator, is very
much a player within the market field (Fligstein highlights the role of the
state in Silicon Valley (2005), Bourdieu in the housing market (2005)).
There is a constant interplay between regulators and market actors in the
framing of the 'field settings' for markets, leading to some ambiguity in
the use of the concept of market as field. Different fields intersect, sometimes including the state, others treating the market field as inhabited
solely by firms: boundaries between fields, overlaps between fields, or
dynamic interactions between fields remain theoretically vague. And in
Fligstein's work, field language about markets frequently drops out
altogether, vying with alternative frames of social movements, politics, and
cultural construction.

Nonetheless, Fligstein provides an elaborated description of markets as fields, defined by four basic organising principles: property rights, governance structures, concepts of control and rules of exchange. Property rights, governance structures and rules of exchange involve states most directly, but the legal institutionalisation of property rights, contract and incorporation, and the governance of markets through laws of competition, trading standards, and so on, are subject to continuous modification in which various parties, firms, workers' organisations, lobby groups, political parties and governments mobilise their resources in their respective arenas in order to shape the market to their advantage. Concepts of control refer particularly to the way in which firms, especially dominant firms, establish shared views in the market field to reduce competitive pressures, mainly through the price mechanism, in order to secure and stabilise their dominance. Concepts of control are central to the cultural construction of the market as a field in which all participants share norms of conduct.

Bourdieu articulates the economic field according to various dimensions of 'capital', a term loosely designating different types of resources. Thus, financial capital in the usual economic sense is just one dimension of capital, alongside which a firm (and in Bourdieu's economic field, the agents are overwhelmingly assumed to be firms) mobilises cultural, technological, juridical and organisational capital (resources/capabilities). The economic field itself (the market) is constituted by the distribution of total capital of all kinds within the field, this unequal distribution then shaping the conduct, and possible conducts, of all the firms contained within it.[12] As an analytical framework, Bourdieu deploys it to a limited and largely implicit extent in his analysis of the large construction companies involved in the new-build sector of the French housing market. But, it has to be said, with this narrow empirical focus and the absence of extended treatment, the framework is underdeveloped.

A striking feature shared by Fligstein and Bourdieu is their emphasis on the stability of markets, and above all the persistence of domination by the principal agents within them. This raises the question as to whether there is something about the concept of field that leads to this kind of analysis.[13] In Fligstein's case, stability of the dominant players is their strategic objective, and an overriding political objective: competition is limited, price war or profit maximisation taking second place to securing dominance (Fligstein, 2001: 17–18). Stability is the strategic priority of the dominant firms to remain dominant.[14] In Bourdieu's case, the argument verges on the tautological, with the unequal distribution of capital creating a forcefield that prevents or inhibits redistribution of economic power. There is a paradox that both these arch-critics of neo-classical theories of market equilibrium promote an alternative position that amounts to a theory of power-equilibrium as the 'normal' state of affairs in capitalism.

Where does this leave the concept of field, either as a metaphor or as an analytical tool for conceptualising markets? Adopting a concept of field in relation to markets cuts out or defines a circumscribed space within which market dynamics occur, rather than viewing markets as a phase in a process of production, distribution, exchange and consumption. The consequences of this conceptual 'cut' are manifold. A primary effect is manifest in the stability theses just noted. Innovation and technological change, 'waves of market destruction and creation' in a Schumpeterian or Marxist perspective, are rendered atypical or marginal to the analysis. To take markets for communication as one example of the blind-spot, the advent of the internet and mobile telephony have not only transformed markets and patterns of consumption, but also notably disrupted and transformed the power relations and the cast of dominant players. Where innovation appears in their analysis, it is presented as exogenous to markets as fields, as if the activity of innovation and the activity of trading by a given economic agent were somehow disarticulated. The field concept breaks the link between transformations in production and markets, and thus makes it difficult to embrace waves of market creation and destruction so typical of capitalism.

If the field concept cuts the firm as producer and market player in two, it also has similar effects in the vertical relations of firms, on the one hand downstream in the production/value chain and on the other to consumers. In the first place, it is clear that neither downstream suppliers nor consumers inhabit the same field as that of a given market and its agents. At best, the vertical division of labour and its coordination is decentred from the analytical frame, with the focus placed on similar agents at the same phase in the production process. The field concept handles the dynamics between like actors much more adequately than between actors vertically differentiated in the value chain. This is most conspicuous, however, in the treatment of end-markets and consumers. In Fligstein's case, the field is not so much a concept explicitly justifying a supply-side vision,[15] as one consigning consumers to being out-of-vision. Consumers are rendered subliminal creatures. In Bourdieu's analysis of the housing market, in spite of having announced the significance of housing as a project for the reproduction of the household, consumers appear primarily as the innocent and gullible victims of market imagery and symbolism purveyed by construction companies.[16] The role of changing patterns of household composition and their impact on the market, indeed architecture, of housing is actively excluded from his field analysis – a paradox when one considers the contrasting but equally intimate linkage between social structure and housing architecture in the Kabylie with which Bourdieu was so familiar. In both cases, the treatment of consumers can be seen as symptomatic of the way the field concept cuts its empirical domain.[17]

If these economic relations and processes are disrupted and underplayed by the field concept, the strangest effect of the conceptual cut is visible in how field theory downgrades markets as institutions of exchange, and hence of coordination and integration between buyers and sellers. Exchange is an ongoing process through which resources circulate, a circulatory system necessary for capitalist economies, yet the field concept cuts these arteries of economic activity. Although an indication only of what is at stake, Fligstein suggests that the stability of fields is maintained by dominant players avoiding the use of price competition – surely in itself a questionable empirical assertion. The price institution ensures the circulation of resources necessary for the economic survival of firms, and their relative positions in markets. Yet price determination and the market institutions that standardise transactions in monetary terms play little or no role in this field conception of markets.

Overall, then, the concept of field, notably of stabilised spaces controlled by dominant players, dismembers economic activity on a number of levels, and in so doing fails to account for specifically economic aspects of market institutions. In Fligstein's version, the result is to portray markets much as any other political–cultural arena, driven by the pursuit and maintenance of power, and the establishment of political coalitions disrupted by social movements of newcomers (Fligstein, 201: 70–6). For Bourdieu, the economic field is identified with the market as the product of a long historical genesis, a space both 'arbitrary and artificial' in which reason is a non-deliberative habitus, born of socially engrained routines of thinking, rather than individual conscious calculation.

Neo-institutionalist economic approaches

In the previous section, we explored how some economic sociology approaches have approached the institutionalisation of markets. This section examines how some varieties of institutionalist economics view economic institutions, and markets in particular. Departing from Walrasian and neo-classical conceptions of institution-less markets, major contributions from within economics have without doubt emerged from the neo-institutionalist trend and game theoretical approaches. In both cases, although the institutions figure prominently in the understanding of the 'rules of the game', formal laws and informal codes, norms and routines that condition and constitute markets, they share the striking feature of remaining within the mainstream economistic mould of behavioural rather than institutionalist explanations of institutions. There remains a distance between such approaches and those of the new economic sociology.[18]

The neo-institutionalist trend, as it has come to be known, emerged in its earliest Coaseian formulations, on a basis that appeared to promise little for an institutionalist analysis of markets. *Given* markets, Coase asked, why do firms exist as organisations operating in a market context (Coase, 1988)?[19] The basis for organisations to emerge, hence fundamentally changing the nature of the agents engaged in market activity, was related to the costs of transacting in the market. If these were higher than the costs of direct organisational and managerial control, in terms of information acquisition, measurement of performance, control and enforcement of contracts between individual agents, then firms would emerge.[20] Subsequently, but still on the same narrow footing, Coase touched on the issue of why laws emerged, expressed in terms of why states might intervene to regulate market exchanges (Coase, 1960). This was posed in terms of social costs, now re-badged as negative externalities, and the relative transaction costs of monitoring and enforcing them by a third party, as against the costs of the externalities themselves. Laws emerge where governmental administrative transaction costs are less than those incurred by the negative externalities, which otherwise are absorbed as a fact of market existence.[21] Quite apart from unresolved problems of measurement in the absence of market testing or other prior standards, this form of transaction cost analysis advances us but little in any institutional analysis of the exchange process or markets as such.

North substantially shifts the ground, both broadening and providing a new foundation for the concept of transaction costs, setting them firmly on now explicit assumptions about human behaviour (1990). Rather than any frontal demolition of neo-classical framing of markets as entailing frictionless and timeless exchanges with perfect information and unconditioned/unlimited rationality, North neatly sidesteps (*and leaves intact*) a neo-classical market at the extreme fringes of historical reality, where such assumptions might just conceivably obtain. In almost all circumstances, human behaviour is characterised by limited rationality with respect to a complex environment, and by shifting and complex motivations.

The complexity of most market (or other economic) environments surpasses human mental processing power, hence imposing a heavy burden of unlimited choice in conditions of uncertainty, combined with possibly shifting human motivations. In these circumstances, reduction of complexity and the relevance of unknowns is needed to oil the wheels of transactions, enabling them to occur between human beings, and facilitating coordination between them.[22] Institutions serve that lubricating function, making up for the deficiencies of human rationality in the face of uncertainty and absence of full information (total comprehension of the world). Norms, habits, routines, institutional frameworks, by restricting alternative actions, all reduce the costs of transacting, by pre-empting the need to acquire information, calculate costs of alternative actions, and by subduing the volatility of desire. In the broadest sense, substantial efforts (costs) are involved in coping with and reducing complexity, and in acquiring and providing information necessary for transacting. Any such effort is a cost of transaction (whether or not expressed in market or monetary terms). For this reason, there is an economy of human transacting with other humans: in a sense, transaction costs are the *economic* foundation of human societies. Institutions must come into being in order to make human transacting possible – and North encompasses the broadest range of types of transacting here.[23] As the social world grows more complex, moreover, transactions become less repetitive and more anonymous, so increasing the information and rational calculability deficits.[24] Institutions become more and more formalised, building on layers of informal habits and routines, with third-party arbitration, measurement and enforcement. The state and law, as an institutional infrastructure, then become necessary to making transacting possible.[25]

For markets, therefore, and especially those that arise out of a complex division of labour where increases of productivity derived from techno-logical progress are a driving force, institutional frameworks of property rights, measurement, standards and enforcement are core features required for their functioning. The costs of transacting in complex societies are sig-nificant in relation to the total wealth produced, hence requiring a complex architecture of hierarchically nested institutions.[26] In the real world of institutionalised markets, the complex play of actors endowed with differ-ent motivations, different power balances, and the vagaries of political institutions result in major path divergencies, a heterogeneity of institution-alised markets. There is no 'perfect market', only a mixed bag of more or less adaptively efficient markets for enabling economic growth.

In some ways, this is an extraordinary vision: institutions only exist because of human frailty and inconstancy in an uncertain and complex environment. They are there to make human interactions less complex and more routinised. And yet, history is one of increasing complexity and scale of interactions *and* institutions. Accepting and extending a notion of path dependency into one of 'varieties of capitalism', institutional proliferation involves inter-relations between divergent institutions, and the emergence of new scales and multiple levels of institutions – even when considering only the phase of market transactions (Braudel, 1979). The historical evo-lution of markets simply does not look like a complexity-reduction, effi-ciency-maximisation exercise undertaken to make life easier (less costly) for individuals inadequately endowed with compute power.

Although abandoning the deficit-mitigating account of institutions based on assumptions about individual human endowments, Greif provides an alternative and significant institutionalist account of the emergence of markets and market behaviour that remains at least in part built up from microfoundations of inter-individual interactions (Greif, 1994, 2000, 2006; Greif et al., 1994). For this purpose, he enrols game theory, as an analyti-cal and empirical tool, especially in order to introduce a concept of motiva-tion, the incentives and pay-offs for different behavioural patterns.[27] His critique of the transaction cost analysis of neo-institutionalists is fundamen-tal and wide-ranging for its narrowly functionalist account of efficiency maximisation; its failure to recognise the significance of culture; and, above all, the absence of an account of why rules of the game are enforceable or self-enforcing. Many times he argues that functional necessity fails to give an adequate account of why rules or norms actually come into existence. A motivational account plugs that theoretical gap, by introducing incentives to motivate individuals to believe in rules and norms, and so endogenise them as a guide to their behaviour.[28]

Greif takes an explicitly 'sociological turn', adding a strongly cultural perspective to his analysis. Crudely expressed, it could be said that culture sets different parameters and initial conditions for the game, and hence determines what games are engaged in where and when, historically and comparatively. Institutions comprise cultural beliefs, rules of the game, organisations and norms, and ultimately are defined by social elements that 'generate regularity of (social) behaviour' (Greif, 2006). In a formulaic manner, institutions are described 'exogenous to *each* individual', resulting in stable – equilibrium – patterns of behaviour of the participants in social interaction. This much insisted-upon 'exogeneity', however, is ambiguously used, both to mean non-restricted (extensive) or transcendent with respect to each individual, and 'outside' or external to each individual, with beliefs, norms and values subsequently being incorporated, through socialisation or transactions, within individuals through endogenous motivation. For Greif, institutions therefore almost go 'all the way down' – that is to say, there is no such thing as non-institutionally guided behaviour, no extra-institutional human being. The players of a game play from the positions – historical and cultural – they are born into. As we shall see, moreover, culture is almost as much taken as a given as are assumptions made by setting the rules of a game within game theory, just pushing back a step, taking empirical cultural differences as givens rather than theorists making assumptions. Thus, in Greif's analysis of market behaviour in the Middle Ages, much rests on a contrast between individualist and collectivist cultures characteristic of Genoese and Maghribi traders respectively, the results of an historical past and tradition that become the starting point for future path dependencies. This polarity of cultures is the taken-for-granted precondition for subsequent divergence of economic performance between the two sets of traders, each playing their games according to culturally pre-given rules.

Yet this is not so much a theory of institutions to account for markets, as a theory for markets that has been generalised into a theory of institutions, and it shows. Developed from the historically powerful case of the growth of markets in the West from the late Middle Ages, it is a theory that places the transaction at its centre. For Greif the deficit-mitigation function of institutions is not with respect to the computational powers, information acquisition capacity or stable preferences of humans, but essentially with regard to a social deficit, the presence or absence of a commitment to interact socially. This deficit model has a similar peculiarity to the neo-institutionalist perspective highlighted above: without institutions, humans would struggle to be social. It is as if there was a real option or risk of a quite radical disconnect between all individuals, not even merely a deficit of trust or commitment, but a disconnect from social relations as such, an evocation of a Robinson Crusoe alternative for everyone. We all need institutions, or we might all end up as Robinson Crusoes, a peculiar functionalist account of institutions indeed.

This 'social-deficit-mitigating' model of institutions emanates from an analysis of mercantile trading at a distance in international trade in the late Middle Ages. It is clearly a development from an understanding of what is deemed to be 'the fundamental problem of exchange' or FPOE (Greif, 2000). On the assumption of a transaction between players where *nothing binds them together*, the problem is to establish the necessary conditions such 'that one can *ex ante* commit to being able and willing to fulfil contractual engagements *ex post*' (Greif, 2000: 254). The development of the economy through exchange relations depends on the extent to which this fundamental problem of commitment between transactors is mitigated by institutions, and the divergent cultural ways in which it is mitigated.

The historical specificity of *mercantile* trading and emergent markets in the Mediterranean basin, especially of distant trading either by use of intermediary agents by the Genoese or by the collectivist social grouping of a dispersed Maghribi 'nation', is under-analysed. What we are dealing with, at most, is a mercantile medieval market problem of exchange (MMMPOE), with distinctive commitment risks and constraints, rather than a fundamental or equivalent problem of exchange common to all historical and comparative instances of market formation. This mercantile model of markets, predicated on economic or social relations where nothing other than the trade binds parties together (not even co-location), is the one which is subsequently generalised into a mercantile market metaphor for all social interaction. Thus, the divisions of labour emergent in industrial capital between specialised producers or the division between capital and labour underpinning capitalist labour markets, where constraints and interdependencies bind parties through complementarities and necessity of coordination, are not captured by a Greif FPOE. Exchange may be predicated on cooperation, or producer–user interactions, rather than vice versa. Exchange may take place by necessity, rather than conditioned by commitment or trust. Indeed, ultimately the attempt to establish a microfoundational basis for institutional analysis of markets leaves us with models of behaviour within markets as given environments, but without means of differentiating markets as institutions, historically or comparatively. The widely and fundamentally varied institutional organisations of exchange escape from grasp, failing to capture the kind of historical depth provided, for example, by Braudel (1979).

The generic market model for institutions is extrapolated to frame almost all human interaction in terms of transactions, where 'A transaction is defined as an action taken when an entity, such as a commodity, social attitude, emotion, opinion, or information is transferred from one social unit to another' (Greif, 2006: C2 18). This perspective culminates in transactions effectively being constitutive of society.[29] The model of trade, of an entity passing from one to another, under conditions where nothing other than trade binds them together, is the ultimate market vision of social institutions. It is for this reason that alternative institutional analysis is required to put markets back in their place, as historically and variously instituted, but also as one phase in a much broader range of economic processes.

The contribution and structure of the book

The preceding discussion of some economic sociology and institutional economics approaches aimed to situate the contributions of the book, and highlight the distinctiveness of the perspectives developed here with respect to some of their closest neighbours, historical and intellectual. This was certainly far from a comprehensive overview of the vast literature on markets, and leaves to later chapters discussion of some important omissions, notably of Braudel, Weber and some mainstream economists.

Clearly, there are widely differing understandings of markets as institutions, and the workshops that led to this book attempted to problematise and advance understanding of processes of institutionalisation with respect to a wide range of empirical, historical and comparative cases: emergent markets for knowledge, venture capital markets, a long duration account of food distribution and the late rise of supermarkets, household service markets, and new technology capital markets, as well as non-market modes of distribution and exchange. A theme that runs through the book concerns the various roles of state, regulation and law as constitutive of markets. But, equally not all 'rules of the game' that constitute markets are state-inspired or constructed. Many modes of market organisation and coordination emerge from dynamics of economic variation, dislocation and destruction. While emphasising the importance of the state in processes of market institutionalisation, it would be bizarre indeed to characterise market forms in contemporary capitalisms as state-planned, even in those contemporary examples of markets that arose from privatisations of state enterprises.

From a historical and comparative perspective, markets emerged from prior organisations of exchange, production, distribution and consumption, not from societies without institutions (whatever that could mean). Institutionalist accounts of institutional transformation do not therefore need to start with assumptions of Robinson Crusoe origins, or of humans endowed with certain motivations, or information acquisition and processing capacities analytically prior to institution-formation. Historical institutions (in the different ways we understand them) are our shared starting point. So several contributions explore the complex relation between different modes of regulation and rule formation, political, economic and cultural. Our focus on different modes of institutionalisation and processes of instituting and organising exchange hopefully takes the discussion beyond the rather bland and general concepts of 'embedding' and social construction. And, while our focus is here on markets, our shared concern is always to situate markets within the wider political economy, rather than treat markets as autonomous spheres of activity with their own self-standing internal dynamics. The contributions reflect an open and unfinished dialogue, however, and the differences of emphasis and orientation will hopefully stimulate further conversations and future enquiries.

Benjamin Coriat and Olivier Weinstein develop a thorough critique of both neo-classical and neo-institutional economics approaches to markets, emphasising both the gains and limitations of the latter (chapter 2). Viewing institutions as 'rules of the game' (North), they develop a more fundamental and expansive concept of rules as enabling rather than constraining, and as constitutive of new fields of economic action (Searle).

Following a discussion and critique of neo-institutionalist conceptions of firms, transactions and markets, this perspective is developed as a theory of markets where rules are only secondarily understood as corrective measures addressing typical 'market failures', but primarily as conditions of existence, and creation, of markets. Formal–legal and conventional–social rules are seen to be necessary in defining what it is that is exchanged, principles of evaluation for qualities of goods and services, and the constitution of social categories involved in regular and repeated exchanges. They argue particularly that new markets for knowledge and services involve the radical development of new rules for defining objects of exchange and for evaluating and coordinating quality and price. This forms the basis of a much more extensive conception of markets than one focusing narrowly on exchanges of property rights.

In chapter 3, Harvey and Randles present a neo-Polanyian analysis of the organisation of exchange processes.[30] Their 'instituted economic process' (IEP) approach informs much of the empirical research and analysis of markets undertaken by CRIC, represented by several chapters in this book. The chapter addresses the anthropological issue of how markets are distinctive forms of organising exchange within societies. Rather than taking markets for granted in capitalist societies, it problematises why, when, and between whom exchange is necessary, and then builds up a step-by-step analysis of the dynamics of market and non-market organisation of exchange processes. By limiting analysis to specifically economic instituted characteristics, the intention is both to broaden the economic sociology of markets, and to situate instituted organisation of exchange processes in a much broader field than market exchanges. The chapter develops a procedure for analysing the variety and dynamics of exchange processes by identifying some key underlying parameters. The separation and formation of classes of economic agent between which exchange occurs; the interdependent nexus of economic agents and exchange processes, market and non-market; and interaction across the exchange process between sellers and buyers upon which exchange processes depend are analysed as a way of understanding systematic differences and variations both between and within labour, product, and capital markets. One significant aspect of this analysis is that it presents the organisation of exchange – especially within markets – fundamentally in terms of a continuing process and between classes of actors defined by their mutual dependency and asymmetric power relations. This contrasts with atomist accounts that suggest independence and equality of power and information between individual buyers and sellers in the ideal market.

Harvey and Metcalfe ask the question (chapter 4):[31] what would have been the conversation if Schumpeter had met Polanyi to talk about markets? The perspectives of two of the most influential non-orthodox thinkers of the twentieth century on the nature and role of markets are counterposed and contrasted. In broad terms, the encounter between the two raises the big question that drives this chapter: what is the relation between market creation and destruction that arises from innovation in products and services and the transformation of the institutions of markets as organisations of exchange, distribution and intermediation? From Schumpeter we understand the market as a device to facilitate the self-transformation of economic activity, as a frame to promote and diffuse novelty and to discover new ways of meeting human needs. It is because the generation of novelty is widely distributed and pervasive that there is a continual need for market institutions to re-impose order and to do so by absorbing novelty. From Polanyi, we can see markets in their own right as organisations integrating diverse societal economic activities over time and space. Too often markets are interpreted as devices solely to establish prices and patterns of exchange whereas in fact they also play a key role in the distribution of goods and services. The relationship between exchange and distribution processes may vary but they are always interdependent and they are reflected jointly in the instituted frame of the particular market. So, in sum, the need for exchange arises from continuously emergent divisions of labour, which firstly involves innovation of new goods and services; secondly, new modes of distribution of these across space and time; and, thirdly, new modes and organisation of the exchange process itself.

To explore the question arising from the encounter, the chapter provides a 'long duration' empirical section on the evolution of food-provisioning markets in the United Kingdom from 1200 to the present day. A Polanyian and a Schumpeterian analysis of the process of order and change are posited and compared. The argument is made that both accounts are necessary, making up for some of their respective shortcomings. New products and services frequently transform the organisation of exchange, modes of distribution and intermediation, including, critically market knowledge, on the one hand. On the other, market-institutional change can readily be seen to involve both innovations in services and infrastructures of distribution and communication in their own right, and these can in turn condition the modes and opportunities for innovation of goods and services across the economy. They conclude that there is therefore a dynamic relationship between intra-market and market-institutional order and change.

Combining a theoretical approach and empirical analysis, Dorothée Rivaud-Danset and Emanuelle Dubocage focus their analysis on the relationships between venture capitalists and entrepreneurs (chapter 5). They base their argument on primary empirical research in France, compared with existing studies of venture capital in the USA. The framework is different from the usual one derived from agency and information theories. It emphasises the importance of specific practices, like the organisation of exchanges based on a network of non-financial intermediaries and the impact of supply-side criteria over the demand side. These practices are at the core of the organisation of exchanges in the venture capital market. Following the ideas presented in chapters 2 and 3, the analysis focuses both on the organisation of exchange and on the informal rules that are established in networks of venture capitalists so essential for the formation of venture capital markets. These rules concern above all the organisation of exchange through a network of intermediaries; the 'formatting' or standardisation of demand, especially through the institution of a 'business plan'; and the regularisation of processes of evaluation, in particular the establishing of prices through negotiation between start-up firms and venture capitalists over respective property rights, the level of venture capital involved, and the projection of returns and strategies for exit through IPO (initial public offering) or acquisition. The importance of these 'rules of the game' comes from the following principle: coordination is difficult because of the highly uncertain context surrounding start-ups, and the complexity of risks, as much as risks as such. Difficulties for firms dealing with uncertainty and dependency on financial markets result in the highly unstable dynamics of venture-capital. Consequently, venture capital markets provide a particular interesting case for questions concerning the institutional conditions and regularising of exchange processes that are the focus of this volume.

In chapter 6, Valérie Revest addresses a topic rarely explored in much of the literature on markets: the failure of a market to establish itself, as against the much narrower concepts of 'market failure'. This is based on a case study of the French New Market, one of many institutional experiments in high-technology financial markets. The other main interest, alluded to in chapter 4, is the dissolution of the market–firm dichotomy: the case study explores the firm responsible for organising the market, i.e. the market firm. So, is it a market failure, or a firm failure, or both? Finally, the chapter addresses a very significant type of market in contemporary economies: the new technology capital markets, in this case the French New Market from the mid-1990s to its failure in 2004.

Empirically, the chapter traces how the need for new technology capital markets became increasingly pressing within Europe, where several such markets were established in emulation, even imitation, of the NASDAQ. It did so against the grain of many of the existing institutional arrangements of capital markets. In line with much of the analysis presented in chapter 2, it is demonstrated that there were considerable difficulties in defining the object (carving out and circumscribing what counted as new technology firms to be exclusively listed on the exchange) and in establishing principles of evaluation – especially the institution of the 'market maker' for price setting.

Analytically, the chapter develops and builds upon both the institutionalism of North, and the organisation theory of March and Simon, by arguing that there was both a failure to develop an institutional framework of 'constitutive rules' governing the exchanges on the new market, and a failure of the organisation of the market firm to develop a coherent strategy to cope with change, and acquire the new capabilities and learning involved in the transformation from established capital markets. By examining the lessons of failure, the often hidden but fundamental requisites for market formation are strongly highlighted. Thus, the chapter offers a valuable input into the debate running through the volume as a whole.

Patrick Haddad then provides a valuable contrast to the high-tech/high-finance markets discussed in other chapters by exploring the market for household services in France (chapter 7). The growth of this tertiary-sector market has been a significant feature in recent years, and has the interest of focusing on personal services, where the relationship between buyer and seller can be very immediate and direct. The provision of these services (home helps, carers, and so on) has evolved considerably over the past few decades, particularly in developing new intersections between formal and informal, market and non-market, exchanges. The role of the state in stimulating, regulating and subsidising these exchanges also means that any analysis needs to go beyond any straightforward state–market dichotomies.

The analytical perspective developed in this chapter shares with others a focus on both the constitutive rule-systems of markets (markets as institutions) and the organisation of actors involved in providing services. A typology of household provisioning exchanges is developed with three dimensions: the formal or informal nature of the transaction; the organisation of supply, whether by individuals, or various types and scales of organisations; and the market or non-market status of the supply organisations. In France four types of organised exchange, each with their own rule systems, are identified: a state-administered market; a state-subsidised private market; individual provisioner markets with state subsidies; and informal markets, outside regulation. These four are dynamically inter-related by competition, and by the different pricing systems at play in each of them, according to their own 'rules'. This variety of co-existing and even complementary modes of organised exchange demonstrates the complexity of the 'order' and integrative processes of coordination involved. Institutions and rules of the game create variety across economic space, rather than homogeneity under a single set of rules.

The final chapter addresses some key questions around one of the central aspects of contemporary capitalist economies, namely the production, distribution, appropriation and use of knowledge in the economy. McMeekin and Harvey argue that there is an unstable and historically shifting fault-line between public and private economies of knowledge. They interrogate the notion of the public economy and public good, insisting that there is a continuous process of innovation and institutional transformation, co-evolving with private property rights and forms of appropriation of knowledge. The processes of differentiation and interdependence between public and private economies at the heart of capitalist economic growth forcefully demonstrate the multi-modal character of capitalist political economies. It is impossible to understand market economic growth independently of non-market economic growth. Empirically, this chapter draws on research into the revolution of biological knowledge and technologies, and the emergence of new forms of knowledge, such as biological databases and bioinformatic software tools. Through the final decades of the twentieth century, there was a continuing flux between new public forms and markets for knowledge. At different times, the total privatisation of the human genome appeared a real possibility, as did the emergence of new public modes of production, distribution and appropriation of biological knowledge and soft instrumentation. As such, the chapter addresses key issues of both market and non-market institutions of economic activity.

New openings and future enquiries

'Putting markets in their place' within multi-modal capitalist political economies calls for a rebalancing of research and analysis of markets – acknowledging their intermediation as a critical phase, with specific dynamics, but disputing their centrality and autonomy. Clearly, this book presents analytical approaches that open up this perspective in a number of ways, and at the same time provides some empirical examples of types of market and non-market organisation of exchange and their interdependencies. We hope that our discussions will stimulate further research and expand the perspectives for understanding why markets are significant for their historically changing, phase-specific and circumscribed place in multi-modal capitalist political economies.

There are a number of directions opened up or promoted by our discussions of markets, and a few are highlighted here. Much further thought and research is suggested to explore different modes of instituting markets, particularly exploring the tension between regulation and political construction of markets. The regulation of sustainability across all product and service markets, and the institution of markets for renewable energies and materials, may well provide a fruitful empirical terrain, given the inadequacy of economically emergent markets to address the twin challenges of global climate change and petrochemical depletion. Secondly, a more thorough engagement with the new economic geography could undoubtedly develop further the shared concern to understand scale formation of markets, historically and comparatively. In spite of concepts of globalisation, very few markets, including financial markets, are characterised by an institutionally integrated, homogeneously regulated, global scale. Even with transnational firms, the scale of markets for many products is far from global: mobile phones are only mobile within certain geographic zones, because of geographic market-scale boundaries. Thirdly, although touched on in various ways by contributions of the book, an exploration of the historical dimension of market creation, growth, stabilisation and destruction, could develop understanding of the perpetual tension between institutionalisation and transformation. It is as important to understand why markets appear and disappear, as to why and how they work when they work. Fourthly, so much of the literature on markets is confined to studies of markets for particular goods or services, possibly as a hangover from the internalist view of markets. The research on supply and value chains, and on distributed innovation processes, all point to the need to understand the dynamics of market interdependency, both vertically and cross-sectorally. This is particularly the case when value chains are radically restructured with new casts of agents, and when sectoral divisions are transformed or blurred, resulting in new patterns of market interdependency. Finally, the widespread and significant non-market modes of systems of provision, and ongoing processes of differentiation and interdependence between market and non-market modes across a wide range of economic activities within contemporary capitalisms, suggest a research agenda for putting markets in a place very much within multi-modal economies.

Such an agenda for interdisciplinary research and discussion continues to recognise the imposing presence, variety and significance of market institutions in contemporary economies, but does so by situating them within a wider frame. Capitalism does not only depend on markets for its economic coordination, dynamism and growth, not even centrally so. Markets and states co-evolve, alongside, and in interdependence with, many dynamic non-market economic activities.

Notes

1 Alan Greenspan's testimony to a House of Representative's Committee: 'I made a mistake in presuming that the self-interest of organisations, specifically banks and others, was such that they were best capable of protecting their own shareholders . . . I had been going for 40 years with considerable evidence that it was working very well . . . The whole intellectual edifice, however, collapsed in the summer of last year.' *Financial Times*, 24 October 2008, front page.
2 For this reason, the approaches represented here invite engagement with the new economic geography (e.g. Coe, 2004; Coe and Hess, 2005; Dicken, 2007; Lee et al., 2004; Leyshon and Thrift, 1997).

3 Indeed, Samuelson (1958) argued that forms of state compulsion were necessary to establish serial exchanges between generations over an extended timescale without stable measurements of value, and that pension arrangements were 'logically impossible in a free market' based on reciprocal exchange. (1958: 477). See Harvey, 2005.

4 A quite frequent usage of embedded has the connotations of 'bedded down', 'sedimented', 'stabilised' or institutionally settled in. This can blur with the idea of undifferentiated from other social or cultural aspects, but not necessarily. In this usage, the US dollar is quite well 'embedded', the euro, much less so; and yet, even though politically instituted, they are both clearly strongly differentiated economic institutions, equally 'disembedded' in the other usage of the term.

5 'The anonymous market of neoclassical models is virtually nonexistent ... Transactions of all kinds are rife with social connections ... All I need to show here is that there is sufficient social overlay in economic transactions across firms (in the 'market' ...) to render dubious the assertion that complex market transactions approximate a Hobbesian state of nature' (Granovetter, 1985). The key ambiguity resides in the phrase 'social overlay in economic transactions', and ambiguity is found again in the phrase 'distinctively social dimensions in the most conventional economic practices' (Yakubovich et al., 2005).

6 Weber's grand ambition (Weber, 1978), and one that should be pursued, as Swedberg has argued.

7 The Wright system that prevailed owed 'its adoption ... from the complex manipulations and exercises of power by the leading industry actors, who mobilised support through their personal networks and domination of industry trade associations' (Yakubovich et al., 581–2).

8 A loose analogy is suggested between the 'closure' of social networks engaged in economic activity, and the closure of controlled experimentation in the natural sciences. The idea of social network closure, however, provides little basis for understanding what makes the economy economic, except in the image of the neo-classical conceptualisation of rational individual calculative agency (Callon, 1998, 2007).

9 'Fields contain collective actors who try to produce a system of domination in that space. To do so requires the production of a local culture that defines local social relations between actors' (Fligstein, 2001: 15).

10 For example, 'The field imposes on everyone, *though to varying degrees depending on their economic position and capacities*, not just the "reasonable" means, but also the ends, of economic action, that is to say: individual enrichment' (Bourdieu, 2005: 8). Or: 'The forces of the field orient the dominant towards strategies whose end is the perpetuation or reinforcement of their domination' (202). This conception of the field as a structure forcefield is linked to that of habitus, a much less strategic or political view of action than Fligstein's, where economic action is interpreted in terms of 'a calculation without a calculator and an intentional action without intention' (203).

11 The concept is notably less static when employed to cultural fields, notably the role of the avant garde and tradition, schools, and fashions, in the artistic world (Bourdieu, 1993). It is worth noting in this respect that here the focus is primarily on artistic and cultural *production*, rather than markets as fields of exchange, which is treated cursorily.

12 Bourdieu writes: 'Agents . . . in this case firms, create the space, that is to say, the economic field . . . It is the agents, . . . the firms, defined by the volume and structure of capital they possess, that determine the structure of the field that determines them, for example, the state of the forces exerted on the whole set of firms engaged in the production of similar goods' (Bourdieu, 2005: 193). And again: 'the structure of the field, defined by the unequal distribution of capital, weighs . . . on all the agents engaged in the field' (Bourdieu, 2005: 195).

13 Compare these two formulations: Fligstein: 'The basic insight is to consider the structure of exchange (i.e. markets) as a field. The social structure of a field is a cultural construction whereby dominant and dominated coexist under a set of understandings about what makes one set of organisations dominant' (Fligstein, 2001: 68). Bourdieu: 'The tendency for the structure to reproduce itself is immanent in the very structure of the field' (Bourdieu, 2005: 196).

14 'The theory of fields explicitly links the formation of markets and firms to the problem of stability and, in doing so, considers how markets become stable' (Fligstein, 2001: 19).

15 'Markets (and this includes almost all modern production markets) are mainly structured by sellers looking for buyers. A given market becomes a "stable market" (i.e. a field) when the product being exchanged has legitimacy with customers, and suppliers of the good or service are able to produce a status hierarchy in which the largest suppliers dominate the market and are able to reproduce themselves on a period-to-period basis' (Fligstein, 2001: 30–1).

16 Bourdieu speaks of consumers being subjected to a 'contract under duress', a duress symbolically maintained by the sales pitch of the perfect house for the perfect household.

17 Of course, consumers can be readily portrayed as constituting their own field – Bourdieu's work on distinction being a prime example. But this only serves to demonstrate the lack of economic ties between vertical fields and their theorisation.

18 See, for example, Nee's critique of North in accounting for the introduction of markets into China, and the inadequacy of a behavioural, incentive-based accounts of institutional change (Nee, 2005).

19 'Our task is to attempt to discover why a firm emerges at all in a specialised exchange economy. The price mechanism . . . might be superseded if the relationship which replaced it was desired for its own sake . . . The main reason why it is profitable to establish a firm would seem that there is a cost of using the price mechanism' (Coase, 1988: 37–8).

20 In this perspective, Williamson developed a more extended account of organisation and governance in a market context, still based on similar transaction cost foundations (Williamson, 1985).

21 The focus of much debate, according to Coase, was misplaced in its attention to circumstances of zero transaction costs, missing the main point of his argument concerning the emergence of public goods (Coase, 1988).

22 'The computational limitations of the individual are determined by the capacity of the mind to process, organise, and utilise information. From this capacity taken in conjunction with the uncertainties involved in deciphering the environment, rules and procedures evolve to simplify the process. The consequent institutional framework, by structuring human interaction, limits the choice set of the actors' (North, 1990: 25).

23 'The costliness of information is the key to the costs of transacting, which consist of the costs of measuring the valuable attributes of what is being exchanged and the costs of protecting rights and policing and enforcing agreements. These measurement and enforcement costs are the sources of *social, political and economic* institutions' (North, 1990: 27, my emphasis).

24 'The greater the specialisation and the number and variability of valuable attributes, the more weight must be put on reliable institutions that allow individuals to engage in contracting with a minimum of uncertainty about whether the terms of the contract can be realised' (North, 1990: 34).

25 It is intriguing to contrast the approaches of Fligstein with those of North in this respect. As we have seen, for the former markets are an extension of politics. For the latter, state institutions are partly an outcome of markets for politics, driven by incentives to reduce the costs of transacting politically: 'The efficiency of the political market is the key to the issue. If political transaction costs are low and the political actors have accurate models to guide them, then efficient property rights will result' (North, 1990: 52). North has a far more radically economic determinist account of institutions than that frequently ascribed to Marxism.

26 Wallis and North (1986) estimate that 45% of national income was represented by costs of transacting.

27 In his recent work particularly, he insists that the game is not a basic unit of analysis, or an appropriate metaphor for institutions, but a useful tool for analysing and theorising motivational effects, through the manipulation of incentive parameters and rules of the game. 'Institutions are not game-theoretic equilibria, games are not the basic unit of institutional analysis, and game theory does not provide us with a theory of institutions. Indeed, the key to advancing institutional analysis by using game theory is precisely to recognise the difference between game-theoretic equilibrium analysis and institutional analysis' (Greif, 2006: 19).

28 'If prescriptive rules of behaviour are to have an impact, individuals must be motivated to follow them. Motivation mediates between the environment and behaviour, whether the behaviour is rational, imitative, or habitual' (Greif, 2006: 8).

29 'One's behaviour is influence by another's past, present or future action only if a transaction is involved. Transacting renders a situation social' (Greif, 2006: C2, 19).

30 Previously published in *Revue d'Economie Industrielle*, 2002, 101, December, 11–30.

31 Previously published in *Journal des Economistes et des Etudes Humaines*, 2004, December, 14, 4, 87–114.

References

Block, F. 2003. 'Karl Polanyi and the Writing of the Great Transformation', *Theory and Society*, 32, 275–306.

Bourdieu, P. 1993. *The Field of Cultural Production. Essays on Art and Literature*. Polity Press. Cambridge.

Bourdieu, P. 2005. *The Social Structures of the Economy*. Polity Press. Cambridge.

Braudel, F. 1979. *The Wheels of Commerce: Volume II Civilisation and Capitalism*. Fontana Press. London.

Callon, M. (ed.) 1998. *The Laws of the Markets*. Blackwell/Sociological Review. Oxford.

Callon, M. 2007. 'What does it mean to say that economics is performative?' in McKenzie, D. Muniesa, F. and Siu, L. (eds), *Do Economists Make Markets? On the Performativity of Economics*. Princeton University Press. Princeton, NJ: 310–57.

Coase, R. H. 1960. 'The problem of social cost', *Journal of Law and Economics*, 5, 1–44.

Coase, R. H. 1988. *The Firm, the Market and the Law*. University of Chicago Press. Chicago.

Coe, N. M. 2004. 'The internationalisation/globalisation of retailing: towards an economic–geographical research agenda', *Environment and Planning A* 36, 9, 1571–94.

Coe, N. M. and Hess, M. 2005. 'The internationalization of retailing: implications for supply network restructuring in East Asia and Eastern Europe', *Journal of Economic Geography*, 5, 4, 449–73.

Dicken, P. 2007. *Global Shift. Mapping the Changing Contours of the World Economy* (5th edition). Sage. London.

Fligstein, N. 1996. 'Markets as politics: a political-cultural approach to market institutions', *American Sociological Review*, 61, 4, 656–73.

Fligstein, N. 2001. *The Architecture of Markets. An Economic Sociology of Twenty-first Century Capitalist Societies*. Princeton University Press. Princeton, NJ.

Fligstein, N. 2005. 'States, markets, and economic growth', in Nee, V. and Swedberg, R. (eds), *The Economic Sociology of Capitalism*. Princeton University Press. Princeton, NJ: 119–43.

Fligstein, N. and Mara-Drita, I. 1996. 'How to make a market: reflections on the attempt to create a Single Market in the European Union', *American Journal of Sociology*, 102, 1, 1–33.

Fligstein, N. and Sweet, A. S. 2002. 'Constructing polities and markets: an institutionalist account of European integration', *American Journal of Sociology*, 107, 5, 1206–43.

Glucksmann, M. 2009. 'Formations, connections and divisions of labour', *Sociology*, 43,5, special issue on sociology of work, 878–95.

Granovetter, M. 1973. 'The strength of weak ties', *American Journal of Sociology*, 78, 1360–80.

Granovetter, M. 1985. 'Economic action and social structure: the problem of embeddedness', *American Journal of Sociology*, 91, 3, 481–510.

Granovetter, M. 1992a. 'The sociological and economic approaches to labour market analysis: a social structural view', in Granovetter, M., and Swedberg, R. (eds), *The Sociology of Economic Life*. Westview Press. Oxford.

Granovetter, M. 1992b. 'Economic institutions as social constructions: a framework for analysis', *Acta Sociologica*, 35, 3–11.

Granovetter, M. and McGuire, P. 1998. 'The making of an industry: electricity in the United States', in Callon, M. (ed.), *The Laws of the Markets*. Blackwell. Oxford: 147–73.

Greif, A. 1994. 'Cultural beliefs and the organisation of society: a historical and theoretical reflection on collectivist and individualist societies', *Journal of Political Economy*, 102, 5, 912–50.

Greif, A. 2000. 'The fundamental problem of exchange: a research agenda in historical institutional analysis', *European Journal of Economic History*, 4, 251–84.

Greif, A. 2006. *Institutions and the Path to the Modern Economy: Lessons from Medieval Trade*. Cambridge University Press. Cambridge.

Greif, A., Milgrom, P. and Weingast, B. R. 1994. 'Coordination, commitment and enforcement: the case of the merchant guild', *Journal of Political Economy*, 102, 4, 745–76.

Harvey, M. 2005. 'Pensions, Retirement and the Historical Formation of Rights over Resources', *CRIC Discussion Paper*, 69. CRIC. Manchester.

Harvey, M. 2007. 'Instituting economic processes in society', in Harvey, M., Ramlogan, R. and Randles, S. (eds), *Karl Polanyi: New Perspectives on the Place of the Economy in Society*. Manchester University Press. Manchester.

Harvey, M., Randles, S. and Ramlogan, R. 2007. 'Working with and beyond Polanyian perspectives', in Harvey, M., Ramlogan, R. and Randles, S. (eds), *Karl Polanyi: New Perspectives on the Place of the Economy in Society*. Manchester University Press. Manchester.

Hopkins, T. K. 1957. 'Sociology and the substantive view of the economy', in Polanyi, K., Armstrong, C. M. and Pearson, H. W. (eds), *Trade and Market in the Early Empires*. Free Press. New York.

Knorr Cetina, K. and Preda, A. 2005. *The Sociology of Financial Markets*. Oxford University Press. Oxford.

Krippner, G. 2001. 'The elusive market: embeddedness and the paradigm of economic sociology', *Theory and Society*, 30, 775–810.

Krugman, P. 2008. *The Return of Depression Economics and the Crisis of 2008*. Penguin. London.

Lee, R., Leyshon, A., Aldridge, T., Tooke, J., Williams, C. and Thrift, N. 2004. 'Making histories and geographies? Constructing local circuits of value', *Society and Space*, 22, 595–617.

Leyshon, A. and Thrift, N. 1997. *Money/Space. Geographies of Monetary Transformation*. Routledge. London.

Lie, J. 1991. 'Embedding Polanyi's market society', *Sociological Perspectives*, 34, 2, 219–35.

Lie, J. 1992. 'The concept of mode of exchange', *American Sociological Review*, 57, 4, 508–23.

McKenzie, D. 2006. *An Engine not a Camera: How Financial Models Shape Markets*. MIT Press. Cambridge, MA.

McKenzie, D. 2007. 'Is economics performative? Option theory and the construction of derivatives markets', in McKenzie, D., Muniesa, F. and Siu, L. (eds), *Do Economists Make Markets? On the Performativity of Economics*. Princeton University Press. Princeton, NJ: 54–86.

McKenzie, D., Muniesa, F. and Siu, L. 2007. *Do Economists Make Markets? On the Performativity of Economics*. Princeton University Press. Princeton, NJ.

Nee, V. 2005. 'Organisational dynamics of institutional change: politicised capitalism in China', in Nee, V. and Swedberg, R. (eds), *The Economic Sociology of Capitalism*. Princeton University Press. Princeton, NJ: 53–74.

Nee, V. and Ingram, P. 1998. 'Embeddedness and beyond: institutions, exchange and social structure', in Brinton, M. and Nee, V. (eds), *The New Institutionalism in Sociology*. Russell Sage Foundation. New York.

Nelson, R. R. (ed.) 2005. *The Limits of Market Organisation*. Russell Sage Foundation. New York.

Nelson, R. R. 2008. 'What enables rapid economic progress? What are the needed institutions?' *Research Policy*, 37, 1, 1–11.

Nelson, R., and Sampat, B. 2001. 'Making sense of institutions as a factor shaping economic performance', *Journal of Economic Behaviour and Organization*, 44, 31–54.

North, D. C. 1990. *Institutions, Institutional Change and Economic Performance*. Cambridge University Press, Cambridge.

North, D. C. 2005a. 'Capitalism and economic growth', in Nee, V. and Swedberg, R. (eds), *The Economic Sociology of Capitalism*. Princeton University Press. Princeton, NJ: 41–52.

North, D. C. 2005b. *Understanding the Process of Economic Change*. Princeton University Press. Princeton, NJ.

Polanyi, K. 1944. *The Great Transformation. The Political and Economic Origins of our Time*. Beacon Press. Boston, MA.

Polanyi, K. 1957. 'The economy as instituted process', in Polanyi, K., Arensberg, C. M. and Pearson, H. W. (eds), *Trade and Market in the Early Empires*. The Free Press. New York.

Polanyi, K. 1968. *Primitive, Archaic and Modern Economies. Essays of Karl Polanyi*. Anchor Books, Doubleday. New York.

Samuelson, P. A. 1958. 'An exact consumption-loan model of interest with or without the contrivance of money', *Journal of Political Economy*, 66, 6, 467–82.

Stern, N. 2007. *The Economics of Climate Change*. UK Cabinet Office, www.hm-treasury.gov.uk.

Swedberg, R. 1994. 'Markets as social structures', in Smelser, N. J. and Swedberg, R. (eds), *The Handbook of Economic Sociology*. Princeton University Press. Princeton, NJ: 255–82.

Swedberg, R. 2003. *Principles of Economic Sociology*. Princeton University Press. Princeton, NJ.

Swedberg, R. 2005. 'The economic sociology of capitalism: an introduction and agenda', in Nee, V. and Swedberg, R. (eds), *The Economic Sociology of Capitalism*. Princeton University Press. Princeton, NJ: 3–40.

Urry, J. 2009. 'The Great Crash of 2008: pouring oil on troubled waters', www.lancs.ac.uk/fass/doc_library/sociology/Urry_the_great_crash.pdf

Wallis, J. J. and North, D. C. 1986. 'Measuring the transaction sector in the American economy, 1870–1970', in Engerman, S. L. and Gallman, R. E. (eds), *Long-Term Factors in American Economic Growth*. University of Chicago Press. Chicago, IL: 95–148.

Weber, M. 1978. *Economy and Society: An Outline of Interpretive Sociology*. Roth, G. and Wittich, C. (eds). University of California Press. Berkeley.

Williamson, O. E. 1985. *The Economic Institutions of Capitalism*. Free Press. New York.

Wolff, E. 2004. 'The unravelling of the American Pension System, 1983–2004'. Paper to the New School University of New York Conference, September

9–11, 'Pension Fund Capitalism and the Crisis of Old-Age Security in the United States'.

Yakubovich, V., Granovetter, M. and McGuire, P. 2005. 'Electric charges: the social construction of the rate systems', *Theory and Society*, 34, 579–612.

Zukin, S. and DiMaggio, P. 1990. *Structures of Capital: The Social Organisation of the Economy*. Cambridge University Press. Cambridge.

2

The market, institutions and transactions

Benjamin Coriat and Olivier Weinstein

Introduction

For a long time, the category of the market, like that of the firm, has occupied a highly paradoxical position in economic theory. Economists have placed both of these concepts at the heart of their constructions: the firm because it is the central agent of production, and the market because it constitutes the essential mode of coordination between agents – often, indeed, the only one considered. And yet these categories are among the least well-studied, and they suffer from the attribution of the most simplistic and unrealistic hypotheses.

In standard theory, the firm is reduced to a simple combination of infinitely malleable factors, entirely driven by its environment. Only recently have certain schools started to open up the 'black box' of the firm to explore its contents. As for the market, dominant theories treat it as a 'space where consumers and suppliers meet', governed by mechanisms which lead to the establishment of so-called 'equilibrium' prices, corresponding to firms' production costs, and where profits are nil.

Surprising though it may seem, these charming fictions, which have persisted despite the important works produced by historians and sociologists, have been accepted by many economists as points of reference. Again, it is only recently, and particularly on the basis of the work accomplished by the institutionalist schools, that economists have started seriously to explore the concept of market. This exploration has been rendered all the more necessary by the marketisation of an ever-growing number of spheres of human activity, a trend which demonstrates the complexity of the processes of market construction and the many and varied arrangements which enable them to exist and operate.

Within this context, our aim in the present chapter is to draw on recent works on this subject to give an ordered view of the basic concepts needed to understand the market, from an institutionalist perspective.

The chapter is divided into two parts. In the first section, we shall explore the contributions and limits of 'individualist' approaches, in particular the schools which define themselves as 'contractual' or neo-institutionalist and which, following on from the works of Coase, have recently made important progress.

We shall explore not only the contributions which neo-institutionalist approaches have made in defining the conditions of existence of a market, but also the dead ends to which these approaches lead. We believe that they pass in silence over many of the essential questions which must be tackled if we are to come to a fuller definition and understanding of the concept of market and its operating conditions.

In the second section, while making use of some of the elements of analysis produced by the neo-institutionalist approaches, we set out to explore some of the paths of research they have neglected, to start laying what should, in our opinion, constitute the foundations of a 'complete' and authentic institutional approach to markets.

1. Institutions, property rights and markets: the sense and insensibility of neo-institutionalist approaches

We should start this section by making two things clear. Firstly, we are proposing a re-reading of the works inspired by new institutionalist economics (NIE),[1] not a simple presentation of the theses put forward by the different authors concerned. Secondly, and this is inseparable from the first point, giving it meaning and consistency, this re-reading is also a reconstruction and interpretation of the theses involved, drawing on the works and results of approaches derived from classic institutionalism (particularly Commons), which diverge, in part, from the neo-institutionalist corpus and theses being examined here. By confronting and comparing these two movements, we hope to shed an entirely new light on the theses involved.

To get this investigation under way, we must start by presenting the hypothesis of the 'double nature of institutions'. This proposition is central to our analysis. We believe that it provides the key to a critical appraisal of the approaches now described as neo-institutional; approaches which, we argue, a complete analysis of markets should both incorporate and surpass.

The double nature of institutions[2]
To understand what an institution is, we could do worse than start with North, who defined institutions as 'the rules of the game in a society or more formally . . . the humanly devised constraints that shape human interactions' (North, 1990: 3). Taken in this sense, institutions should be considered as the series of institutional constraints under which agents operate and coordinate with each other.[3] These institutions – or 'rules of the game', as North calls them – are necessary and therefore accepted by agents, to

the extent that they create regularities, thus reducing uncertainty and enabling agents to adopt more efficient behaviour. Today, this representation of institutions and their role appears to be well accepted by all the schools of thought within the institutionalist approach, even if they differ on other points.

However, we believe that this representation is too one-dimensional; it needs to be completed. To this end, it should be noted that once they are established, the 'rules', or more precisely the 'systems of rules' imposed by institutions, do more than simply function as 'constraints' imposed on agents. Equally important is the role they play as 'resources' that can be mobilised by agents, to be used in the formulation and deployment of the strategies adopted to achieve their objectives.

On this point, it can be observed that this approach, which emphasises the 'public good' dimension of institutions, is perfectly in tune with some of the attributes used by Commons to characterise institutions. For Commons, institutions should be defined as 'collective action in control, liberation and expansion of individual action'. And collective action

> is more than control of individual action – it is, by the very act of control . . . a liberation of individual action from coercion, duress, discrimination, or unfair competition, by means of restraints placed on other individuals. . . . And collective action is more than restraint and liberation of individual action – it is expansion of the will of the individual far beyond what he can do by his own puny acts. (Commons, 1990: 73)

We can go even further along the path suggested by this quote from Commons, and observe that, far from simply constituting a system of rules and constraints that facilitate human action in *existing* domains, there is at least one category of institutions which *give rise to and create (in a manner of speaking) entirely new fields of activity*. By establishing new environments and regulatory frameworks, certain institutions open up new domains of action, in which individuals and groups can deploy their initiative and exercise their capabilities. This quality of certain institutions was suggested by Searle (1995), who proposed a distinction between regulatory rules and constitutive rules. According to this approach, rules of the first type are established to help regulate existing activities, which can, in any case, function even in the absence of the newly established rules. A clear distinction must be made between these rules and those which *create* new fields of activity. These 'constitutive' rules give rise to new statuses, new positions and new behaviour. Many institutions which play key roles in the economic sphere must be analysed from this perspective. For example – and we shall explore this point in detail later (see section 2) – it is essential to differentiate between the institutions at the origin of the market, which found its very *existence*, and those institutions which enable and ensure the *functioning* of the market. One illustration of this type of institution and the rules they establish can be seen in the role played by certain scientific institutions.

Thus, the establishment of universities as publicly financed bodies, or again the creation of big public research laboratories, opened up a new 'game' for players involved in the production of innovation (and especially firms): the aim of this game is to appropriate, through competitive means, the 'resources' (engineers, researchers, products of discoveries and new knowledge) created by these new institutions.

On the basis of this definition, institutions can be categorised in several different ways. In this chapter, we have chosen to adopt the classification proposed by Aoki (2000), because it places markets and their definition at the heart of the analysis. In one of his recent works, Aoki proposed that institutions should be divided into four large groups or series:

1. money and the market
2. the legal and political framework of the State and its apparatuses
3. contracts and organisations (with private status),[4]
4. social norms and shared beliefs. (Aoki, 2000: 161)

By exploring this categorisation in greater detail, we can begin to grasp the concept of market.

The market as the central institution of capitalism and the need for complementary institutions

In our economies, often defined as 'market economies' – based on a very high level of task specialisation and division of labour – one of the many institutions needed to ensure the widespread exchange of goods and services calls for particular attention. This specific institution is the market itself. The market is the central operator through which society as such reproduces itself, because it is through market mechanisms (including the use of money) that the exchange of goods and services is made possible. In this sense, the market must be considered one of the central institutions, if not the institution *par excellence*, of so-called modern economies.

But if the market is to fulfil this role as central operator, then *the property rights governing all the goods subject to exchange must be perfectly defined, and agents must recognise and accept the legitimacy of these definitions*. As Aoki observed: 'For this institution [the market] to evolve and function, property rights to economic assets need to be clearly defined and enforced' (2000: 171). Property rights theorists emphasise – quite rightly, we believe – the fact that property rights, defined as 'socially enforced rights to select uses of an economic good' (Alchian, 1987) are of an institutional nature. As Alchian pointed out, on the subject of private property rights: 'its strength is measured by its probability and costs of enforcement, which depend on the government, informal social actions, and prevailing ethical norms' (1987: 1031). Thus, a series of institutional arrangements concerning the definition of property rights and the conditions of their recognition by agents are fundamental components of market economies.

For our authors, this involves the establishment of a set of arrangements whose purpose is to guarantee that these rights are themselves respected, which presupposes the introduction of what Aoki calls a 'third party'. For Alchian, this is the 'government'; for Aoki it is 'the legal and political structures of the state'. This third party is made up of a set of political and administrative bodies (including, in particular, the police and the judiciary) responsible for enforcing property rights and, more generally, the 'rules of the game' governing their exchange.

When all these conditions are satisfied (a 'complete' definition of property rights and the conditions of their exchange and transfer between agents, a third party guaranteeing the effectiveness of transactions), the economy can be organised on the basis of a set of interdependent markets. We are then in something very similar to the Walrasian universe. Under these conditions (which are totally unrealistic and unrealisable, as we shall see below), a certain number of theorems on the efficiency of market allocations can be established, and these make it possible to reach what is called a situation of equilibrium.

However, if property rights for products have not or *cannot be* completely defined and established – in other words, if imperfections or situations of 'market failure' or 'missing markets' exist – then the need arises for complementary institutions, the purpose of which is to go beyond or transcend the imperfections of the market. According to the NIE approaches, two different sets of causes are responsible for the formation of these new institutions required for the good functioning of markets.

Firstly, the existence of organisations has been founded on and justified by the cost of bargaining transactions. This dimension was highlighted long ago by Coase (1937), before being further developed by the neo-institutionalist school. It is used to explain the emergence and affirmation of alternative (to the market) means of coordination between agents, especially through the formation of hierarchies and organisations. These organisations can and should be considered as *institutional constructions*. As Aoki observed, they constitute 'humanly-devised constraints', in that the coordination which they establish – particularly through the key relation of authority – is socially determined. The relation of authority draws its essential characteristics from the nature of the work contracts prevailing in society. All the attributes of the relation of authority – the way in which it is exercised, its field of application and the boundaries it cannot cross – are of an institutional and social nature (Coriat and Weinstein, 2002). In this way, organisations, as alternative modes of coordination between agents, act as institutions that are 'complementary' to the market, playing a decisive role in the mechanisms of production and allocation of resources.

Secondly, and on this point neo-classical theory (including its most standard versions) is absolutely explicit, various types of indivisibility and externality, linked to the 'collective good' nature of many goods and services, can be found in many domains of market coordination. In all these cases, the system of property rights cannot be completely defined or, as Arrow (1962) first observed, can only be defined at a prohibitive cost to the efficiency of the system. Efficient markets (of the Walrasian type) cannot, therefore, be envisaged.[5] One consequence of this fact is that a series of 'additional' institutional arrangements (additional to those which ensure the exchange of property rights in the market) is required. As opposed to the 'first order' arrangements required to ensure the establishment of markets (constituted by systems of property rights), we shall refer to these additional arrangements as 'second order' ones.

We can even go one step further, and observe that these second-order arrangements belong to two separate 'classes', although the neo-institutionalists do not make this distinction.

1. In certain cases, the market cannot function without certain 'additional' rules of the game, imposed by the visible hand of regulators. This is the case for the big network markets (communications, electricity, rail transport, etc.), for example, where specific rules must be laid down to ensure that agents can continue to carry out the transactions necessary to the pursuit of their activities without the risk of a breakdown in supplies. It is also the case for the markets governing the production and exploitation of inventions. In this case, specific laws regulating the allocation of 'patents', i.e. temporary monopolies granted to firms at the source of inventions, are needed to make up for the market shortcomings inherent to this type of activity. Here, the system of intellectual property rights gives rise to an 'incentive structure', intended to transcend the contradiction generated by the indivisibility of information as a good (Arrow, 1962; Nelson, 1959), and thus avoid the risk of sustained under-investment by firms in research.

2. In other cases, the incentive structures created by institutional arrangements, like the *ad hoc* regulations issued by agencies, are incapable, on their own, of making up for the shortcomings of the market. Other types of institution are then required, the function of which is not only to specify the regulatory and legal framework of transactions, but also and above all to provide agents with 'tangible' resources which the market alone is incapable of providing in sufficient quantities to ensure the successful reproduction of society. A good example of this is basic research, for the production of which specific institutions must be created (universities, public research laboratories, etc.). These types of institution are the only solution that has been found to provide society with a sufficient quantity of the intellectual resources needed for its reproduction, by overcoming the market failures inherent to the production of these goods (Arrow, 1962).

Ultimately, all these phenomena render 'pure' markets (in other words, markets without 'complementary' and 'additional' institutional constructions) very mediocre tools of coordination. On their own, if indeed this expression has any meaning, they are totally incapable of ensuring the production and allocation of the resources needed for the reproduction of society.

We can follow this line of thought further, by investigating the nature and characteristics of the institutions needed for the good functioning of markets.

Types and structures of institutional arrangements 'complementary' to the market

We can bring together the points developed above, concerning the institutions needed to 'complete' the functioning of the market, and formulate them in three propositions.

Firstly, a first series of institutions is constituted of laws, regulations, contracts, and so forth. In brief, in the situation where it is impossible completely to define the type of property rights system required for the efficient functioning of market allocations, their role consists in introducing complementary 'rules of the game' to make up for the shortcomings of the market. Deficient market allocations are, as it were, 'corrected' by the specific rules and regulations introduced in the fields concerned.

As we have argued elsewhere (see Coriat and Weinstein, 2002), these rules and regulations can be divided into two types:

1. those of universal scope and vocation, situated at a level above the agents, as is the case with the system of laws issued by the political authorities, the most significant illustration here being the system of rights and obligations laid down by the Constitution ('the legal system', to paraphrase Coase). These laws or systems of laws usually have a 'national' basis and field of application; and
2. those which are the result of contracts and agreements concluded between agents or particular groups who have agreed to place their interactions under the aegis of certain rules which they undertake to respect. We have designated the first class of institutions as 'type 1' and the second as 'type 2' (Coriat and Weinstein, 2002).

One of the key questions in the analysis of institutions and their evolution concerns the ways in which these two types of rules interact. Here, marked differences can be observed, according to national traditions.[6] We believe that in every case (from the 'hierarchical' French model to the more 'horizontal' models close to common law traditions), the 'rules of the game' which eventually become established generally possess two characteristics:

1. they are the result of *compromises* between the demands of different agents with divergent interests and objectives; and
2. they are always guaranteed (at least for a given period of time) by a 'third party', which maintains the regularities enabling agents to interact at a tolerable level of costs for the system of exchange.

So, even in the case of systems based on common law, responsibility for a change in the basic rules is generally taken by the political organs of the State. In the field of innovation economics, the passing of the Bayh–Dole Act in the USA provides a good example of this point of view. A change as profound as that introduced by this Act (authorising the granting of patents on products of publicly funded research and the transfer of these same patents to private firms in the form of exclusive licences) could never have been introduced without prior political deliberation.[7]

Secondly, although this point is not made in the neo-institutionalist analyses, it is worth noting that in many cases a second class of institutions is required. The purpose of these institutions is to provide individual agents not only with rules of behaviour, *but also with 'real' and 'tangible' financial and/or non-financial resources*. This is necessary to the extent that, as we have already observed, the simple 'adding-on' of *ad hoc* institutional rules is often insufficient, on its own, to overcome the shortcomings of the market and the free-rider behaviour to which they give rise. Some non-market bodies in charge of the production of resources are required, if the economy is to operate 'not too far from the optimum' (Arrow, 1962). These institutions appear when goods have a collective nature, and when externalities and indivisibilities lie at the heart of the transaction. This is the case for basic research, education, justice, certain health and security services, defence, and so forth. In most cases, these institutions bring into play State apparatuses, and the State thus becomes the main operator. These resources are then delivered in the form of 'public services' by particular bodies, whether or not in liaison with market organisations participating in the delivery of the said services. But it may also happen that private agents and organisations 'in the market' decide to associate some of their assets to produce (and share out among themselves) certain of these resources, following non-market principles (in accordance with agreements, contracts or conventions concluded between themselves). This is the case for 'clubs' formed to make use of private security services, for example. It is also the case, in another field entirely, for research consortiums formed between firms and institutions to share the costs of a given investment.

Finally, we propose that the economic institutions required for the functioning of market economies can be defined as the series of institutional constructs designed to provide agents with the resources and rules of the game necessary to their interactions.

Figure 2.1 presents the overall structure and the main links between the different types of institution needed for the functioning of markets, following our interpretation of neo-institutional contributions to the question.

The following comments may help to clarify Figure 2.1.

1. The horizontal and vertical rectangles ('Systems of property rights', 'Third party') represent what should be considered, according to the neo-institutionalists, as 'first-order' institutions. They form the cornerstone on

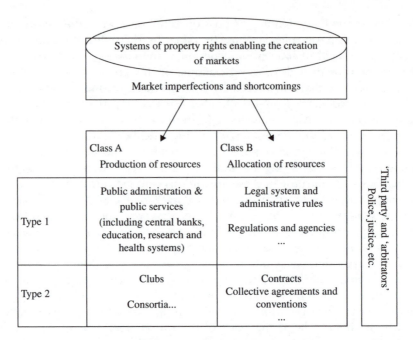

Figure 2.1 Institutions and markets in the neo-institutionalist approach: summary and typology

which market economies are constructed, again according to the neo-institutionalists. The other rectangles (1A, 1B, 2A, 2B) then represent the 'second-order' institutions responsible for providing markets with the 'additional' or 'complementary' resources they need in order to operate.

2. Rectangle 1A deserves special attention. Here, we have the heaviest institutions and institutional systems. They deal with subjects such as health, education and security – or, to put it another way, fields which lie within the sphere of inter-generational reproduction, where the market displays structural shortcomings.[8] This also explains why the institutions which operate here are not only responsible for the allocation of resources, but also and equally for the production of resources made available to agents. Despite their vital importance, little space has been devoted to them in neo-institutionalist literature, which focuses more on institutions of the type 1B, those which deal not with the production but with the *allocation* of resources.

As the conclusion to this section, we shall attempt briefly to characterise the limits of these approaches, the key theses of which we have just examined. Although these approaches place the question of property rights at the heart of the existence of markets, one of the central characteristics of the constructions proposed is that they consider the market as the 'primary', almost natural form of coordination between individuals. Other forms of coordination are derived from it, either generated by its existence or made necessary by the defects in its functioning. This view was succinctly expressed by Williamson when he said 'in the beginning was the market' (Williamson, 1986). Organisations and institutions are then seen as a response to the failures and 'imperfections' of markets, whose existence, once a system of property rights on products has been established, no longer seems to be in any doubt. And this was the perspective adopted by Coase (1937), as we have already remarked, when he presented the firm as being firstly a response to the 'costs of the price system'.[9]

We believe that this kind of approach, although it certainly sheds useful light on the types of institution 'surrounding' the market, has one crucial failing: *it overlooks the question of the very 'nature' of transactions and markets*. Now, well beyond the simple definition of property rights (the focus of attention in new institutional economics), 'markets' cannot operate and repeated transactions between agents cannot occur without a complex series of arrangements which both brings them into existence and guarantees their long-term viability.

In the hope of overcoming these failings, the second part of our chapter will be devoted to an analysis of the systems and arrangements which found market transactions and make them possible.

2. Transactions, exchanges and markets: towards new foundations

We believe that the market cannot be treated as a 'natural' form – the spontaneous product of interactions between 'free' individuals – but must be considered as an institutional construction. This opens up a vast field of reflection to grasp and describe the forces and mechanisms which underlie and organise this construction. Here, we follow the path opened up by Coase (1988), who argued that the market and the firm should no longer be considered as 'alternative' modes of coordination but as complementary institutions 'which, together, constitute the structure of the economic system',[10] markets being 'the institutions that exist to facilitate exchange' (Coase, 1988: 7). As we mean to show in this section, taking these propositions seriously means investigating more deeply (than the neo-institutionalist approaches examined above) the question of what *transactions* and *relations of exchange* actually are, especially when they operate in a framework as complex as that of the economic systems of generalised exchanges which characterise modern economies.

So what are the significance and implications of the decision to consider markets as institutions? To tackle this question, we shall have to confront two problems, which, though connected, must be separated on an analytical level:

1. the need to distinguish between exchange (or bargaining transaction) and market; and

2. the need to situate markets as specific institutional forms within the capitalist economic systems in which they operate today.

The concept of bargaining transaction and its foundations

First of all, let us state precisely what we mean by bargaining transaction. Here, Commons provides a good starting point, with the distinction he makes between the standard view of exchange as the physical transfer of a good, and what he calls *transaction*, meaning the legal transfer of ownership (Commons, 1990: 50). He goes on to specify that a transaction, defined in this way, constitutes a transfer of the future property rights on certain objects, a transfer which takes place after negotiation between the parties involved, following a certain number of rules, which constitute the institutional basis of the transaction. A *bargaining* transaction, which is one particular form of transaction, is also characterised by what we can describe as an equality in the positions and desires of the parties involved (especially when compared with the 'managerial' transaction, which is based on the subordination of one party to the other) (Commons, 1990).

So, the realisation of bargaining transactions presupposes that:

1. agents possess economic goods which they can exchange with each other – they enjoy private, socially recognised rights over these goods; and
2. that they have the possibility *not to* trade, in other words to choose whether or not to alienate the goods they possess,[11] which also implies that a relation of exchange between individuals (or organisations) can come to an end – it does not create any irreversible dependency between the parties.

Furthermore, for what interests us in this chapter, it must be noted that a bargaining transaction is also, necessarily, a *monetary* transaction. This aspect is, of course, essential: coordination 'through prices' (often argued to be constituent of market coordination) cannot be anything other than coordination through money. So at the heart of a bargaining transaction lies the question of the conditions of the determination, according to variable terms and conditions, of the price or, more generally, *the monetary compensation for the transfer of certain rights*; price, in the standard economic representation of the market, being no more than one simple, particular example.

Having said this, we must immediately observe that the concept of bargaining transaction, as we have defined it here, covers very diverse types of relation. In particular, it goes well beyond the standard view of a market exchange, considered as an isolated relation involving the instant transfer of a good between the parties involved, a conception that can seen just as clearly in the Walrasian vision of the market as in the 'classic contract' by which Williamson characterises it.

We shall now attempt to define more precisely the institutional conditions of a bargaining transaction.

Neo-institutionalist analysis highlights two basic conditions.

1. Perfectly defined property rights must exist; they must be accepted and respected by the agents.
2. There must be a set of mechanisms to ensure that parties respect the contractual commitments on which the exchange is based.

In this approach, the question arises of what it is, exactly, which ensures that the parties respect their commitments (delivery of an object or service corresponding to the undertakings, payment) and that an 'honest trade' can take place. In the neo-institutionalist view, the answer lies in the definition of an 'exchange governance mechanism' or, in the words of Aoki, a 'contract enforcement mechanism' (Aoki, 2000: 61). This view has the advantage of bringing to prominence a wide diversity in the methods of exchange governance, in terms of the rules and types of sanction governing a type of transaction, and a wide variety in the conditions of enforcement and in the nature of the agents or bodies responsible for enforcement.[12] This representation may be productive, but it appears to us to have several shortcomings.

Firstly, it assumes that the object of the transaction is pre-defined. But the first step in a bargaining transaction consists in the *definition and delimitation of the object of exchange*. This precedes (in the sense that it conditions) the specification of the parties' rights over the object and the specification of the monetary compensation. In the case of simple exchanges, concerning well-defined objects or services (or a range of objects or services), this aspect (the delimitation of the object of exchange) can probably be ignored, as it is in most market theory. But, for a certain number of transactions, definition of the object of exchange cannot be taken for granted, *it must be constructed*, and this construction constitutes one of the major stakes in the transaction. As Chamberlin (1953) demonstrated, in most markets, *the product is an economic variable*, in the same way as the price is. This leads to exploration of the specificity of 'markets of quality' (Karpic, 2002). But there is more: today, in many markets, the exchange no longer involves well-defined products, but *complexes of rights and obligations*, defined by contracts, which may be either standard or personalised but which are most often incomplete. As Coase (1992: 717) observed: 'what are exchanged in a market are not, as economists often assume, physical entities, but the rights to perform particular actions'. The labour market, insofar as it includes a relation of submission or authority, is the most complete example of this type of market, but the same property (the object of exchange being a complex of rights and obligations) can be found in many other configurations of exchange: rental contracts, insurance contracts, and so on. We can add that the question of the construction of the object of exchange is of particular importance in the complex market systems that exist today, especially when it involves the development of new market spaces, resulting either from the emergence of new activities or from the marketisation of activities previously run by other forms of organisation. One of the key questions is then the construction of 'composite' objects adapted to the constraints of market circulation and to the objectives of certain players, the choice of the character of these objects, and the choice, within a set of inter-connected activities, of the places where the bargaining transactions will be carried out. The privatisation and opening up to competition of many public services which we have witnessed since the late 1980s provide numerous illustrations of the very difficult question of the 'perimeters' involved in the marketisation of these services. In the railways, for example, should the infrastructures be privatised and opened up to competition, or not? If the answer is yes, then under what conditions? And how should the 'price' of access to infrastructures be fixed, for companies whose activity is limited to the provision of services? In quite another domain, the patentability of human genes, which has given rise to the formation of a veritable market of scientific knowledge (through the sale of licences on these gene patents), has provoked a fierce debate, with crucial issues at stake. By making genes, or even partial gene sequences, the object of bargaining transactions, we may have created a market which threatens to impede the very production of knowledge itself.[13]

So, as these examples drawn from the formation of new markets suggest, the construction of the exchange is in fact a highly complex and risky process, involving far more than the simple identification of suppliers and consumers. The very objects of the exchange need to be defined. In passing, it is worth noting that the constructions required bring into play not only the social division of labour, but also the *conditions of the organisation of production*. We shall come back to this point later.

A second shortcoming of the neo-institutionalist approaches derives from the fact that they focus on *bilateral* contractual exchanges, and thus on the conditions of realisation of a particular given transaction. This has several consequences. Firstly, it fails to deal (explicitly, at least) with the question of the functioning *of a veritable market*, in other words the *conditions of coherence and durability of a set of transactions* between a moving set of agents. Investigating the market as an institution means investigating it as a *durable system* bringing into play a whole multiplicity of players (not constituted simply of suppliers and consumers) and not (as the neo-institutionalist approaches tacitly assume) as a set of bilateral relations.

It is a mistake, for several reasons, to believe that transactions can be understood by analysing them in isolation, as bilateral relations. As Commons wrote (1990, 1995), every bargaining transaction involves at least four parties (the buyer and the seller, of course, but also the other buyers and sellers with whom they could transact). But there is more: the involvement of money means that the conditions of each transaction are dependent on the conditions of realisation of the other monetary transactions. In other words, each bargaining transaction can only find its full significance when situated within the bargaining system as a whole. So, in a certain manner, each exchange is built on the whole institutional system which underpins the bargaining system. This aspect is all the more important when bargaining relations occupy an important position in the economic system, which is obviously the case in today's society.

Each transaction must therefore be situated within a broader framework, and firstly within the market. The concept of market remains to be defined and delimited more completely, by giving their full importance to the 'institutional arrangements' which make exchange possible and on which, ultimately, exchange is founded. Then, we must situate these market transactions within the more global context of the system of production and exchange in which they operate.

The permissive conditions of the transaction: the founding role of the institutional arrangements of markets

In what follows, we intend to develop the idea that modes of market organisation should themselves be considered as 'institutions' per se, appearing as a set of constraints and opportunities open to the initiative of the agents, as the possible parties to the exchange.

The literature of the new institutional economics provides a particular perspective on this question, by exploring how different, alternative modes of coordination between agents (or different modes of governance) can become established, with the market, or different forms of market, representing one specific mode of coordination. However, as we have underlined, these approaches only take certain aspects of the market into consideration, without really considering *markets* as such. But it is important to make a clear distinction between the definition, given above, of a bargaining transaction and the definition of what is, strictly speaking, a market. Of course, it is useful, following Commons once again,[14] to consider the transaction, and more precisely the bargaining transaction, *as the primary unit of analysis*. From this perspective, it must then be noted that if the realisation of 'transactions' implies a more or less sophisticated institutional infrastructure, it does *not* necessarily presuppose the existence of a precisely defined and organised market (Harvey and Randle, 2002). To speak of a *market* entails going beyond a simple consideration of the conditions of a bargaining transaction: a market is based on a particular constitution, insofar as that the existence of a market presupposes the possibility of aggregating different transactions, and treating them as elements of the same entity. Now, taking these considerations into account, how can we define a market?

There are two possible approaches.

1. The first approach is that adopted by standard microeconomic theory. This corresponds to the Walrasian view of the market. It defines a market as an abstract space in which *a given product* is exchanged, and in which *a price* is formed. Thus, perfectly identical transactions take place, following identical conditions and involving identical prod-

ucts. This view presupposes the existence of a rigid order which strictly imposes the characteristics of each transaction, including the characteristics of the products or provision of services. A priori, it eliminates any singularity or individualisation of transactions. This representation corresponds to a very specific conception of the market, involving the total anonymity of transactions and the absence of any direct, personalised relation between the parties involved. Looked at more closely, this view appears to be almost completely opposed to the contractual view that now predominates. It is not simply in contradiction to the characteristics of most markets as they can be observed today – even when products display a high level of standardisation – it is also in contradiction to any conception of markets as socially constructed institutional realities. By considering, like Coase (1988: 7), that 'markets are institutions which exist to facilitate exchange', we can say that ultimately, what we have here is not a theory of markets in any strict sense of the term, but rather a theory of exchange *without* markets.

2. If we go against the assumptions of the Walrasian approach, and take bargaining transactions as our point of departure, and if we admit diversity in the forms of transactions and products, and even more if we consider – along the lines of the view developed by Chamberlin[15] – that the *individualisation of transactions and products is one of the major dimensions of the competitive game*, then the concept of market becomes much more difficult to pin down. Doubtless, we could try to stretch the conception described above (as Chamberlin himself appears to do), by defining a market not on the basis of one sole good by on the basis of a set of highly substitutable goods with similar 'characteristics'. This is simply an attempt to save the above conception, in a context where it has become much more unsuitable, especially if we no longer take the set of products as a given. And we continue, as in the Walrasian approach, to leave the precise conditions under which transactions take place totally in the dark. We therefore remain within a 'theory of exchange without markets'.

For all these reasons, it appears that we can only define and identify organised markets through the adoption of an institutionalist view. In this view, there is a market insofar as a set of particular transactions, and the agents involved in these transactions, are subject to the same system of institutional rules and constraints, providing a durable structure for interactions. The market is then constituted of this set of rules and the ways in which agents exploit them. It is only under these conditions that the market can be understood as it really is: *a durable system governing the relations between a moving set of agents*.

This approach has another interest. It enables us to escape from the vision of the market as an almost-natural 'given'. Unlike the representations which prevail in the neo-contractual approaches (described in the first section) the market is seen as the result of interactions between individual and collective agents – including public bodies – who seek to regulate and stabilise the development of a category of transactions, seeking thus to stabilise the functioning of the market itself.[16] Of course, when transactions take place, the agents and groups of agents will try to organise them in such a way as to extract the greatest possible benefit from them. But they will also display a common, shared interest in respecting certain collective disciplines necessary for the successful reproduction of transactions over time. In any case, these interactions will give rise to a set of collective procedures, usual practices, routines and formal rules governing transactions. A process of institutionalisation is thus set in motion which – generally – favours the constitution of specific agents and organisms. These intervene in the functioning of the market on various different grounds, either in the progress of the transactions themselves (this is, notably, the case of intermediaries, 'experts' and consultants), or as 'third parties' responsible for supervising transactions, controlling practices, defining the conditions of application of rules and possibly modifying them – what can be called market regulatory bodies. A constellation of diverse players then appears as constituents of the very existence of markets, intervening both in their 'construction' and their operation. We thus move away from the rather rough 'model' of the neo-institutionalist approaches, constituted solely of 'buyers', 'sellers' and 'third parties' entrusted with the task of enforcing the rules governing exchange and promoting 'honest trade', as Aoki put it. It is no longer solely in the event of market shortcomings or of the impossibility of guaranteeing property rights that a collection of players and operators becomes necessary. *When we take into account the nature of the transactions that are to take place in it, then every market requires the establishment of a series of specific institutional arrangements, as much to ensure the very existence of the market as to enable its good functioning and long-term viability.*

In this approach, it remains for us to define the main features characterising the forms of market organisation. This leads us to reconsider what is called, especially in neo-institutionalist works, modes of 'market governance'.

A priori, there exists a huge diversity of possible modes of governance, especially if we take into account the 'technological' specificities of different activities and the possibility of adopting different forms of market organisation for one same type of activity. The neo-institutionalist approaches, when they tackle this question, focus strongly on one particular dimension of governance: the conditions of enforcement of the rules governing the market and the nature of the agents responsible for this function.[17] On the basis of this dimension, for example, Aoki identifies different 'mechanisms of governance' (Aoki, 2001: 79). Likewise, these approaches are also led to explore the conditions ensuring the *information* of the players (the 'information structure' of the game). Quite apart from the fact that this information structure is most often considered as given, the use of this twin dimension (information structure and mode of enforcement) appears to be a very limited way of characterising markets. When the analysis is restricted to these two elements, other aspects of market organisation, which involve the very nature of trading relations and which we believe to be essential, are completely overlooked. If we are to flesh out this skeletal representation of markets, to arrive at something closer to their real nature, then at least three areas need to be explored in greater detail.

Firstly, we must consider *the organisation of interactions between agents.* Understanding how a market functions means, first and foremost, considering how agents can meet, how the 'negotiations' preceding the transaction can be carried out, the exact definition of the contents of the transaction, the monetary conditions of the exchange, the monitoring of the progress of the transaction, and so on. This dimension, which has been the subject of recent developments in market microeconomics, is itself built on basic organisational and institutional choices which relate to the market per se, and not simply to the conditions of an isolated transaction. At this level, there is a wide variety of possible organisations, of which the Walrasian market is simply one example, which can take various forms depending on the way in which sellers and buyers meet and depending on the precise mechanisms of price determination. The choices made in this sphere have major implications for the operation of the market and for the positions of the different parties involved. We shall give two examples which highlight the extremely varied conditions of market structuring.

The many works on fish markets have demonstrated both the diversity of possible organisational forms in these markets and how the organisation and structure of the market has a profound impact on its functioning and its results.[18] In this type of market, the way in which 'specific and durable' inter-relational networks are built up between buyers and sellers, as the result of the learning which accompanies the processes of interaction, plays a leading role in the organisation of the market. This is a case of which one can say that the structure of the market is largely an 'emergent property' of informal interactions between individuals. But of course the formal, 'constitutive' rules, which define the initial conditions under which the auctions and price determinations take place, also play an essential role.

Now let us consider a profoundly different type of market: the technologies markets and more precisely the conditions under which transactions involving patents and licences are organised. Major problems of coordination arise here, because different aspects of knowledge relating to the same field (and necessary for the design of a given product) may be divided into a large number of different items, with each item being the subject of specific rights. To resolve these problems, specific institutional arrangements will prove to be necessary. Merges (1996) provided an example of this, in the constitution of 'collective rights organizations' – in other words, private, club-type organisations entrusted with the task of organising and supervising the relations between suppliers and users of knowledge, such as 'patent pools'.[19] This example demonstrates the importance, from the point of view of the determination of a market's character, of the way in which the goods which are to be the object of transactions and the rights over these goods are defined and delimited. Here, the development of intellectual property rights and corporate strategies to deal with these rights, in other words the manner in which firms exploit the institutional rules, plays a leading role.[20]

Secondly, we must consider the specific nature of market relations, starting from what Orléan has called the 'market question'. When we look beyond the naive anthropology of rational agents meeting to negotiate a price, a formidable question arises: 'how do separate individuals manage to construct common points of reference enabling them to exchange and to regulate their exchanges?' (Orléan, 2002). In other words: what are the conditions which make it possible for a 'shared' evaluation of goods to be made between separate agents, and for this evaluation to enable the transaction actually to take place? This question has two dimensions:

1. that of the 'quality' (i.e. the 'real') evaluation of the contents of the commitment undertaken in a bargaining transaction; and
2. that of the price and, more generally, the evaluation and definition of the monetary conditions of the exchange.

It must then be noted that the specificity of market relations lies precisely in the fact that the relations between agents form around *monetary* evaluations and calculations. The parties facing each other in a market are calculating agents or, to borrow the terminology of Callon (1998), 'calculative agencies'. The procedures, norms and techniques used to evaluate and determine the 'value' of things are also a key component of the functioning of markets.

The question of the *conditions of 'price' determination* is, of course, a central element in all bargaining forms. Yet, paradoxically, it has been particularly poorly understood, if not totally ignored, in institutionalist (or neo-institutionalist) approaches. The conditions of price determination have been studied mainly for markets of a particular type: through auction mechanisms, defined for a particular transaction, or in markets where a given, well-defined, homogeneous good – either material or immaterial, like shares – is exchanged repeatedly.[21] The question becomes much trickier when we move away from simple, given products, and when the individualisation of transactions is an important feature of the market. As we have already said, this is the most widespread and frequent situation. In this context, the conditions under which the 'value' of complex goods is determined and the monetary conditions of the transaction are decided must themselves become the object of institutional arrangements which can take diverse forms. These arrangements concern the conditions of negotiations between the parties, the precise definition of the contents and type of transaction (such as sale by piece versus subscription or sale versus licence). These can also, in a large number of cases, involve the direct or indirect intervention of specialist agents (intermediaries, credit rating agencies, experts, etc.).

More fundamentally, we must take into account the fact that a market is necessarily based on a *principle of evaluation* – in other words, on a shared representation of that which founds the 'value' of things. This aspect is particularly important when we situate the market within the context of the wider social system in which it operates, especially when we consider the market in fully developed capitalist societies, as we shall see in the following section. On the whole, evaluation in general, and monetary evaluation in particular, occupies a central role in the functioning of a market, involving specific rules and institutional forms.

So, the institutional conditions of markets go well beyond the elements considered in neo-institutionalist approaches. Table 2.1 is a first attempt to clarify the different dimensions of the institutional basis of bargaining exchange and *of markets per se*, by making use of the distinction drawn earlier between type 1 and type 2 institutions.

The third key area is that of the market's 'architecture'. A market always involves a certain structuring of agents. In this sense, it is based on a 'social architecture', meaning the definition of groups of agents operating in the market and the forms of the relations between these groups (on this point, see Fliegstein, 2001; Harvey and Randle 2002). As we have seen, the market cannot be reduced to a simple confrontation between buyers and sellers, with the eventual addition of a third party charged with enforcement. The construction of a market is based on the formation of a complex social structure. Firstly, the formation of a market goes hand in hand with the differentiation of economic agents into separate groups[22] and is thus indissociable from a process of division of labour and a certain mode of development of structures of production. We shall return to this important feature later. There is, of course, the separation between buyers and sellers, to which must be added different categories of intermediaries and agents who play a role in supporting transactions – such as consultants, specialist financial institutions, experts – as well as professional associations, standardisation agencies, regulatory bodies, and so on. Or again, the 'market mediators', the 'designer, packager and merchandiser' so well analysed by Barrey et al. (2000). For its part, the history of the formation of markets for technology in the United States in the nineteenth century demonstrates the essential role played by the emergence of specialist intermediaries (jurists and patent agents), particularly in the evaluation of the value of inventions (Lamoreaux and Sokoloff, 2002).

So, in addition to the simple buyers and sellers, the market is constituted of all these players, their characteristics, their modes of intervention and their interrelations.

Box 2.1 presents an example which demonstrates how the 'market' for one same type of good can exist with radically different forms of organisation.

To go further forwards in our analysis, one essential step remains to be taken. We need to situate the market, and the forms it can take, within the

Table 2.1 Exchange and market institutions

	Type 1	Type 2
Institutions that are conditions of the bargaining exchange	• Legal system: systems of property rights, contracts, etc. • *Public* governance mechanisms responsible for enforcement. (Judiciary system, moral codes, etc.) • Monetary institutions.	• *Private* governance mechanisms responsible for enforcement. (Professional norms, personal trust, etc.) • Arbitration systems.
Institutions which regulate the markets		
Interactions between agents	• Formal regulations governing the conditions of intervention of players (buyers, sellers, intermediaries, market makers, etc.) e.g. financial markets.	• Constitution of informal networks. • Social networks (family relationships, community relationships). • Intermediation and arbitration systems. • Private organisations (clubs, collective rights organisations, etc.)
Monetary conditions of the exchange	• Regulation of the method of price determination (e.g. the definition of an auction system). • Price control, competition regulations (e.g. prohibition of discrimination).	• Experts and consultants. • Credit rating agencies.
Quality and information	• Obligatory information. Public norms and labels. Public control of products (e.g. health controls; marketing conditions).	• Private norms and labels.

more general framework of the economic system in which it operates, and more precisely, as far as we are concerned, within the context of capitalist economies.

Market and capitalism: markets as components of social systems of production

Historians have clearly established this point: the market is a very ancient institution, but the nature and characteristics of markets have seen profound changes over the course of time. We cannot retrace all these evolu-

Box 2.1 Alternative forms of market organisation: the case of the 'table strawberry' market in Sologne

For this example, we have drawn from the work of Marie-France Garcia (1986). Our aim is not to present her fascinating analysis of the 'social construction of a perfect market', but to use this work to show how the transactions for a same type of product – 'table strawberries' produced in a district of the Sologne region of France – were organised in three different ways which succeeded each other over time.

1. Before 1979, transactions took place essentially 'according to personalised relationships, with brokers, shippers and agents' (1986: 7). Most of the production was sold by the growers to brokers, local traders working on commission, who then sold the strawberries at the wholesale market of Rungis. An association of strawberry growers of Loir-et-Cher, created in 1973, had the task of creating a brand image for the strawberries of the region, in the form of a label of quality.
2. In 1979, a strictly organised market was created out of nothing. This was the *marché au cadran* (a type of Dutch auction) of Fontaines-en-Sologne, clearly inspired by the economists' model of the perfect market. The material organisation of the market gave it the following characteristics:

   • Totally anonymous transactions: the very architecture of the auction house was designed so that buyers and sellers could not see each other during the auctions.
   • A strictly defined system of price determination, following a degressive auction principle.
   • Standardised products: the strawberries were classified according to three criteria (label of origin, variety and quality) controlled by third parties (such as the economic committee of the Val de Loire), but – and this is obviously essential to the functioning of the market – according to criteria independent of the identities of the growers. So, as Marie-France Garcia observed, homogeneity, and therefore the definition of the products, was 'the result of a work of organisation of the production stimulated by subsidies or punished by the department of fraud prevention' (1986: 7).

   One key reason behind the raison d'être of this type of organisation involves the agents who argued in favour of it: essentially, it appears, these were farmers who were dissatisfied with the previous system and who hoped to gain independence from the intermediaries through the new organisation of the market.

3. The *marché au cadran* of Fontaines-en-Sologne no longer exists. Why? It appears that the main reason lies in the general transformations in food distribution circuits in France, and the predominant position of supermarket distribution. Today, most transactions take place between the growers and the big distribution companies. This means that personalised contracts have become the linchpin of market organisation. This marks a return to a system based on personalised relations, but in a totally different context from that of the pre-1979 period.

For the purposes of this chapter, the developments we have just summarised call for two comments:

1. everything happens as if the organisation of the market was following the evolution in microeconomic thinking: from the Walrasian-type perfect market to a contract economy; and
2. this case shows how the organisation of a particular market is dependent on the more general conditions which structure systems of production and on the role played by companies, in this case the large supermarket chains.

tions, so our aim in this section will be to help give a more precise picture of what markets are in modern economies, in other words in fully developed capitalist economies where firms are the dominant players.

Fernand Braudel has laid particular emphasis on the fact that capitalism transforms markets and creates new forms of market relations. Thus, he considers that there are 'at least two different forms of so-called market economy (forms "A" and "B")'. In form A, exchange concerns the usual commerce, and particularly the traditional markets in which exchanges are 'regular, predictable, routine, open to both little and big traders', whereas exchanges in the B category, on the contrary, constitute what has been referred to as 'private markets', representing a much more closed and opaque form of market which 'replaces the normal conditions of the collective market with individual transactions, the terms of which vary arbitrarily according to the respective situations of the parties involved' (Braudel, 1985: 57) and, concludes Braudel 'these two types of activity are governed by neither the same mechanisms nor the same agents, and it is not in the former, but in the latter that the sphere of capitalism is located' (Braudel, 1985: 66).

The domination of capitalism over the markets, and the way it shapes them, has implications of essential importance. Two of these are of particular relevance to the subject of this chapter.

Firstly, most markets are, if not totally dominated by firms, then at least *essentially structured by them*.[23] Companies have the perfectly natural objective of organising transactions and markets to suit their own ends. Following what Braudel observed, this can be interpreted as a tendency to favour market organisations closer to form 'B', founded on individualised and personalised relations, rather than form 'A', founded on homogeneity and transparency. This may justify the establishment of institutions of market regulation with the purpose of imposing a type of market operation more in keeping with the (supposed) virtues of form 'A'. In passing, it is worth noting that the form 'B' bears a certain resemblance to the notion developed by Chamberlin, at a time when big firms were beginning to predominate.[24]

More fundamentally, *the interdependencies and complementarities between markets and firms* lie at the heart of our economies. This point has been masked by the 'post-Coasian' views which focus heavily on the opposition between firm and market. And yet it is essential for an understanding of the characteristics of markets – and firms (Azoulay and Weinstein, 2001). In particular, the development of the division of labour and the growing complexity of technologies and systems of production has led to a proliferation of transactions and markets *between firms*. To grasp the nature of market economies as we know them, we must bear in mind the fact that a large proportion of today's markets are corporate markets, the characters of which are highly conditioned by the behaviour – and the structures – of firms.

Secondly, the existence of interdependencies between firms and markets means that there is also interdependency *between the organisation of markets and the organisation of production*.[25] From this point of view, it is important to recognise that the process of marketisation of an activity (or profound transformations in the institutional conditions of marketisation) does not simply mean the transformation of a product or service into a commodity offered on a market. In most cases, it also means the reorganisation of the whole structure of production, which may go as far as the creation of a *system of highly interdependent transactions and markets*, especially intermediate markets resulting from the process of specialisation and vertical disintegration. In most cases, marketisation also means the transformation of products. This may, in particular, take the form of the breaking-down of the product or service into different components, each one being the object of a specific transaction, or the grouping together of goods or services into complex packages. This aspect is perfectly visible, for example, in privatisation and deregulation of public services, such as electricity or the railways. We can then clearly see:

1. how the definition of the objects of transactions, and through that, the organisation of a system of markets, is the result of a process of collective choice (itself made within the context of a certain institutional framework); and
2. how this process is connected with certain methods of structuring production.

As Baldwin and Clark (2003) observed, to understand how markets are structured we must consider how and why production is divided in a certain way into different units, and more particularly between different firms (and other types of organisations). This gives us a further illustration of the degree to which the definition and characteristics of markets are dependent on corporate structures and strategies, and more generally on the character of systems of production.

The third key feature specific to market organisation in a capitalist economy concerns the central role played by particular markets: *the markets for means of production, and the markets for assets (tangible or intangible)*. In industrial capitalism, these markets are located at the heart of the systems of production. This was noted by Polanyi, for certain particular goods: 'labour, land and money are essential elements for industry; they must also be organised into markets; in fact these markets form an absolutely essential part of the economic system' (Polanyi, 1983: 107). For this type of good, especially, the market is in no way a 'natural' given. This is what Polanyi expressed when he said that 'labour, land and money are not merchandise', but that their circulation should nevertheless be organised as a market: 'the fiction of merchandise supplies . . . a vitally important principle of organisation, which concerns the whole of society' (Polanyi, 1983: 107). A long programme of institutional construction is therefore needed to set up this type of market. We could say that the marketisation of scientific and technological knowledge, which now occupies a central position in the evolution of systems of production and innovation, follows the path analysed by Polanyi.

As regards the analysis of current forms of market organisation, and their institutional conditions, these reflections lead us, beyond the *complementarity* between firms and markets – considered as institutional forms – to situate the analysis of markets within the more general framework of institutional systems and social systems of production and innovation in which they operate. Here we must bring into the picture the progress made in comparative institutional analysis and observations on 'institutional complementarities'. The literature in this field analyses the institutional foundations of an economy as a combination of different institutional 'subsystems' or 'domains', which are interdependent and organised into a hierarchy.[26] This means that the institutional characters within a domain can only be understood through their relations with other institutional forms, and that the effectiveness, or even viability, of an institution is highly dependent on its interactions with other institutions.[27]

This calls for two further observations.

Firstly, the characteristics of a market, its operating conditions and 'efficiency' are generally dependent on the *existence and characteristics of other markets*. It has been shown, for example, that the marketisation of scientific knowledge that we have seen since the late 1980s, especially in the United States, could never have developed without concomitant, 'complementary' developments involving financial market regulations, and in this particular case those which govern transactions on the NASDAQ.[28]

But the characteristics of a market, or system of markets, are also highly dependent on *non-market institutional forms*: these include the characteristics of firms, of course, but also other forms of organisation and other forms of interaction between economic agents. In particular, the most recent works studying the concrete functioning of markets shows the importance of networks of personal relations between agents, operating within a certain number of groups and formal or informal networks. Braudel's 'form B' markets are precisely those in which this type of relation plays an important role.

So the marketisation of an activity involves much more than the simple construction of a 'place' where suppliers and consumers can confront each other. It generally involves the construction of a system of complementary institutions. This means that the existence (or not) of bargaining transactions and markets in a given field, the delimitation of the spheres in which these transactions are possible, the characteristics of these transactions, and, more broadly, the institutional arrangements which shape the markets, are components of choice and of global institutional constructions, whether intentional or not. This feature is essential for understanding how processes of marketisation, as witnessed today in many fields, can develop.

3. Conclusion

We shall conclude this article with a brief summary of the approach taken and of the main points that we have established.

Our approach starts from the observation that as soon as we look beyond the 'naive' representations of the market as a place where suppliers and consumers can meet, it appears that agents can only form relations of exchange with each other in the presence of a series of precise institutional conditions. Neo-institutionalist authors have described two main sets of conditions: firstly, the specification of perfectly defined (private) property rights, and, secondly, the existence of mechanisms of enforcement, to ensure that the parties involved in the exchange respect their obligations.

Despite the interest of this first entry into the 'black box' of the market, these representations fall well short of dealing with all the problems raised. In particular, they continue to treat the market as a form whose existence, once property rights on products have been defined and enforcement mechanisms have been established, is never in doubt. Everything happens as if, given these two conditions, the market were a quasi-natural form of relations, and as if the organisation and functioning of the market were a spontaneous result of the interaction between individuals.

This completely overlooks the question of the conditions which enable *transactions actually to take place*, in other words the conditions under which agents can actually meet and agree on the terms of the exchange.

To tackle this question, we must stop considering a market transaction as a simple face-to-face meeting. Transactions are only possible when they take place within constructed frameworks – in other words, *in markets*. As we hope to have demonstrated, markets are themselves organised systems founded on specific institutional arrangements, arrangements responsible, in particular, for determining the terms of interaction between agents and the conditions, especially monetary, of the exchange.

By taking into consideration, in this perspective, all the institutional conditions necessary for the creation and durable operation of markets, we have brought to light the wide diversity of institutional and organisational forms hidden behind the generic term of 'market'. This diversity is evinced by the empirical works that both economists and sociologists have started to accumulate on the subject. This has led us on to show that market forms can only be fully understood within the framework of the broader institutional systems in which they operate, and more especially, as Braudel and Polanyi have proposed, within the context of the capitalist system. This means taking into account the close ties between conditions of exchange and conditions of production, and between *markets* and *firms*, in other words between the central institutions of capitalism. This, we believe, is the path that must be explored if we wish to shed more light on the black box of markets, and of 'market economies'.

Notes

1 We refer to the NIE in the widest sense of the term. In this article, it includes not only the approaches of the transaction costs school (North, Williamson), but also those of property rights theorists (often referred to as 'neo-contractualists'). It also includes Aoki's recent work on these subjects, adopting an approach he himself refers to as 'comparative institutional analysis'. Despite certain differences, these approaches have certain things in common: i) they cling to a representation of transactions dominated by methodological individualism; ii) they give true importance to the institutional dimensions of the coordination between agents.

2 This section draws on previous works by the authors. In particular, see Coriat and Weinstein, 2002, as well as Coriat and Weinstein, 2004.

3 Obviously, acceptance of the idea that institutions help to define the 'rules of the game' doesn't in any way mean that we accept the whole of North's theorisation.

4 Not everyone agrees that organisations should be treated as institutions. North himself, and most NIE theoreticians, draws a distinction between institutions (the rules of the game) and organisations (the players). The authors of the present paper have argued elsewhere (Coriat and Weinstein, 2002) that organisations (especially the firm) should be considered as institutions.

5 This argument, present within the literature produced by property rights theorists, is presented in Barzel, 1989.

6 For a discussion on this point, see our article: Coriat and Weinstein, 2004.

7 For a discussion of the political and social context in which this law was passed, see Coriat and Orsi, 2002; Mowery et al., 1999; Mowery and Rosenberg, 1993).

8 The establishment of purely market mechanisms to ensure the efficient production and allocation of the goods and services involved here is impossible. Transactions must therefore be organised by the Visible Hand of the State. The role played by the State here goes well beyond that of the 'third party' guaranteeing the durability of agreements and rules. To satisfy the needs and interests of agents and to contain their levels of opposition within acceptable limits, the action of public authorities consists in laying down a complex series of institutions entrusted with the task of delivering some of the basic resources needed, and guaranteeing their survival through a complex system of taxes and transfers. In these cases, the State, heavily involved in the delivery of goods and services, appears as the main player in the mechanisms of production and allocation of resources. The theory of regulation then refers to the State as the operator and guarantor of 'institutionalised compromises'.

9 His later works led beyond this point of view: for Coase, the market, like the firm, only exists because there are transaction costs: 'In an economic theory which assumes that transaction costs are nonexistent, markets have no function to perform' (Coase, 1988: 7). They are thus placed on the same level.

10 To which we should add the State.

11 The importance of these conditions is also highlighted by Aoki (see Aoki, 2001: 23).

12 In this perspective, Aoki (2001: 79) distinguished between ten types of 'exchange governance mechanisms'.

13 Here, we refer to the debate instigated by Heller and Eisenberg (1998) on the 'tragedy of the anticommons'. For a discussion of the conditions of formation of a market of scientific knowledge in the field of genome research, see also Coriat and Orsi, 2002; Coriat et al., 2003; Orsi, 2002.

14 And others, such as Callon (2002), Callon and Muniesa (2002), and Harvey and Randle (2002).

15 On this point, see Callon, 2002 or Callon and Muniesa, 2002.

16 Fliegstein (2001) emphasises this aspect: the search, *by firms*, for stable markets, especially by limiting price competition. We shall return to this point in the next section.

17 See, for example, Coase (1988), for whom 'Markets . . . require the establishment of legal rules governing the rights and duties of those carrying out transactions' and 'The main problems faced by exchanges in this law making are the securing of the agreement of the members of the exchange and the enforcement of rules'.

18 See Kirman, 2001 for a synthesis of the different works on this question.

19 The ASCAP – American Society of Composers, Authors, and Publishers (in the United States) or the SACEM (in France) provide other illustrations of types of solutions that can be adopted.

20 The case of the proliferation of patents on gene fragments cited earlier provides a particularly eloquent illustration of the complexity of the procedures at work.

21 And especially for financial markets, in the literature on 'market microstructures'. See, for example: O'Hara, 1995; Schwartz, 1988; and, for a review of the different theses, Revest, 2001.

22 See Harvey and Randle (2002) for developments in this perspective.

23 For Fliegstein (2001): 'markets are mainly structured by the sellers'. We believe it would be more apt to say that markets are structured by firms: most of the markets in which firms are the buyers are structured by the firms, not by the suppliers. This is true for labour markets and markets for technologies, when the suppliers are individual inventors or small companies.

24 Although the distinction must still be made between the differentiation between products proposed by different firms, and the personalisation of the relations between a firm and its different customers, achieved through differentiation in products and conditions of transaction for different buyers.

25 Polanyi (1983: 110) emphasised the fact that, whereas, until the end of the eighteenth century, 'industrial production . . . was a simple appendix to trade', the development of machinism, with industrial capitalism, 'completely transformed the relation of the trader with production'. The need for *continuity* in industrial production entailed, in particular, regularity in the supply of the means of production, thus ensuring their marketisation, as we shall see.

26 See Aoki, 2000, 2001; the literature on 'varieties of capitalism', such as Hall and Soskice, 2001; and that on the theory of regulation, such as Amable, 2000.

27 'The concept of complementary institutions is based on multilateral reinforcement mechanisms between institutional arrangements: each one, by its existence, permits or facilitates the existence of the others. . . . The constraints and possibilities defined by a given institution favour other institutions' functioning (Amable, 2000: 656).

28 On this point, for the case of biotechnologies, see Coriat et al., 2003.

References

Alchian, A. A. 1987. 'Property rights', in Eatwell, J., Muray, M. and Newman, P. (eds), *The New Palgrave: A Dictionary in Economics*. Macmillan. London and Basingstoke.

Amable, B. 2000. 'Institutional complementarily and diversity of social systems of innovation and production', *Review of International Political Economy*, 7(4): 645–87.

Aoki, M. 2000. *Information, Corporate Governance, and Institutional Diversity*. Oxford University Press. Oxford, New York.

Aoki, M. 2001. *Towards a Comparative Institutional Analysis*. The MIT Press. Cambridge, MA.

Arrow, K. 1962. 'Economic welfare and allocation of resources for inventions', in Nelson, R. R. (ed.), *The Rate and Direction of Inventive Activity*. Princeton University Press, Princeton, NJ: 609–25.

Azoulay, N. and Weinstein, O. 2001. 'Nature et formes historiques de la firme capitaliste: prolégomènes à une nouvelle représentation', paper presented at the *Forum de la Régulation*, Paris, September.

Baldwin, C. Y. and Clark, K. B. 2003. 'Where do transactions come from? A perspective from engineering design'. Prepared for the Saint-Gobain Centre for Economic Research 5th Conference, Paris, FR, November.

Barrey, S., Cauchois, F. and Dubuisson-Quellier, S. 2000. 'Designer, packager et merchandiser: trois professionnels pour une même scène marchande', *Sociologie du travail*, 42, 457–82.

Barzel, Y. 1989. *Economics Analysis of Property Rights*. Cambridge University Press. Cambridge.

Braudel, F. 1985. *La dynamique du capitalisme*, Arthaud, Paris.

Callon, M. 1998. 'Introduction: the embeddedness of economic market in economics', in Callon, M. (ed.), *The Laws of the Market*. Blackwell Publishers/The Sociological Review. Oxford.

Callon, M. 2002. 'Pour en finir avec les incertitudes', *Dossier-Débat: La qualité. Sociologie du travail*, 44, 261–7.

Callon, M. and Muniesa, F. 2002. 'Economic markets as calculative and calculated collective devices'. Paper presented at the New York Conference on Social Studies of Finance, Columbia University and the Social Science Research Council.

Chamberlin, E. H. 1953. 'The product as an economic variable', *Quarterly Journal of Economics*, 67(1) (February), 1–29.

Coase, R. H. 1937. 'The nature of the firm', *Economica*, 4 (November).

Coase, R. H. 1988. *The Firm, the Market and the Law*. The University of Chicago Press. Chicago and London.

Coase, R. H. 1992. 'The institutional structure of production', *American Economic Review*, 82(4), 713–19.

Commons, J. R. 1990. *Institutional Economics*. Transaction Publishers. New Brunswick, NJ and London.

Commons, J. R. 1995. *Legal Foundations of Capitalism*. Transaction Publishers. New Brunswick, NJ and London.

Coriat, B. and Orsi, F. 2002. 'Establishing a new regime of intellectual property rights in the United States. Origins, content and problems', *Research Policy*, 31, 8–9 (December), 1491–507.

Coriat, B., Orsi, F. and Weinstein, O. 2003. 'Science-based technological regimes and institutions: does biotech reflect a new science based regime?' *Industry and Innovation*, 10(3) (September), 231–53.

Coriat, B. and Weinstein, O. 2002. 'Organizations, firms and institutions in the generation of innovation', *Research Policy*, 31, 273–90.

Coriat, B. and Weinstein, O. 2004. 'National institutional frameworks, institutional complementarities and sectoral systems of innovation', in Malerba F. (ed.), *Sectoral Systems of Innovation: Concepts, Issues and Analyses of Six Major Sectors in Europe*. Cambridge University Press. Cambridge.

Fliegstein, N. 2001. *The Architecture of Markets*. Princeton University Press. Princeton, NJ and Oxford.

Garcia, M.-F. 1986. 'La construction d'un marché parfait: le marché au cadran de Fontaines-en-Sologne', *Actes de la recherche en sciences sociales*, 65 (November), 2–13.

Hall, P. and Soskice, D. (eds) 2001. *Varieties of Capitalism*. Oxford University Press. Oxford.

Harvey, M. and Randle, S. 2002. 'Markets, the organisation of exchanges and "instituted economic process" – an analytical perspective', *Revue d'Economie Industrielle*, 101, 11–30.

Heller, M. A. and Eisenberg, R. S. 1998. 'Can patents deter innovation? The anti-commons in biomedical research', *Science*, 280, 698–701.

Karpic, I. 2002. 'Que faire des singularités', *Dossier-Débat: La qualité. Sociologie du travail*, 44, 279–84.

Kirman, A. 2001. 'Market organization and individual behavior: evidence from fish markets', in Rauch, J. E. and Casella, A. (eds), *Networks and Markets*. Russell Sage Foundation. New York.

Lamoreaux, N. R. and Sokoloff, K. L. 2002. 'Intermediaries in the U.S. market for technology, 1870–1920', Working Paper 9017, June, NBER Working Paper Series.

Merges, R. P. 1996. 'Contracting into liability rules: intellectual property rights and collective rights organizations', *California Law Review*, 84(5) (October), 1293–384.

Mowery, D. C., Nelson, R. R., Sampat, B. N. and Ziedonies, A. A. 1999. 'The effects of the Bayh-Dole Act on US university research and technology transfer', in Branscomb, L. M., Kodama, F. and Florida, R. (eds), *Industrializing Knowledge: University-Industry Linkages in Japan and the United States*. The MIT Press. Cambridge, MA.

Mowery, D. C. and Rosenberg, N. 1993. 'The US national innovation system', in Nelson, R. (ed.), *National Innovation Systems. A Comparative Analysis*. Oxford University Press. New York.

Nelson, R. 1959. 'The simple economics of basic scientific research', *Journal of Political Economy*, 67, 297–306.

North, D. C. 1990. *Institutions, Institutional Change and Economic Performances*. Cambridge University Press. Cambridge.

Orléan, A. 2002. 'Pour une nouvelle approche des interactions financières: l'économie des conventions face à la sociologie économique', in Huault, I. (ed.), *La construction sociale de l'entreprise. Autour des travaux de Mark Granovetter*. Management et Société (EMS). Paris.: 205–27.

Orsi, F. 2002. 'La constitution d'un nouveau droit de propriété intellectuelle sur le vivant aux Etats-Unis. Origine et signification d'un dépassement de frontières', *Revue d'Economie Industrielle*, 99, spécial 'Les droits de propriété intellectuelle: nouveaux domaines, nouveaux enjeux', coordinated by B. Coriat: 65–86.

O'Hara, M. 1995. *Market Microstructure Theory*. Blackwell Business. Malden, MA and Oxford.

Polanyi, K. 1983. *La grande transformation*. Gallimard, Paris. (Originally published as *The Great Transformation*, 1944).

Revest, V. 2001. 'Une réflexion sur la place des institutions au sein des théories de la microstructure', *Revue d'Economie Industrielle*, 96, 105–23.

Schwartz, R.A. 1988. *Equity Markets: Structure, Trading and Performance*. Harper and Row. New York.

Searle, J. R. 1995. *The Construction of Social Reality*. Free Press. New York. (French translation: *La construction de la réalité sociale*. Gallimard. Paris.)

Williamson, O. E. 1986. *Economic Organization*. Wheatsheaf Books. Brighton.

3

Markets, the organisation of exchanges and 'instituted economic process': an analytical perspective

Mark Harvey and Sally Randles

Introduction

The objective of this chapter is to develop an analytical framework for understanding the organisation of economic exchange in contemporary economies. The rationale for choosing the term 'organisation of economic exchange' rather than 'market' is twofold. Firstly, it enables the analysis to explore a number of organised economic exchanges without making the initial presumptions of a well-defined market as an economic space within which exchanges may take place, or of markets as characterised *a priori* by a set of rules (property rights, governance, etc.) that include some organised economic exchanges but exclude others. So, for example, it might be possible to question whether some labour markets are markets at all, if, for argument's sake, the price menu is fixed by collective bargaining between a single representative body of employers and a single representative body of employees, underwritten by the state and given the force of law. But such an arrangement, market or not, is certainly an organisation of a multitude of exchanges. So the first reason for the choice of this more generic term is to adopt a more anthropological stance, and to allow markets to be placed and defined as a sub-species or several sub-species of different modes of organisation of economic exchanges.

The second reason is to allow the analysis to embrace specifically *non*-market forms of economic exchange. There are very many empirical instances of economic exchanges in contemporary societies involving the transfer of property rights over labour, goods and services in exchange for money, mediated by compulsory monetary transfers imposed by states (e.g. tax, insurance, obligatory private insurance). It is difficult for almost any person or organisation to purchase anything without paying some kind of taxation. There are relatively few 'pure market' exchanges. This empirical fact appears widely ignored, which is puzzling in view of widespread and diverse affirmations that the market has become a dominant allocative and co-ordinating institution in modern society.[1] It is as if market exchanges alone matter with taxation as a *ceteris paribus* to be bracketed off without serious consequence to analysis.

Theoretically, non-market exchanges also involve reciprocal transfers of property rights, payments in return for rights to public goods (education, health care, pensions, law enforcement, and so on). The 'organisation of exchange' concept allows one to situate both unequivocally market and unequivocally non-market organisations of economic exchanges in a common analytical space. The advantage for so doing is twofold. In the first instance, it sharpens the analysis about what is distinctive about each, and about the many 'hybrids' in between. But, more significantly, it provides the opportunity for exploring significant interactions between the two domains on the grounds that these may be a basis for understanding the dynamics of economic growth in contemporary economies. After all, empirically, it is difficult to find a contemporary economy whose economic growth over the past century has not witnessed a growth similar in scale in both market and non-market exchanges.

To conclude, the choice of the term 'organisation of economic exchange' allows us first to explore a range of organised economic exchanges within which only some may constitute markets, and second to examine the possibility of dual or multiple economies, defined by their different modes of organising economic exchange.[2]

Having set out the main objective, the concept of 'instituted economic process' (IEP) (Polanyi, 1944, 1947, 1957; Randles, 2001) will be developed to address it. Each component of this phrase needs to be emphasised: exchange is a process (specifically a reciprocal transfer) that is economic and variously institutable (and de-institutable).

The notion of **process** directs us to looking at (exchange) activities continuing over time, so that even in the extreme case of exchanges of unique objects, they are viewed as instances of similarly reciprocal transfers rather than as unique or timeless events.

By **economic** is meant the combined processes of production, exchange, distribution and consumption necessary for the reproduction of societal resources on the same, lesser or greater scale (economic stability, decline/ collapse, growth). Following Polanyi, however, the extent to which the economic is a distinct and specific set of connecting processes, governed by their own distinct logic and causality, is itself a consequence of historical institution, varying from society to society over historical time.

> The study of the shifting place occupied by the economy in society is therefore no other than the study of the manner in which the economic process is instituted at different times and places. (Polanyi, 1957: 250)

When we adopt this analytical approach a number of important consequences follow, which distinguish it from much contemporary economic sociology of markets. Exploring these differences will help also define and refine the use of the concept '**instituted**' when applied to the 'economic', and to suggest why something more is required than adopting an institutional approach (North, 1990, 1996; Powell and DiMaggio, 1991). Broadly three types of analysis can be identified which fail or refuse, in one way or another, to address the issue of the institutionalisation of the specifically economic. The first can be characterised as social contextualisation of the economic, and exemplars of this approach have often adopted another Polanyian concept, embeddedness, where economic processes are said to be embedded in broader social contexts and institutions, and indeed where there may be said to be no easily drawn boundaries between the economic process and the socio-institutional context (e.g. Callon, 1998a, b; Granovetter, 1985, 1992a, b; Granovetter and McGuire, 1998). The second can be characterised as deploying generic social terms such as norms, habits or routines, to analyse the economic, where the force of a norm (habit, routine), and hence its explanatory power, is also generic, lacking in economic specificity (e.g. Hodgson, 1988, 1994, 1997). The third can be characterised as the erasure of the economic, and its replacement by non-economic explanations for all institutionalised phenomena that occur even in stronghold 'economic' domains such as markets. Thus, to caricature slightly, Fligstein's (2001: 98) view of 'markets as politics' involves seeing *economic* worlds as *social* worlds operating according to principles *just like* those other social worlds (Fligstein, 2001: 70; Baker et al., 1998).[3]

Adopting an IEP approach requires the analysis of power as specifically economic power, of norms as specifically economic norms, as well as motives, strategies and rationales. This is not to argue that contextual embeddedness, non-economic norms, legal property rights or political politics are unimportant, nor that the economic is insulated or isolated from their influence or impact. It is to argue that the economic is left underspecified without an analysis of its own 'laws'. For that reason the focus of the present analysis is on the instituted nature of the specifically economic and in this chapter we focus on economic exchange.

The framework for analysis of instituted exchange processes

The challenge for this approach is to be able to comprehend the full range and distinctiveness of different exchange processes within an overall theoretical framework, although here we delimit ourselves to exchange processes in more or less modern capitalist economies. In order to build this framework, we first explore two conceptual dimensions, each with three aspects. We then exemplify the framework by indicating how it might be applied to labour markets and product end-markets. The first dimension represents the analytical steps necessary to understand the institution of exchange process irrespective of whether applied to labour, product or capital exchanges. The three interlocking aspects of the exchange processes are:

- the separation and differentiation of classes of economic agent between which exchanges occur;

- the organisation between different classes of economic agent as a condition for any exchange between any two classes of economic agent (including, but not only, the interdependence between different exchange processes/markets); and
- the exchange process itself.

The second dimension identifies three interdependent aspects of exchange processes where the *specificities* of the nature of these aspects is seen as essential to the understanding of any given organisation of exchange. The three dimensions are:

- the nature of the parties to the exchange (private enterprises, state organisations, NGOs, workers, end consumers, citizens);
- the nature of entities that are traded (labour, goods and services, property rights, etc.); and
- the nature of the modalities of exchange in time and space.

It is argued here that these are instituted specificities, rather than universal characteristics.

Dimension 1. The first three analytical steps, general parameters of instituted variation

A useful starting point for the analysis of exchange process is Weber's (1922) paradigm, as elaborated by Swedberg (1994, Figure 3, Table 3; Swedberg, 1998).

Buyers	Single exchange events	Sellers
O		X
O	←——————————→	X
O		X
O	←——————————→	X
O		X

Figure 3.1 Exchanges as single events between atomistic agents

It is a model that has also been widely adopted, if often implicitly, in which the main parameters involve degrees of concentration on the buy or sell-side, and questions of relative monopoly and monopsony. Power relations between the buy and sell-side are treated largely in terms of relative numbers, and degree of collusion. Whilst no doubt this is an important feature of exchange processes, it does not provide strong analytical grounds for differentiating structurally between different exchange processes, and in many ways adopts the 'perfect market' assumption of the market as a coordinating device between a multiplicity of approximately equivalent independent agents on the buy and sell-side. Thus Chamberlin (1933) posits two directions for departure from the perfect market with similar outcomes: relative concentration on either side of the exchange relation and product differentiation, either or both resulting in monopoly and monopolistic competition, regarded as a normal condition. Chamberlin's interpretation of product differentiation, moreover, accentuates the normality of monopoly by regarding *any type* of departure from a commodity identical in all respects as entailing the creation of a new market, within which the product differentiator holds a monopoly position (1933: 8–9).

In Weber's and Swedberg's account of the elemental model of a market, competition for exchange (an essential characteristic of markets for price setting and resource allocation), occurs between agents on either side of exchange, but not across it; between a buyer and a seller. The corollary of this account is that restrictions on competition over exchange lead to market imperfections – in market coordinating terms. A further deep assumption of this model is that exchanges, however often repeated, are discrete one-way events. That is, entities pass from sell-side to buy-side, and vice versa, and each transaction is a complete and terminal event, in the sense that property rights are unequivocally and absolutely transferred. A corollary to this assumption is that all 'economic' entities are equally amenable to such an absolute exchange of property rights: there are no inherent limits to marketisation. Again, departures from this model may be viewed as imperfections.

Here we critically modify the point of departure, analytically starting prior to the separation of the world of economic agents into a buy-side and a sell-side, on the one hand, and arguing that such a separation is constituted only by repeated exchange events – an exchange process. The analysis takes place in three steps.

Step one

As a first step, it posits that processes of separation and differentiation of classes of economic agent are co-constituted with the institution of exchange processes between them (Figure 3.2).[4] The notion of a 'class' of economic agent is that members of the class share distinct economic functions with each other, on the one hand, and contrast with economic functions of other classes, on the other hand. To emphasise the level of analysis that this supposes, one can differentiate a class[5] of retailers and a class of consumers on the one hand, and likewise a class of employers and a class of employees on the other, both sustained by exchange processes between them. Employees and consumers are of course commonly the same individuals, and, indeed, labour markets and consumer markets may be dynamically related to each other. Yet both in terms of organisation and function the class of employees is very different from the class of consumers.

Processes of separation and differentiation give rise to new opportunities for exchange between parties previously unseparated or differentiated as to economic function. In contrast to a Coasean or Williamsonian problematic (Coase, 1996; Williamson, 1994, 1996, 1997, 1999), the question of why exchanges exist needs to be posed at the same level of analysis as why firms exist. For exchanges to exist, there need to be different types of agent and vice versa. Yet Coasean and transaction cost analysis of different forms of

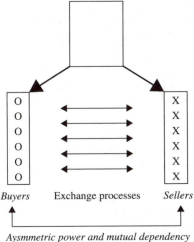

Buyers   Exchange processes   Sellers

Aysmmetric power and mutual dependency

Figure 3.2 Analytical step 1. Separation and differentiation of classes of economic agent

coordination and governance take for granted the prior existence of markets, as can be seen from the following original formulation of problematic:

> Our attempt is to discover why a firm emerges at all in a specialised exchange economy. (Coase, 1996: 74)

On the basis of this first analytical step, it becomes possible to distinguish between labour, product, and capital markets, on the grounds that they result from different processes of separation and differentiation. It further becomes possible to distinguish between processes of differentiation and separation within each of these three types of markets. This enables us to analyse processes of institution of the three different types of market as being of a different order to processes of differentiation within each type.

Separation and differentiation of classes of economic agent, however, can only be one side of a process, which at the same time creates a functional interdependency between them, essential to the dynamics of exchange processes. Separate classes of economic agent engaged in exchange processes between each other are held together by various relations of *asymmetric power and mutual dependency.* The continued economic existence of a separate class of economic agent depends on exchanges with other classes of economic agent, although, in both cases, not necessarily with any particular member of the other class.[6] End-product manufacturers depend on exchanges with retailers for their economic existence, in order for their products to find an end market, and, conversely, retailers depend on manufacturers in order to have something to sell to consumers. Their mutual dependency is at the level of class to class, rather than at the level of particular members to particular members, between which there may or may not be competition for exchange.

Likewise, asymmetries of power are at the level of *relations between classes*, and this concept of power must be distinguished from that of power as wielded by virtue of monopoly or oligopoly – where relative power resides in the restriction of the possibility of alternatives for exchange *within* a given class of economic agent. Asymmetries of power between classes of economic agent refer to the different *qualitative* kinds of power that one class can wield over another. Baker et al. (1998) have argued that there is an asymmetric power between any class of sellers and any class of buyers, on the grounds that sellers need to sell, whereas buyers do not need to buy, at least not from any given alternative. The difficulty with such an argument is that it posits a generic 'need to sell' and hence also a market driven by the supply-side.[7] The analysis developed here, however, argues that there are qualitatively different types of power and power asymmetry, between qualitatively different classes of economic agent. There is inherently no point of balance or equilibrium between them, given that different kinds of power are not calibrated by any common measure. Two examples may illustrate this notion of qualitative asymmetries of power: the relations between manufacturers and retailers, and those between employers and employees. Thus, manufacturers may exercise power over retailers by virtue of their capacity to innovate and produce, or of their brand reputation. Retailers may exercise power by virtue of their organisation of end markets and control of access to them. These two kinds of power do not cancel each other out, and may be in continuous tension, as a consequence of mutual dependency. However much power retailers or manufacturers wield, they still depend on the existence of each other.

The long history of industrial relations in capitalist societies points to a similar account of the different kinds of power that can be wielded by employers, on the one hand, and employees, on the other. Fluctuations in the ability to dictate terms of the exchange between them reflect the inherently and qualitatively different types of power each is capable of exerting, as well as mutual dependency within capitalist economies.

Step two

The second step of the analysis extends the principle of separation and differentiation of classes of economic agent by affirming that any one instituted exchange process between two classes of economic agent is interdependent with others *on either side* of the exchange. In the first place, this can be seen to involve an interdependence between markets. But secondly, as represented in Figure 3.3, market exchanges can also be dependent on non-market exchanges of two broad types. Firstly, there is the reliance of some exchanges on public good infrastructures sustained by taxation (transport, education, health, etc.), where economic flows are visible in monetary terms (type 1). Sellers need to purchase inputs in order to sell; buyers need to buy some commodities to be able to buy others. Secondly, there is the reliance on some non-monetary, but nonetheless economic, exchanges or

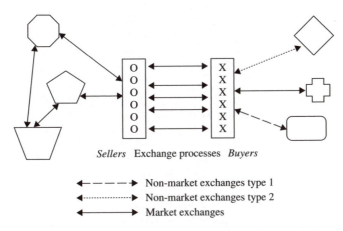

Sellers Exchange processes *Buyers*

◄ ─ ─ ─ ►   Non-market exchanges type 1
◄ ············►   Non-market exchanges type 2
◄───────►   Market exchanges

Figure 3.3 Analytical step 2. Interdependency between market and non-market exchanges

reciprocations for monetary exchanges to take place. The contribution of household economies providing necessary outputs (e.g. labour) for the market economy, and of unpaid skill acquisition (e.g. riding a bicycle) or habit formation necessary for the appropriation of inputs (commodities) from the market economy, constitute an *economic* prerequisite for monetary exchange processes (type 2).

The general point is that no one set of economic exchanges is economically self-sustaining. Figure 3.3 gives a focus on one central exchange process. But it could equally well have taken any of the other indicated exchange relations, rotating the constellation of economic agents.

This analytical step complements a view of innovation as a process distributed between different classes of economic agent (Coombs et al., 2001). Whether one takes an end-market for air travel or clothing, a complex nexus of innovation – and transformed exchange processes – across several classes of economic agent is necessary for new market formation. Such processes of innovation can involve many interdependent changes in exchange processes in all the successive inputs necessary for an end-product/ service to enter an end market. Moreover, changes in the structure of retailing outlets can reverberate upstream on design, production, and raw materials. As a consequence, power asymmetry and mutual dependency extend beyond the immediate exchange processes between any two classes of economic agent to relative power positions of all classes of economic agent involved in a nexus of interdependent exchange processes on either side of any given exchange process (Randles, 2002).

Step three

The third and final step in this analysis will be that in many, but by no means all, instituted exchange processes there are interactions between different classes of economic agents *across* an exchange relationship that may

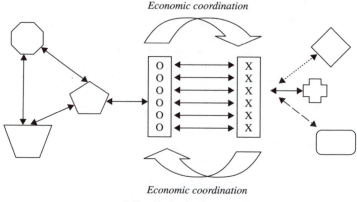

Economic coordination

Sellers Exchange processes *Buyers*

Figure 3.4 Analytical Step 3. Interaction across the exchange

significantly shape and condition that relationship. Exemplary in this respect are the user–producer interactions described by Lundvall (1988) in product markets, open-book accounting between agents in given supply chains, or collective agreements in labour markets. Co-design and specification of products between sellers and buyers may be a necessary economic form of coordination for the 'coordination of the market'. The form of the price mechanism, the nature and duration of contracts, processes of quality specification in relation to price, or accounting procedures, in many cases may be the outcome of negotiation as a condition for exchange. This is not to deny the importance, additionally, of many social interactions between buyers and sellers (golf clubs, friendships, and social networks generally) or of legal frameworks. But this third analytical step of instituted economic exchange process entails those supplemental coordinating interactions economically necessary in order for the exchange process to occur.

Dimension 2. The three analytical specificities of classes, entities traded, and space/time exchange modalities

So far we have been building an analytical tool of progressive levels of complexity for exchange processes in general, as if it did not matter between whom exchanges take place, what is exchanged, or time–space dimensions of exchanges. But, specificities on each of these three aspects do matter, and matter in the sense of conditioning the institution of exchange processes in fundamental ways. So in this section we explore three sets of systemic differences, one based on the nature of the agents between which exchanges take place, another based on the nature of the entity exchanged, and the third based on the time–space modalities of the exchange process. The argument will be developed that the institution of exchange processes involves interactions *between* these three sets of systemic differences.

Broadly speaking, we will first distinguish between exchanges between labour and capital/employers (labour markets), firm-to-firm exchanges between buyers and sellers of products/services (intermediary product markets) and firm-to-end-consumer exchanges (end-product markets), and exchanges between buyers and sellers of financial arrangements and property rights (financial and capital markets). Moreover, changes in the nature of these classes of economic agent can fundamentally change the nature of exchange processes, contributing to the creation and destruction of markets.

Secondly, differences in the kind of entity exchanged form an important part of our approach. Innovation may be more than market disruptive in the narrow sense of altering market share within existing markets, but may also destroy markets and some exchange processes altogether, whilst creating new ones. Qualitative characteristics of the entity traded may affect the nature and organisation of the exchange process, even the possibility of trading. Within product markets, one could contrast houses and bioinformatic algorithms and suggest that the nature of the commodity profoundly affects the way exchanges are organised. Within labour markets, sellers of legal services might be contrasted with sellers of the services of manual skills. Within capital markets, important distinctions might be made in exchange processes for venture capital, financial arrangements of mergers and acquisitions, or trading in derivatives.

Thirdly, in terms of exchange processes, differences in terms of the medium of exchange from the buyer and the distribution of the entities exchanged by sellers affect the transaction process itself. Many models of markets and exchange process – whether talking about the supply of goods, labour or capital – abstract the pricing process or the monetary transaction process from the temporal and spatial process of distribution in the broad sense. For product markets, distribution is often treated as a cost of production rather than as an inherent part of the value formation of the commodity. This approach underestimates the significance of markets as organisations of distribution as much as of exchange: one does not take place without the other. Differences in modes of distribution or mobility in product, labour, and capital markets, however, clearly are significant aspects of the interactions between these markets. Innovations or transformations in modes of distribution and transaction (e.g. Internet) and logistics, coupled with changes in the nature of entities changed (e.g. intangibles) can affect the nature and organisation of economic agents involved in the exchange process and the organisation of the market, but they do not eliminate distribution in time and space (Leyshon and Thrift, 1997).

In advancing these three aspects of specification in the institution of exchange processes, the approach distinguishes itself from the position either that all markets are essentially the same once one arrives at a sufficiently high level of abstraction, or that there are some transcendent, essential differences in the entities to be exchanged. Thus, an IEP approach attempts to demonstrate why there are systematic or structural differences in one or each of the three dimensions which underpin differences in exchange processes which mean that it is *not* possible, at any level of abstraction, to state that all factors are commensurable by a unique pricing system in a single market. Exchange processes cannot be instituted in the same way for all types of market. The differences have nothing to do with 'market imperfections' held up against a standard of perfect markets, nothing to do with the difference between formal models and 'real existing' markets (Boyer, 1997).

At the same time, it is *not* being argued that there are some inherent universal characteristics of the traded entities that underlie this differentiation. In this respect, we distance ourselves both from Polanyi's original position, and, for example, Boyer's adoption of a neo-Polanyian view (Boyer, 1997: 68–9). In relation to labour, land and money we shall argue that there is something institutionally specific about capitalist economies markets that underpins the difference. There is not something intrinsic to humans that makes them untradable as other commodities, such as biological or universal societal characteristics. Similarly, with land and money, we do not regard these as 'fictitious commodities' in contrast to 'true commodities', by virtue of putative inherent universal properties. Rather, we would aim to analyse why there are systemic differences in the historically instituted exchange processes for these entitities.

In order to exemplify specificity across these three dimensions and its significance in conditioning the general nature of exchange processes, we apply the three analytical steps to two cases: labour markets and end-product markets. The intention here is not to analyse specific historic cases of either, but to develop the analytical tools for analysis of exchange as IEP.

Two exemplifications of the analytical framework

1. Labour markets and the organisation of exchange
In analysing the institution of exchange processes in labour markets, the three analytical steps will be taken in turn: the process of formation and separation of distinct classes of economic agent, the interlocking nexus of agents 'behind the scenes', and the exchange relation itself, all within the dynamics of asymmetric power and mutual dependency.

Much has been written in classic political economy about the separation of a class of employing agents and a class of labour-selling agents. In Marx's formulation, labour-power is exchanged in a capitalist labour market as a commodity *like any other*, with its value determined in the same manner as any other. Price is formed in (a not necessarily direct) relation to a common standard, the socially necessary time required for its production. For a Marxist account, the specificity of labour comes later in production, with the uniqueness of labour-power being that it in use it creates more value than its own value. In respect to the exchange process as such, there is little difference between a Marxist model and a neo-classical model of factor inputs.

However, there are differences in the exchange process that mark out labour as unique, and which have at least been partially recognised (Moncel, 2001; Swedberg, 1994). One difference resides in the inseparability of the seller of the entity from the entity sold. The purchase, in capitalist economies, is of the use of labour capacity, not of the bearer of the labour capacity. The bearer retains the labour capacity, only selling its use to the engagers of labour, in terms to be defined by the exchange process. In this respect, in historically and variously instituted capitalist labour markets, labour capacity, as possessed and retained by the sellers of labour use, is *not traded*. Capitalist labour markets are different from slave ones, where bearers of labour and their differential capacities are traded as commodities. Slave markets are labour markets of a different kind. In capitalist economies, human labour skills and capacities are not traded in the manner of talking parrots or guide dogs, where the value inputs involved in the training process are exchanged as an integral part of the commodity purchase. The educators have limited property rights over the way the educated trade in the use of acquired skills. Ownership of capacities resides in the trader of skills. Moreover, the doubling-up of the economic function of wage earner and consumer can be seen as essential to capitalist economic reproduction and growth, in contradistinction to slavery or feudalism (Genovese, 1967). Thus, without recourse to any Polanyian essentialist notion of human labour – contradicted by slave labour markets or some contemporary child labour markets – these aspects of labour markets can be seen as historically *instituted differences*.

Let us consider the significance of this double difference: the non-sale of the labour capacity as such and the inseparability of the entity sold from the seller. If labour capacity is not exchanged but retained by the bearer, and hence open to the bearer to offer its use for exchange elsewhere (mobility and distribution of labour power), or to decline to offer its use to sale (leisure or withdrawal of labour-use, etc.), the central question becomes how that labour capacity is produced or created as a non-tradable entity. The answer seems to be of central significance: unlike other commodities its production takes place largely through non-market processes, in which there is no possibility of successive market values being accumulated and transferred. This is precisely why labour capacity can never be analytically akin to capital, and why human capital models are erroneous (Becker, 1975; Rubinson and Browne, 1994): the accumulation of capacity is not achieved through successive transferable market value inputs, and the full 'worth' of the capacity is thereby uncashable.

It is perhaps worth at this point emphasising that capacities, cognitive or physical, are formed and produced by historically specific processes. They are not naturally occurring, universally present and evenly distributed –

unlike air.[8] This leads us into the second step of the analysis. The production of labour capacity rests on a nexus of economic agents behind the scenes of the exchange on the supply side, notably the household economy, and, with increasing significance from the middle of the nineteenth century onwards, education systems and health systems. These institutions and the processes of capacity creation and maintenance are assured by non-market forms of production, and outside market forms of exchange. As a counterpart to the non-tradability of labour capacity by the sellers of labour services in the exchange process, those involved in its production[9] also have no property rights over what they produce. In the case of the household economy, the process is one largely of unpaid labour.[10] In the case of education and health, there are differently instituted systems, but taxation or compulsory insurance form a central means of ensuring the resource flows necessary to sustain and expand these systems. The classes of economic agent behind the scenes that are necessary for the appearance of labour capacity on labour markets thus include a changing and variable range of agents, each with their own dynamic. Households, education and health systems develop in relation to the market economies with which they are coupled.

The central conclusion from the analysis of this first aspect of the specificity of exchange processes in labour markets is that dual or multiple market and non-market economic processes are integrally linked. Market and non-market processes are an inherent part of capitalist labour markets, and *capitalist economies are hence dual-, or indeed multiple-, process economies, and need to be analysed as such.* That the exchange price of labour includes tax or compulsory insurance is not an accidental or contingent phenomenon, but intrinsic to instituted processes of exchange by virtue of the connection between the exchangeable and non-exchangeable characteristic of labour capacity and its use.

Turning to the formation of the class of buyers of labour power, the ability to purchase labour services requires ownership of resources and capabilities to organise those services' use in such a way as either to create revenues from the sale of services or products or to create public goods. Firm- or organisation-internal divisions of labour generate demand for different labour-service capabilities. Internal capability differentiation is linked with industrial divisions and mutual dependencies between different classes of employing economic agents, behind the scenes of any particular class of agents' labour-service demand. The concept of IEP implies that these configurations of demand-side employing agents are open to major restructuring, as innovation brings about the emergence of new classes of employing agents and the disappearance of old ones. The formation and restructuring of economic agents creates new demand above the level of individual buying agents in a way quite remote from the elemental model of exchange. It also suggests a much more robust economic notion of the inter-relatedness of differential demand as a condition for instituted processes of exchange than social network models of supply or demand-side interactions (Baker, 1984; Granovetter, 1985, 1992a, b; White, 1981).

To take the third analytical step, given the inseparability of sellers of labour services from the entity sold, and hence the indissoluble linkage between the owner of labour capabilities and the use of labour services following the exchange processes outlined above, there is a strong incentive for both sellers and buyers to engage in interactions beyond and above the exchange. Property rights over the use of labour can never be unambiguously and absolutely transferred in a way possible with many products in product markets. The fact that sellers of labour power are ever-present during its use and after its exchange, and can organise amongst themselves in a way that products cannot (buyers of labour-use can do likewise), suggests that, in conditions of asymmetry of power and mutual dependency, negotiated interactions of some kind are quite likely to occur as a condition for continuing exchanges of labour services.

2. Product end-markets

From the analysis of processes of exchange of labour services, certain immediate contrasts can be drawn with processes of exchange of products/services. The first is that the producers (unlike educators, households, etc.) have property rights over the entity to be exchanged. The second is that these property rights are transferred, often completely and irreversibly, through exchange processes. Thus, *even in the case* where the product traded is a labour service, the firm owns the use of that labour service (not of course the labour capacity itself), and frequently adds value before trading it on, either as a 'pure' labour service, or as a continuing contract of labour service associated with a product. This is stating the contrast baldly. There are many cases where property rights can be ambiguous, both in their ownership and in their exchange: the vagaries of contractual law and compulsory state purchase point to the absence of absolute property rights, even within normalised economic processes.

Let us consider the historical emergence of mass production and consumption in terms of steps 1 and 2, the formation and differentiation of classes of economic agent either side of the exchange process. On the sell-side, mass production entails the co-emergence of mass distribution and retailing and a transformation of spatial and temporal scales of the markets. On the buy-side, it involves the development of new patterns of demand through urbanisation and an expansion of the wage-based economy over self-subsistence and paid or unpaid labour in the household economy. The significance of various 'retailing revolutions' in the process of mass consumption has been under-recognised (Harvey et al., 2000, 2002; Jefferys, 1954). The consequence of this dual transformation of retailers and consumers profoundly changes the organisation of exchanges between them.

On the sell-side, different product end markets are characterised by differentiated and contrasting structures of retail outlets, and historical processes of the extent and range of products in any one type of retail outlet have been subject to continuous restructuring. The rise and fall of department stores, the emergence of malls, the development of new forms of sale and distribution with the use of e-commerce intermediation, point to competition between different forms of organisation of end markets as much as competition between the branded products of major global manufacturers (Benson, 1986; Strasser, 1989).

If, therefore, from the sell-side there is a structuring of complementary retail outlets, from the buy-side also, demand is highly structured, in terms not only of differentiation and stratification within the class of consumers as economic agent, but of complementarities between demands for different products (such as ready-made foods and microwave ovens). The organisation and differentiation of 'lifestyles' is predicated on complementarities between whole ranges of interdependent products (Harvey, 2002; McMeekin et al., 2002).

Then, on either side of the exchange in end-product markets, the asymmetries and mutual interdependencies behind the end-exchange also demonstrate interdependency in the organisation of exchanges. For retailers in different product markets there are substantial variations between producers/manufacturers and retailers, differently structured developments of branding and marketing, and modes of quality standardisation and recognition. Producer-owned franchised outlets; franchising without producer-ownership of retail outlets for producer brands where prices may be fixed or not by manufacturers; retailer-branded manufacturing to retailer specifications where prices are fixed by retailers; or relatively independent trading between manufacturers and retailers, are suggestive of a range of possibilities. The organisation of exchanges in end markets by retailers is hence inextricably and variously linked to the organisation of exchanges between retailers and their suppliers.

On the buy-side, consumers' relations to other economic agents are likewise a condition for their purchasing activities in end-markets. Nowhere is this more clear than in the characteristics of consumer knowledge underpinning the organisation of end-market exchanges, with different forms of knowledge acquisition involving different and widely varying other classes of economic agent (formal education, household reproduction, informal peer-to-peer learning, and so on). Striking examples are perhaps compulsory driving teaching and testing, and the learning of cooking skills, both of which clearly demonstrate the dependence of market exchange on non-market processes. It is difficult to think of any end-market exchange that does not presuppose the interdependence of end-market consumers on a wide range of other social institutions, an interdependence that frequently is intermediated by an organisation of exchanges through taxation and state institutions. Cars and road infrastructure make the point, and not only for car end-markets.

In terms of analytical step three, there are many types of interactions between consumers and retailers that condition the nature and organisation of exchanges between them, consumer protection movements and organisation, protest and political representation, as well demonstrated by the creation and destruction of GM food markets in Europe (Harvey et al., 2002).

Conclusion

This chapter has chosen to focus on the organisation of exchange as an IEP. Acknowledging the importance of developments in economic sociology that have explored and elaborated on non-economic (political, legal and social) dimensions to markets, this limiting focus was intended to emphasise that the organisation of exchanges is a much broader field of enquiry than markets. From an anthropological standpoint, it stressed the need to situate markets both within the broader field of organised purchases of good and services, and non-discretionary exchanges in return for public and private goods and services, mediated by taxation, compulsory insurance and other such devices. Interaction between these different forms of organised exchange is seen as central to the dynamic for *economic* growth.

However, the insistence on the specifically (but not exclusively) economic character of exchange processes is accompanied by an emphasis on the historically and spatially specific instituted nature of exchange processes. In order to embrace the variety and continual transformation of exchange processes, an attempt has been made to create an analytical instrument able to interpret and explain this richness and diversity. An analytical process was developed which addressed different dimensions of variation. The formation and differentiation of economic agents is co-constituted with the exchange processes between them, as a condition of economic reproduction. Any one set of economic exchange processes is interdependent with others, both market and non-market, forming nexuses of exchange processes and interactions between different markets, as a condition for any given exchange process between a class of sellers and a class of buyers. Specifically economic interactions between parties to an exchange, including negotiations over the nature and conditions of exchange, are seen as a prerequisite for many exchange processes. Structural differences between consumer end-markets and labour markets were exemplified in this regard.

In addition to these sources of variation, differences in the specificities of exchange processes were analysed across three aspects: the nature of the entities traded, the specific characteristics of the agents engaged in the exchange processes, and the spatial and temporal specificities of exchange processes. These abstract aspects of specification are offered as general tools for analysing the source of variation, and not posited in order to contrast formal (economic) with real markets. They suggest that the specific nature and organisation of agents, of the goods and services that pass between them, and of the spatial and temporal dimensions of the exchange are necessary aspects of any transfer of property rights involved in exchange processes, whether these property rights are individual or collective.

Notes

1 Slater and Tonkiss (2001) and Carrier (1997) usefully cite a number of these, whilst adding themselves to the list.
2 This is not to foreclose on a discussion of dimensions of difference between market and non-market economic organisation in addition to exchange, such as production systems of public goods, modes of consumption of collective goods, and so on. But that is not the focus of this chapter.
3 Thus Fligstein argues that markets are examples of fields, and that 'the theory of fields is a generic theory of social organisation in modernity . . . The theory of fields assumes that actors try to produce a 'local' stable world where the dominant actors produce meaning that allow them to reproduce their advantage' (2001: 29). The analysis both assumes that stability of existing power relations accounts for the existence of markets – substituting for an equally problematic economic stability theory of equilibrium – and at the same time suggests that this power balance has nothing specifically economic about it. It is just that the powerful always seek to remain so.
4 It should be stressed that this is an analytical account, not an historical or geographical one. It is quite possible, empirically, for exchange processes to occur between separated economic agents without them having to be previously integrated or undifferentiated. The basis of the exchange nonetheless rests on a differentiation of economic function.
5 The singular is used here just for the sake of argument, not to suggest that there is a single, homogeneous class on either side of these exchange processes.
6 This elaborates on Fourie's (1991) concept of the necessary contra-positionality of exchange parties.
7 This position is also reflected in Fligstein, where he argues that 'Markets (and this includes almost all modern production markets) are mainly structured by sellers looking for buyers' (2001: 31), on the grounds that the firm's survival depends on securing a stable customer base. But, conversely, consumers' survival depends on being able to buy commodities. And, to refine this consumer need further, this 'survival' may mean buying a pair of Nike trainers rather than any other make, even in the presence of apparent alternatives.
8 In normal circumstances, air is non-commodifiable for these reasons, until one flies in an airplane where supply of air is part of the purchased commodity in a pressurised container.
9 It can be argued that for much educational work in the reproduction of generic capacities, there is co-production by teachers and taught.
10 Of course, child care can be purchased, but there is little evidence that this enhances the value of the labour capacity on the market, or constitutes a value input in the same manner that purchased services would constitute costs of production in products for product markets. The same argument applies essentially to private education, even if this accrues labour market advantages.

References

Baker, W. E. 1984. 'The structure of a national securities market', *American Journal of Sociology*, 89, 775–811.

Baker, W. E., Faulkner, R. R. and Fisher, G. A. 1998. 'Hazards of the market: the continuity and dissolution of interorganisational market relationships', *American Sociological Review*, 63, 147–77.

Becker, G. S. 1975. *Human Capital*. Columbia University Press. New York.

Benson, S. P. 1986. *Counter Cultures: Saleswomen, Managers and Customers in American Department Stores*. University of Illinois Press. Urbana.

Boyer, R. 1997. 'The variety and unequal performance of really existing markets: farewell to Doctor Pangloss', in Hollingsworth, J. R. and Boyer, R. (eds), *Contemporary Capitalism. The Embeddedness of Institutions*. Cambridge University Press. Cambridge, 55–93.

Callon, M. (ed.) 1998a. *The Laws of the Markets, Introduction*. Blackwell. Oxford.

Callon, M. 1998b. 'An essay on framing and overflowing: economic externalities revisited by sociology', in Callon, M. (ed.), *The Laws of the Markets*. Blackwell. Oxford, 244–69.

Carrier, J. G. (ed.) 1997. *Meanings of the Market: The Free Market in Western Culture*. Berg. Oxford.

Chamberlin, E. H. 1933. *The Theory of Monopolistic Competition. A Re-orientation of the Theory of Value*. Harvard University Press. Cambridge, MA.

Coase, R. 1996. 'The nature of the firm', in Buckely, P. J. and Michie, J. (eds), *Firms, Organisation and Contracts. A Reader in Industrial Organisation*. Oxford University Press. Oxford.

Coombs, R., Harvey, M. and Tether, B. 2001. *Analysing Distributed Innovation Processes*, CRIC Discussion Paper 43. CRIC. Manchester.

Fligstein, N. 2001. *The Architecture of Markets. An Economic Sociology of Twenty-first Century Capitalist Societies*. Princeton University Press. Princeton, NJ.

Fourie, F. C. 1991. 'The nature of the market: a structural analysis', in Hodgson, G. M. and Screpanti, E. (eds), *Rethinking Economics: Markets, Technology and Economic Evolution*. Edward Elgar Publishing. Aldershot.

Genovese, E. D. 1967. *The Political Economy of Slavery: Studies in the Economy and Society of the Slavery*. Vintage Books. New York.

Granovetter, M. 1985. 'Economic action and social structure: the problem of embeddedness', *The American Journal of Sociology*, 91(3), 481–510.

Granovetter, M. 1992a. 'The sociological and economic approaches to labour market analysis: a social structural view', in Granovetter, M., and Swedberg, R. (eds), *The Sociology of Economic Life*. Westview Press. Oxford: 53–81.

Granovetter, M. 1992b. 'Economic institutions as social constructions: a framework for analysis', *Acta Sociologica*, 35, 3–11.

Granovetter, M. and McGuire, P. 1998. 'The making of an industry: electricity in the United States', in Callon, M. (ed.), *The Laws of the Markets*. Blackwell. Oxford, 147–73.

Harvey, M. 2002. 'Markets, supermarkets and the macro-social shaping of demand. An instituted economic process approach', in McMeekin et al. (eds), *Innovation by Demand*. Manchester University Press. Manchester.

Harvey, M., McMeekin, A., Randles, S., Southerton, D., Tether, B. and Warde, A. 2000. *Between Demand and Consumption: A Framework for Research CRIC*

Discussion Paper No 40, ESRC Centre for Research on Innovation and Competition, University of Manchester/UMIST. Manchester.

Harvey, M., Quilley, S. and Beynon H. 2002. *Exploring the Tomato: Transformations of Nature, Economy and Society*. Edward Elgar. Cheltenham.

Hodgson, G. M. 1988. *Economics and Institutions: A Manifesto for a Modern Institutional Economics*. Polity Press. Cambridge.

Hodgson, G. M. 1994. 'The return of institutional economics', in Smelser, J. and Swedberg, R. (eds), *The Handbook of Economic Sociology*. Princeton University Press. Princeton, NJ.

Hodgson, G. M. 1997. 'The ubiquity of habits and rules', *Cambridge Journal of Economics*, 21, 663–84.

Jefferys, J. B. 1954. *Retail Trading in Britain. 1850–1950*. National Institute of Economic and Social Research, Economic and Social Studies, XII. Cambridge University Press. Cambridge.

Leyshon, A. and Thrift, N. 1997. *Money/Space: Geographies of Monetary Transformation*. Routledge. London.

Lundvall, B.-A. 1988. 'Innovation as an interactive process: from user–producer interaction to the national system of innovation', in Dosi, G., Freeman, C., Nelson, R., Silverberg, G. and Soete, L. (eds), *Technical Change and Economic Theory*. Pinter. London and New York.

McMeekin, A., Green, K., Tomlinson, M. and Walsh, V. 2002. *Innovation by Demand*. Manchester University Press. Manchester.

Moncel, N. 2001. 'Labour markets as instituted economic process. A comparison between France and the United Kingdom'. Paper to the Market and the Organisation of Exchanges Workshop, University of Paris Nord, November.

North, D. 1990. *Institutions, Institutional Change and Economic Performance*. Cambridge University Press. Cambridge.

North, D. 1996. 'Markets and other allocation systems in history: the challenge of Karl Polanyi', Swedberg, R. (ed.), *Economic Sociology*. Edward Elgar Publishing. Cheltenham.

Polanyi, K. 1944. *The Great Transformation*. Beacon Press. Boston, MA.

Polanyi, K. 1947. 'Our obsolete market mentality', commentary, 3 February, in Swedberg, R. (ed.) 1996. *Economic Sociology*. Edward Elgar Publishing, 109–17. Cheltenham.

Polanyi, K. 1957. 'The economy as instituted process', in Polanyi, K., Arensberg, C. M. and Pearson, H. W. (eds), *Trade and Market in the Early Empires*. The Free Press. New York.

Powell, W. W. and DiMaggio, P. J. 1991. *The New Institutionalism in Organisational Analysis*. University of Chicago Press. Chicago.

Randles, S. 2001. *On Economic Sociology, Competition and Markets: Sketching a Neo-Polanyian IEP Framework*. Draft CRIC Working Paper, presented as part of the CCP seminar series, University of Manchester, November.

Randles, S. 2002. 'Complex systems applied: the merger that made GlaxoSmith-Kline', *Technology Analysis and Strategic Management*. September.

Rubinson, R. and Browne, I. 1994. 'Education and the economy', in Smelser, J. and Swedberg, R. (eds), *The Handbook of Economic Sociology*. Princeton University Press. Princeton, NJ.

Slater, D. and Tonkiss, F. 2001. *Market Society. Markets and Modern Social Theory*. Polity Press. Cambridge.

Strasser, S. 1989. *Satisfaction Guaranteed. The Making of the American Mass Market*. Pantheon Books. New York.

Swedberg, R. 1994. 'Markets as social structures', in Smelser, N. and Swedberg, R. (eds), *The Handbook of Economic Sociology*. Princeton University Press. Princeton, NJ.

Swedberg, R. 1998. *Max Weber and the Idea of Economic Sociology*. Princeton University Press. Princeton, NJ.

Weber, M. 1922. *Economy and Society: An Outline of Interpretive Sociology*. University of California Press. Berkeley.

White, H. 1981. 'Where do markets come from?' *American Journal of Sociology*, 87(3) (November), 517–47.

Williamson, O. E. 1994. 'Transaction cost economics and organisation theory', in: Smelser, J. and Swedberg, R. (eds), *The Handbook of Economic Sociology*. Princeton University Press. Princeton, NJ.

Williamson, O. E. 1996. *The Mechanisms of Governance*. Oxford University Press. Oxford.

Williamson, O. E. 1997. 'Hierarchies, markets and power in the economy: an economic perspective', in Menard, C. (ed.), *Transaction Cost Economics: Recent Developments*. Edward Elgar. Cheltenham.

Williamson, O. E. 1999. 'The new institutional economics: taking stock/looking ahead', *ISNIE Newsletter*, 2(2) (Fall), 9–20.

4

The ordering of change: Polanyi, Schumpeter and the nature of the market mechanism

Mark Harvey and Stan Metcalfe

Introduction

In this chapter we address three questions – namely: 'What is the market?', 'Where do markets come from?' and 'How do markets work?' – to explore an approach to the market economy which draws together a Polanyian perspective on the instituting of markets with a Schumpeterian, evolutionary perspective on the role of markets as promoters of economic and social change. The familiar view of markets in particular and the market system in general is that they are institutions for solving a problem – that of allocating scarce resources to the satisfaction of multiple competing ends – and they achieve this by a process of self-organisation, a 'spontaneous order', to use Hayek's term. What is less well recognised is the market as a device to facilitate the self-transformation of economic activity, and as a frame to promote and diffuse novelty and to discover new ways of meeting human needs (Witt, 2003). Self-transformation depends on self-organisation, in that order is necessary before change can be conceived of and implemented, while it evolves the pattern of a market order; and rather than emphasising calculation by economic actors it points to their use of imagination and, fundamentally, to the link between market activity and the growth and application of knowledge. Among the arguments we shall mount, the following are of particular relevance.

First, the traditional view of markets, that they serve to impose equilibrium in the allocation of resources to meet given ends, seriously misrepresents the wider significance of the market. That a market-clearing price implies that every sale matches an equivalent purchase with no production unsold or demand unmet does not mean that this situation is one that can remain undisturbed until external circumstances alter. For the prices so established only serve to stimulate the question 'Can economic arrangements be improved?' Markets establish particular patterns of economic order and it is a confusion of language to call these orders 'equilibria'. It is a characteristic of any equilibrium that all internal reasons to change have been exhausted so that any disturbance of that position can only be achieved by the imposition of external and largely unpredictable forces that cannot be part of the explanation of equilibrium. Thus a market paradox arises: it is only in the presence of novel and thus unanticipated events that markets are needed. If the future states of preferences, resources and technologies were fully foreseen then prices for all time could be known today and markets would become redundant. It is because the generation of novelty is widely distributed and pervasive that there is a continual need for market institutions to re-impose order and to do so by absorbing novelty (Loasby, 2003; Witt, 2003). Moreover, the patterns of change are generated within the market process: not only do markets lead to self-organisation of economic orders, but the particular pattern of spontaneous order shapes the possible patterns of spontaneous transformation (Metcalfe and Ramlogan, 2005) – the two phenomena are inseparable.

Second, markets do not appear as if by magic. They are created by instituting processes and these processes mean that real resources have to be devoted to developing and maintaining market relationships. 'Who forms the market and why?' is the question, and that the answer varies across different markets is a matter we will address below. There are many forms of market organisation, differing fundamentally in terms of the presence and functioning of 'market traders' and other intermediaries, and the boundaries between market and non-market means of allocating resources is capable of major alteration over time. Different societies draw these boundaries differently in terms of public and private provision and the scope and regulation of market activity.[1]

Third, it follows from the above that markets are to be judged not solely in terms of allocating given resources either at a point in time or over time. The traditional economists' model of intertemporal general equilibrium deals with this question very well but it is the lesser of the ways in which we ought to judge market institutions, for it postulates a result without explaining the causal processes which make available the necessary resources and knowledge that underpin economic activity. Much more fundamental is the significance of markets in promoting economic change and in the discovery of new uses for resources and new ways of meeting new consumer needs. Markets are important precisely because they are arrangements in which novel actions are possible and indeed are encouraged. The crucial attribute of a market system is that it is an open system in which all established positions are open to potential challenge by superior methods or means of supplying goods and services. Moreover, it is not simply that they are open; they are also adaptable in that market systems facilitate structural change and the transfer of resources to new activities. Here the market economy is to be judged as an adaptive experimental system, a system in which innovation processes are of central importance.

Fourth, markets as instituted patterns of activity do not stand alone; they coexist with other instituted arrangements in society. Social norms and practices, for example, have a major influence on where the market boundary is drawn, as do political regulatory processes. It is therefore helpful to see the market in the context of a continuum of possible arrangements for changing the allocation of resources with a shifting boundary between market and non-market processes. Markets for health care, for example, operate very differently in the UK and the USA in terms of the balance of tax-funded and insurance-funded treatment and in terms of the private versus public provision of medical services. Both systems are heavily regulated by professional bodies and by government, particularly in respect of the process of innovation adoption. In both systems, ethical and moral suasions legitimise medical practice and draw clear boundaries to the scope of markets – for example, in terms of the possibility of markets in body organs. The social and political dimensions of market systems – fairness, power distributions, status, inequality – all influence self-organisation and self-transformation. In recent years, the spread of globalisation has shifted the boundary in favour of the market but this is not without challenge, and the grounds under which the scope of the market is limited provide considerable insight into a market economy. Thus, for example, there is much discussion in the WTO about extending competition law to developing economies, but this begs the question of how markets should be regulated to facilitate economic change and indeed how competition is a regulator of development. The point to be stressed is that the particular norms and rules of the game are specific to each market context and the evolution of these arrangements parallels the more usually investigated evolution of the products and their production processes. Too often markets are interpreted as devices solely to establish prices and patterns of exchange, whereas in fact they also play a key role in the distribution of goods and services. The relationship between exchange and distribution processes may vary but they are always interdependent and they are reflected jointly in the instituted frame of the particular market. So in sum, the need for exchange arises from continuously emergent divisions of labour, which firstly involves innovation of new goods and services; secondly, new modes of distribution of these across space and time; and, thirdly, new modes and organisation of the exchange process itself. Each of these three domains – along with practices of consumption – can be seen as domains of innovation in its own right, interdependent with each other. None of them presupposes the emergence of either market or non-market forms of organisation, so we could argue that 'markets' entail particular forms of interdependency between these three domains.

To explore these themes we draw upon the work of two of the intellectual giants in the social sciences, Joseph Schumpeter and Karl Polanyi, who in their very different ways provide a basis for understanding markets as devices to order economic change. We shall draw upon a range of our empirical and conceptual work to illustrate the connection between Polanyi on the one hand and Schumpeter on the other. In particular, the study of retail and wholesale markets in the UK provides an instructive example of how the way in which markets are instituted may be transformed very significantly over time. In this way, we expect to address the three questions posed in the opening paragraph.

The chapter is organised as follows. We begin with an exposition of Schumpeter's arguments that it is the self-transforming attributes of capitalism that distinguish it from other possible economic systems. However, self-transformation requires a context of self-organisation; change requires order against which alternative economic worlds can be imagined entrepreneurially. This leads us directly to Karl Polanyi's particular approach to the instituted nature of economic order, which is explained and subjected to critical assessment in the next section, following which we explore the evolution of the markets for food in the UK as an example of Polanyian change in the methods for creating economic order. We conclude with an attempted synthesis of the positions of Schumpeter and Polanyi, suggesting that missing bits from each are needed if the restless nature of market capitalism is to be understood more clearly.

Schumpeter and the inner dynamic of a market economy

Of all Schumpeter's work, his *Theory of Economic Development* published in 1911 provides the most compelling starting point for this account (Schumpeter, 1934). For in this essay Schumpeter raised and provided an answer to a central question in economic understanding, 'Why does the economic world change at the rate and direction at which it historically seems to do?' A brief outline of his approach will help fix our ideas.

The first and most significant aspect of this work from our viewpoint is that Schumpeter spends little time on the instituted basis of the market economy – it is, as it were, taken for granted and beyond a need for explanation. Markets are there without explanation, even though one of the classes of possible new combinations that he identifies is the discovery of new markets. Rather, Schumpeter's concern is with why that instituted system produces continuous economic change, a transformation in terms of human activity that is not explained by the prevailing economic theory, essentially the Walrasian account of market equilibrium or, we prefer to say, market order.

What are the elements of the Schumpeterian scheme? As is well known, he begins by contrasting the circular flow of economic life with the process of economic development. The former is his depiction of a self-reproducing pattern of economic activity in which the same activities are carried out in repeated interlocking cycles in patterns that reflect the ordering properties of the price mechanism. In this equilibrium or quasi-stationary situation, prices exactly cover the contracted costs of the productive inputs used in each activity and there is neither profit nor loss. Here, the role of markets is to establish prices and coordinate decisions to buy and sell; that is, to say to establish an economic order in terms of patterns of production, consumption and the allocation of resources. How those prices are established is left unexplained. Moreover, this is a world, as its label implies, in which time passes but nothing happens. Either its inhabitants are entirely devoid of imagination and unreflecting on their circumstances or, more plausibly, this is a logical construct out of real time: it may change but it cannot develop.

Thus, the circular flow is not a representation of capitalism in practice but a thought experiment or benchmark against which to judge the real processes at work. This benchmark may accommodate population growth, saving and the accumulation of capital, but otherwise it is a conservative system in which all the present activities have been in practice for time immemorial. In Isaiah Berlin's imagery such worlds are 'still, immutable, eternal'; they are effectively dead in terms of human agency. Consequently, although we can conceive of change in this order, we can only do so as a thought experiment in which a new order is a response to events that are from an economic view uncaused. Moreover, these effects can be analysed using the apparatus of the circular flow, the comparative static method – but these exercises are only meaningful if it is also assumed that the market order is stable. Stability of the price system, a market order in the narrow sense, is however a quite different matter from the stability of the overall economic order. Indeed, the stability of the former may be the precondition for the instability of the latter. Consequently, the great contribution made by Schumpeter is to raise and answer the question, 'How can an existing order be invaded by new activities and how does the acceptance of those activities result in the decline and disappearance of formerly healthy economic activities?' It is through these processes that development takes place, and standards of living are transformed in a very uneven fashion; self-organisation is necessary for this but it is not sufficient. Structural change, the growth of new activities, and the decline and disappearance of formerly established ones are the signatures of this process, and those signatures reflect the ordering dimension of markets and the instituted frames in which they operate.

The charge implicitly made by Schumpeter against the Walrasian theory of markets and its descendents is that it cannot explain the principal feature of modern capitalism, the knowledge-based transformation of activities so characteristic of the system from the 1750s onwards if not before. What that frame does not allow for is development from within that has an economic cause, and the central purpose of Schumpeter's account is to show how the most important form of change in capitalism is caused by the market process – it is not separate from it. Hence, Schumpeter's lasting contribution is not only to ask how the capitalist market system transforms itself from within, but to ask how this self-transformation is a product of the particular mode of self-organisation.

The endogenous element that generates self-transformation is innovation, the economic application of new combinations of productive resources, and the vehicle for the introduction of innovation is the entrepreneur or, more accurately, the enterprise. Innovation is a process of ongoing modernisation which is quite separate from inventive activity and is distinguished by its association with a new business plan; a plan which reflects the entrepreneurial conjecture that the economic world can be organised differently. Thus enterprise is associated with new economic conjectures that can only be partially based in current knowledge; the invention may be known but the viability of the business plan remains to be established. As the carrier of change, the entrepreneur must not only conjecture, he or she must also implement, and in doing so exercise the economic leadership to marshal and organise the necessary productive resources.[2] The consequences of this view are considerable.

First the entrepreneurial process must be associated with radical uncertainty. The success of a venture cannot be known, and since each new innovation is unique, a risk calculation is not possible: there is no logical basis for a probability judgement since the set of possible outcomes of the innovation cannot be closed in advance, a point that we recognise in terms of the unintended and unanticipated consequences of human action.[3] Markets become the context in which this uncertainty is resolved.

Second, in exercising leadership the entrepreneur must overcome the hostility of the interests that are threatened and the natural inclination in the population at large to proceed along existing routine channels of behaviour. These enterprise attributes are special and, according to Schumpeter, are held by a small proportion of the population against which the rest can only be judged as followers or imitators. Since the market order depends on an extended division of labour and knowledge, and within each activity a degree of understanding in common as to what is the most appropriate pattern if economic conduct, we see the entrepreneur in a new light as the agency that destroys existing patterns of understanding by establishing new patterns of economic knowledge. It is perhaps not surprising that in his later work Schumpeter coined the phrase 'creative destruction' to capture this process.

Thirdly, the mechanism of innovation-based transformation is closely connected to the price mechanism. The prevailing pattern of prices and quantities produced provides the basis for a tentative judgement of the economic viability of any new combination. Once the innovation is introduced, the prevailing pattern of prices for existing activities determines the actual profitability of a unit of production using the new method; profit emerges as a surplus associated with the superior productivity or superior desirability of the new combination.

Finally, profit acts as the inducement for others to follow by investing where the entrepreneur has led, so generating a swarm of imitation that diffuses the new method into the economy and in the process establishes a new set of prices and dispositions of resources consistent with the post-innovation economic order. As a consequence of this diffusion, the initial profitability of the innovation is destroyed and profit becomes, in Schumpeter's words, 'The child and the victim of development'. Thus, in the process of market adaptation to innovation profits appear as transient signals of an order that is far from equilibrium; transient not only in terms of imitative behaviour but transient also in terms of the induced competitive challenge posed by further, as yet unknown, competing innovations. This is a quite different perspective on abnormal profits which from an equilibrium perspective can only be explained as abuses of market power possibly mediated by strategic interaction.

Thus the Schumpeterian economic process is one of the creation of, and adaptation to, new opportunities, a process of internally changing market order in which the price and profit mechanism is central to its operation. That is to say, innovation and enterprise find their significance in the context of market order.

An appraisal

We begin by noting that Schumpeter's is not the only theory of enterprise in the context of the market process. Israel Kirzner (1973) has proposed a quite different conception, the entrepreneur as market trader cum arbitrageur, aware of the opportunities that arise when the same commodity or factor is sold at different prices, and buying and selling until the profit opportunity is extinguished. No innovation is entailed here, no imagination, no leadership, only alertness to the possibilities for profitable trade when those profit opportunities are created elsewhere in the system. Kirzner's entrepreneur is an answer to a different question from that posed by Schumpeter. It addresses a different problem: the establishment of market order not the transformation of market order. It is no less important for this because the problems of 'Who sets prices?' and 'Where do prices come from?' cannot be avoided, especially if we hold that the processes and patterns of self-transformation reflect processes and patterns of self-organisation. This is the first clue that the instituted nature of the economic process has a profound influence on the processes of change from within.

This leads to the idea that innovation is intrinsic to the competitive process in market capitalism. If business rivalry drives the competitive dynamic then rivalry depends on businesses following different courses of action, and this they do by innovating. No business gains a competitive advantage by copying its rivals or by holding to the same plans and expectations. This dynamic is, as Schumpeter realised, the dominant form of competition. It is not the perfectly competitive equilibrium of the circular flow that is responsible for the long-term increase in living standards but the competition from a new product or process. Crucially, it involves the displacement of inferior activities so that growth overall cannot be explained without recognising that many activities must decline and disappear in the process. Thus, for this kind of competition to work the system as a whole must be receptive to novelty and adaptive in the presence of novelty. Here lies the importance of the instituted frames of a market economy; enterprise and markets go together. The open nature of markets means that every established position is open to innovative challenge, while the price and profit mechanism generates the incentives and rewards from implementing novel conjectures. Market processes are from this view a 'low-cost' method of reallocating resources and demand relative to the alternative of centralised bureaucratic control and will be relied on and selected for when they are the most efficacious way of generating change. Yet there is a deeper foundation to this evolutionary process. What is involved in innovation-induced transformation is the growth of knowledge and the fact that the market process is the context in which economic knowledge is generated as conjecture turns to fact for the good or ill of the promoters. But if enterprise plans differ they cannot be reconciled; there are winners and losers; there is growth of some ventures and complementary decline in others. We cannot expect that in the face of such events knowledge and beliefs remain unchanged, and thus we must expect adjustments to entrepreneurial conjectures which maintain the system's transient states. This is exactly what is meant by saying that the competitive, market process is autocatalytic: it continually generates new knowledge of market prospects. Indeed, the central message of the Schumpeterian scheme is that it is the endogenous growth of knowledge that gives capitalism its dynamic properties, properties that are inherently historically dependent. This is, no doubt, why modern societies devote considerable resources within the market process to support the capacity to produce and use knowledge in the form of R&D, and expenditures on capability formation more generally. The fact that complementary expenditures on knowledge generation occur outside the market process, in education and public research activities, simply points to the particular epistemic foundations of restless capitalism. Clearly the market process operates within a wider instituted frame of knowledge generation and application in which public and private activity and market and non-market means of establishing order interact.

Karl Polanyi and the instituted economic process framework

We have seen that the idea of endogenous change within markets, generated by entrepreneurial innovation and the restless capacity of knowledge to conjure alternatives, was central to Schumpeter's critique of self-regulating – in the sense of equilibrating – markets. This critique, and the Schumpeterian evolutionary alternatives, can be seen to be 'from within' the market, primarily from the standpoint of the entrepreneur or firm. Karl Polanyi was equally determined to develop a critique of self-regulating markets, but, taking an historical and comparative anthropological stance, his critique was by contrast 'from without'. He was almost unconcerned with the capacity of innovation activities within markets to generate change, or to see markets as an environment shaping innovation through selection. Rather, he was concerned to situate historically at the beginning of the nineteenth century both the 'self-regulating market' – as an outcome of the 'Great Transformation' – *and* a self-regulating market ideology viewing 'the economy' of all societies through its own distorting lens. Thus, for Polanyi, the self-regulating market as economy and ideology were historically instituted and located, rather than universal or natural economic 'laws'. As such, the market, and its place within society, could be historically transformed, and these processes of institution and transformation were his empirical and theoretical interest. We could crudely contrast Schumpeter as identifying the source of change as being intra-market endogenous, and Polanyi as market-organisation endogenous. Comparing the two enables us to see each for their limitations and to consider a more complex combination of levels of change and order, a point that we shall develop later.

Polanyi viewed the emergence of the 'self-regulating market' and its ideologues in terms of a double shift. Firstly, markets became hegemonic, pervasive throughout the substantive economy for provisioning people's needs and wants. In particular, this meant that, aside from commodities that had long been traded in markets, land, labour and money were marketised to an historically unparalleled extent. Other forms of provisioning, for example through reciprocal obligations, were squeezed out, and the market became dominant. Secondly, and equally important, the place of the economic in society shifted. Here an ambiguity creeps into Polanyi. He suggested that as markets became 'self-regulating' – that is to say, functioning without social or political intervention – they became 'disembedded' from society, and the economy ran itself. Being dominant, moreover, the market economy ran society, rather than society or the polity running the economy.[4] However, this was also the ideological representation of supporters of the free market, of a laisser-faire self-regulating economy, an economy best left to the hidden hand, to automatic equilibrating processes. It was a belief system that the economy should be self-regulating that aided and abetted the institution of a market that functioned *as if* it were self-regulating.[5] If the self-regulating economy was ideologically represented as running itself without political intervention, in fact it could only be instituted by political action and, once instituted, it required the full state apparatus of law and regulation to maintain it.[6]

This ambiguity is further intensified by Polanyi's main dynamic theory of market change, the theory of the 'double movement'. In the process of historical institution, market forces voraciously absorbed everything into their orbit, and in so doing were essentially destructive – the contrast with Schumpeter here is quite instructive – especially of land, labour and money. The unrestrained marketisation of the natural world would lead to ecological disaster. The unlimited marketisation of labour would destroy the human capacity to survive if every aspect of life became dependent on market exchanges, if nothing was left outside its orbit. The unfettered marketisation of money – treating the means of payment as if it were a tradable commodity like any other with free fluctuations of its price – would result in catastrophic economic turbulence.[7] This trebly destructive potential from the historical outset provoked a reaction, a countermovement of regulation. So, legislation to protect labour, especially that of children and women, and laws to protect the urban environment and prevent pollution emerged to prevent an otherwise headlong rush to disaster. The implication is that a non-market (public or domestic) economic domain was from the outset an historical necessity for the development of capitalism. The double movement, force and counterforce, underpinned the 100 years of peace that followed the Napoleonic Wars in Europe.[8] This is in many ways a remarkably static account of the transformations that took place over the century, like two counterposing armies locked in a war of position, one temporarily gaining or losing some territory at the expense of the other, until the collapse of the Gold Standard, and the eruption of competitive economic wars of the early twentieth century. The century of peace is explained in terms of what definitely would have happened had it not been prevented from happening. The self-regulating market was an impossible utopia, never an actually instituted economy.[9] Well, Polanyi leaves us a bit uncertain on this count.

It is helpful, however, to place the concept of markets as found in *The Great Transformation* in the broader context of Polanyi's later work. Although never claiming to achieve a 'complete theory of economic institutions' (Polanyi, 1960: 309), Polanyi gave a centrality in all his writing to movements 'locational or appropriational or both' (1960: 307): economic processes are restricted to two core processes of motion: spatial distribution of goods and services, and transfers of ownership, however socially organised.[10] Polanyi argues that these distributional and property-exchange processes are the integrative principle underlying all economies, and he identifies three primary modes of integration in historical societies: reciprocity, redistribution and market exchange. For example, reciprocity characterised many societies organised through kinship, and redistributional systems could be achieved by a monarchical or religious institutional centre. For exchange to become the integrative principle, price-making markets were the prototypical organisational form.[11] In this respect, Polanyi understands markets as coordinating devices necessary for socio-economic integration across geographical space and time. In Joan Robinson's terms, they are the critical intermediating institutions between scattered buyers and sellers (Robinson, 1979: 148). The three forms of integration can perfectly well sit side by side.[12] But it is clear for Polanyi that something happened towards the end of the eighteenth century that resulted in the market form of integration driving out other forms of integration in England, and progressively the rest of Europe and eventually the world. Markets were the core integrative functions of the economy within a regime of the self-regulating market. Societies were economically distinguished by their modes of integration through distribution and property-exchange, their circulating principle. Capitalism was defined as a market society, rather than markets being defined as capitalist, pre-capitalist, or – as Joan Robinson has done – socialist. Markets made capitalism, rather than capitalism made markets. The strength and weakness of this Polanyian account is that on the one hand he understood exchange processes – or other reciprocal or redistributional processes – as instituted processes operating according to their own principles, and on the other he thereby limited the possible sources of change, effectively excluding intramarket changes arising from innovation, and only considering a model of a market that hovered somewhere between a liberal utopia (or his dystopia) and historical reality, all change arising from the oscillations of regulation and deregulation.

Braudel's excoriating and somewhat misdirected critique of Polanyi (1979: 227–8) arises from his long-duration historical approach, which identifies no fundamental break in terms of market organisation at the beginning of the nineteenth century, unjustly accusing Polanyi of the methodological error of arbitrary anthropological comparisons between nineteenth-century England and examples plucked from anywhere, any time.[13] The force of his critique, however, lies in his demonstration of the historical evolution and widespread, even pervasive, presence of self-regulating markets across Europe certainly, as well as in China, India and the Islamic world. Moreover, Braudel traces the proliferation of what he calls 'layers' of markets, as well as market-to-market interdependence within a layer. The elementary or even 'natural' (Polanyi, 1957a: 21) form of market, a first layer, are direct producer-to-consumer markets, in the German term, *Hand in Hand, Auge in Auge Handel* – hand-to-hand, eye-to-eye trading. But from a very early stage, certainly by the thirteenth century, the fairs and exchanges developed an overlaying layer, both in terms of more internationally traded and high-value merchandise, but more importantly in terms of markets for credit and money markets, with paper currencies and bills of exchange.[14] The circuits of this superior layer were critical for the functioning of the inferior layer as well. By the beginning of the sixteenth century two further developments had substantially created further levels of market intermediary institutions: the enormous expansion of the wholesale warehouse trade often dealing in commodity futures and the establishment of a permanently based, and relatively centralised, stockmarket and exchange market in Amsterdam first, soon followed by London, Geneva, Lyons, Bordeaux and Nantes in the eighteenth century: the 'big business hexagon' (Braudel, 1979: 104). Denounced by moralists as 'Windhandel' (trading in wind), such was the complexity of commodity futures trading, derivatives trading and hedging in bills of exchange, that Joseph de la Vega described these markets in a book entitled *Confusión de confusiones* (1688). But the key implication from Braudel, to which we shall return, is the interdependency between new upper-layer forms and instruments of exchange, including price institutions, and the expansion of the time- and space-frames of distribution of goods and services.

Braudel's account of the interdependency and progressive layering of markets[15] prior to industrial capitalism provides an important context for an understanding of the market economy. However, in denouncing Polanyi's 'self-regulating market' as a 'figment of the imagination' (Braudel, 1979: 227) – we have already seen that Polanyi also considered it to be a figment but of the liberal economists' imagination – Braudel adopts a strangely narrow, and at the same time ahistorical concept of 'the market economy'. The market economy emerges whenever 'prices in the markets of a given area fluctuate in unison, a phenomenon the more characteristic since it may occur over a number of different jurisdictions and sovereignties' (1979: 227).

This fairly abstract and surprisingly ahistorical concept exposes a weakness shared by Polanyi and Braudel, but comes to the core of what might be called 'the order of the market', relating directly also to Schumpeter's circular flow. It is a concept of a 'self-regulating' circuit of supply and demand governed by a fluctuation of prices that occurs regardless of, or indeed supervenes over, any regulation formal or informal. This concept highlights the key difference between 'regularities' and 'regulations', in a way obscured by the term 'self-regulating'. These regularities, the cycles of exchange and distribution, with the different periodicities of 'hand-to-hand' and trading in credit or paper money, can also be distinguished from 'norms' or rules, whether formal or informal. They have a specifically economic constraint, and are necessary for economic integration and order, a level of stabilisation of economic processes. Without wishing in any way to underestimate the importance of historical changes in formal market regulation, laws of competition and property, essential to any comprehensive analysis of historical order and change, this chapter analytically restricts itself to consideration of 'regularities' and order and change in relation to these, in the encounter between Schumpeter and Polanyi.

And this notion of regularities of economic processes is where the seminal, but rather undeveloped, Polanyian concept of 'instituted economic process' comes back in. The processes of exchange and distribution – including very varied institutions of price-making and -taking, and of price competition – are continuously subject to historical change. There is no general, ahistorical, ageographical, market mechanism. It is a shared deficit of both protagonists that neither Braudel nor Polanyi developed an analysis of different forms of pricing institution, or different organisations of supply and demand, or competition. In spite of everything, they made more or less the same assumption about a 'self-regulating market', as Schumpeter, and had little more to say beyond a concept of supply and demand governed by fluctuations of price without, or in spite of, regulatory intervention. Indeed, Braudel adopts an extreme Chamberlinian[16] stance by even branding capitalism as 'anti-market', and by arguing that the emergence of large power firms, advertising, branding and monopolisation subvert the 'true' autonomous market regularities of price determination.[17]

Yet, by developing a concept of instituted economic process, it is possible to differentiate between 'self-regulating' markets in terms of differently instituted forms of circular flow, intermediation, supply, demand, organisations of exchange, price fluctuations and competition. It is for this reason that we prefer the more neutral and differentiating concept of the 'organisation of exchange', and instituted processes of exchange, to avoid definitional and superfluous arguments over the term 'market' (Harvey and Randles, 2003, and chapter 3 in this volume). For it is certainly clear that there are varied organisations of exchange and pricing, related to flows of goods and services, in labour markets, capital markets, inter-firm trading and end-product markets of all different kinds, and whether analytically one calls them markets is neither here nor there. Moreover, as we have argued elsewhere, adopting a more anthropological concept of the 'organisation of exchange' also allows us to embrace Polanyian examples of economies based on redistribution and reciprocity, as well as forms of exchange mediated by taxation and the state. Indeed, if it is often said that there are no markets without regulation, it is also the case that there are very few markets without taxation. This is so of most of the examples of markets to be found in Braudel's historical treasury of markets, as of Polanyi's redistributive monarchical economy in Dahomey (Polanyi, 1966). Indeed, it has been powerfully argued that a large part of the British colonial administration throughout the nineteenth century could not have existed but for the opening up of the opium markets, and the tax farms and regimes that benefited from it (Trocki, 1998).[18] Opium was not only in value one of the most significant commercially traded global commodities through much of the nineteenth century, but also, along with sugar and tea, pioneered factory organisation and commodity production for the market, which heralded a new phase of marketisation of many economies. At the same time, opium taxation was an essential pillar of Empire. It exemplifies the mutual interdependency between growth of the state and growth of the market, quite the antithesis of any conception of state versus market.

Thus, developing a concept of organisation of exchange enables us to analyse different modes of exchange and their interdependency. It means that different forms of 'regularity' of economic processes and how they are instituted becomes an object of analysis in their own right. Furthermore, this view draws attention to the many kinds of economic individuals other than firms and consumers that may lie outside the market narrowly defined yet which are essential to the operation of the market system as a whole. This in turn contributes to our attempt to sharpen the motivating question behind this chapter, namely the relation between intra-market order and change and market-institutional order and change, the Schumpeter–Polanyi encounter. However, in order to make this discussion more than an abstract

Table 4.1 Configurations of the exchange organisation of Covent Garden, 1200 to 1970

	Supply organisation	Price institution	Exchange process	Demand organisation
1200–1530	Monastic agricultural surplus	'Just price'?	Producer–consumer direct trade	Urban elite
1530–1700	Chartered guild of market gardeners	Regulated prices	Market producer–traders to end consumers	Aristocratic elite
1680–1830/50	Commercial growers, international trade	Fluctuating market prices?	Retailer-organised sales to consumers	Merchant, bourgeois, aristocratic households
1830–1970	National agriculture and international trade	Commission agent sales, blind pricing, market clearing	Wholesalers to retailers exchanges, centralised wholesale market, with secondary wholesale markets	Urban populations, all classes, wage earners
1970–THE END of Covent Garden as intermediating institution	Integrated supply chains	Supermarket price ranges	Open-book accounting upstream, consumer catchment area end market	Segmented hierarchically differentiated lifestyles

one, we first provide some empirical illustrative material, related to the satisfaction of that most basic of human wants, food.

A case study of the evolution of the organisation of exchange and distribution of food

The empirical grist to the analytical mill has been chosen to in order to pose the question of the relationship between market organisational order and change, and intra-market order and change. The historical example is that of the 800-year history of London's central fruit and vegetable market, Covent Garden, and its final demise, and the historical evidence will be presented in a schematic and stylised fashion.[19] The first presentation of the case will be entirely 'Polanyian', as it is unproblematic to present the material entirely in terms of order and change with respect to the organisation of distribution, intermediation and exchange. It is an account which is convincing almost without any consideration of the flow of food, or changes in the nature of food over these eight centuries: order and change irrespective of product innovation. The second part of the presentation, however, looks at the same story from the Schumpeterian standpoint, order and change driven by product innovation. The concluding discussion will then attempt to go beyond either perspective, by synthesising the two levels of order and change.

The Polanyian account

The history of the Covent Garden[20] organisation of exchange will be analysed with four dimensions: the organisation of supply, the organisation of the distribution and exchange process, the price institutions (where there is the historical evidence), and the organisation of demand. Broadly, the history of Covent Garden can be divided into five periods, each with a distinctive organisational configuration and economic function. Each configuration, it is argued, involves a transformation and establishment of a new order of regularities between the four dimensions, as summarised in Table 4.1.

1200–1530

The market acquired its name as the New Convent Garden, and was essentially supplied by the agricultural surplus produced by the large London estates of the monasteries and convents until the dissolution of the monasteries in 1530. The supply was supplemented by similar surplus-to-needs production from large feudal estates. The trade was direct producer–to–consumer trade, but it seems that the main consumers were the urban elites, so quite different from the peasant markets described by Braudel, that were also a major feature of the wider market activity in England throughout this period. No direct evidence exists for price institutions, but given the monastic provenance and the dominant religious concepts of just price, it is difficult to see these markets as driven by commercial profit-seeking activities.

1530–1680

The Gardners Company was given a Royal Charter after many years operation, acting as an incorporating guild, having at that time 1,500 market gardeners, with 400 apprentices, and dedicated commercial production-for-market from gardens surrounding the capital.[21] The Gardners Company was selling produce to the urban elite, as producer–distributor–retailers, but in 1670 Lord Bedford, a major English aristocratic–political family, was granted a Charter free of royal taxation, but with rights to exact tolls from all traders and regulate the entrants. By 1704 there were regular retail markets three times a week on the Covent Garden chartered site. Consumption was increasingly by the urban middle classes, and especially following the Great Fire in 1666 there was an enormous expansion of the urban population, which doubled in London between 1600 and 1700 from 250,000 to 500,000.

1680–1830/50

A third phase, reflecting the expansion of urban populations and the scale of commercial agriculture required to meet its needs, saw the end of the combined producer–distributor–retailer. Extensive and large-scale distribution channels with dedicated wagons to carry quantities of produce from further afield led to the establishment, the first by Sarah Sewell in 1712, of retailers in business on their own account. These were increasingly supplied from the various wharves on the Thames with exotic produce from across the world, as well as from the agricultural catchment area of the Lea Valley, and other areas with canal or wagon transport access to central London. The retail outlets were permanent outlets, replacing the cyclical markets, and this in turn no doubt affected the pricing fluctuations of the market, as a result of continuous trading. Retailers were continuously active in excluding 'higglers', mostly itinerant traders offering cut-price goods. So a form of competition arose between itinerants and fixed-outlet retail traders. In terms of demand, the urban populations were now far more variegated, with artisans, crafts and professions, as well as the established aristocratic and merchant households that surrounded the actual market.

1830/50–1970

Everitt (1985) has recorded the growth of the distinction between wholesale trading and retailing, and certainly Braudel has demonstrated that for many areas of trade the eighteenth century witnessed the concentration of trading power in warehousing so emphasised by Sombart. Wholesaling became a functionally differentiated intermediary operation that eventually brought about a revolutionary change in the operation of Covent Garden, requiring different circuits of exchange and credit. Along with the growth of canal and then especially rail transport radiating from the capital, Covent Garden ceased functioning as a retail market selling to London consumers, and became a highly centralised national hub for the wholesale marketing of fruit and vegetables. A large percentage of the flow of this produce went through this one central market, to be distributed to secondary wholesale markets across the country. As a consequence, there was high level of national price integration, dictated by the Covent Garden market price, probably unparalleled in Europe for this kind of produce. The pattern of trading, in terms of the organisation of exchange, was described in the Runciman Report (Runciman Committee, 1957), as one of dispersion–concentration–dispersion, with 70,000 primary producers feeding into 320 primary wholesalers, which in turn sold produce on to 150,000 retailers. As the central hub, Covent Garden's share of the market was seven time greater than the size of the next wholesale markets of Manchester, Birmingham, Glasgow or Liverpool. The price institution itself was essentially producer-driven commission sales on behalf of growers, a percentage added to the price gained in the market. The price-setting institutions were quite distinctive, stalls displaying produce but no prices, operating on a spot-market daily basis, with no transparent current price information, again a feature of wholesale concentrated power over fragmented retailers. The commission salesman was the pivotal agent, 'on a pedestal', and the market was designed to clear irrespective of quality: for a price, anything could be sold. It is worth emphasising the institutional distinctiveness of this pricing process. By contrast, the equally centralised wholesale fruit and vegetable market in The Netherlands operated a producer-driven clock auction, where the price was visible to all traders, starting from the top of price expectations and decreasing until the market cleared (Harvey et al., 2002: 80–92). Different articulations and organisations of supply, distribution and demand were hence linked to quite different price institutions, including the instituted 'governing principle' of price fluctuations, and competition. This clearly indicates the necessity to develop a differentiated analysis of 'self-regulation' beyond the ahistorical assumptions shared by Braudel, Polanyi and, indeed, Schumpeter.

1970–

Jefferys has described the revolution in retailing that occurred from the late nineteenth century as equivalent to the revolution in industrial production, in terms of its organisation of the productive activity and its impact on consumption. Covent Garden, until that time, had largely supplied street markets as the retail outlet. Grocery stores that traded mostly in non-perishable foods such as tea and sugar had existed from the seventeenth century as fixed and permanent outlets. But fresh food retailing in greengrocers was a relatively late phenomenon, beginning in the early twentieth century. Jefferys describes the first wave of concentration and national integration of retail chains, pioneered by the Co-operative Society. This first 'revolution' laid the groundwork for the second, qualitatively different, level of concentration with nationally integrated retail chains, the 'multiple' supermarkets. From the late 1960s onwards these progressively developed their own dedicated integrated supply chains, so that by the mid-1970s Covent Garden progressively ceased to function as a market for fruit and vegetables after nearly 800 years. It was simply bypassed, and the various successive integrating function of the market during its many phases became a relic of history. The whole organisation of distribution and intermediation was superseded eventually by monopsonistic retailer-led integrated supply chains (Harvey et al., 2002). With its passage, an historical evolution of organisation of exchange and the pricing institutions and a mode of distri-bution also came to an end. Whereas wholesale markets were typically spot-markets with market-clearing prices, supermarkets have profoundly different organisation of pricing, both upstream to suppliers with open-book accounting, and downstream to consumers, with segmented and quality differentiated population catchment areas, and high levels of price-quality differentiation. This demonstrates the instituted nature of processes of exchange and modes of price fluctuation, the very governing principles of regularities of economic processes.

In a Polanyian account, it is possible to interpret these five configurations as 'instituted economic processes' of exchange and distribution, each with distinctive price institutions, as well as distinctive forms of competition between different organised agents. It is a perspective that encourages one to go beyond a supply–push, or demand–pull view of markets, and rather to inspect and analyse different articulations between organisations of supply, demand, exchange and intermediation. The configurations thus establish the historically distinctive interrelated *modus operandi* for each of the classes of economic agent involved from production through to con-sumption, the framing conditions of the economic activity. Table 4.1 sum-marises each configuration, showing the interdependencies between different organisations of supply, distribution, exchange, and pricing institution for each historical epoch. The purpose of the summary is to focus on configu-rational change as what is in need of explanation. There is no implication of this being more than a particular and English case, no suggestion of any universal historical process of economic growth and differentiation. Indeed, elsewhere the history of the tomato suggests quite the opposite, a variety of historical trajectories (Harvey et al., 2002). It is an illustrative case to sharpen the questions to be posed in our constructed Schumpeter–Polanyi encounter.

Moreover, in addition to the 'order' and integrating function of each configuration, one can construct a Polanyian type of explanation for the sometimes quite revolutionary transformation of configurations. In the first place, the expansion of urban populations, and those entirely dependent on markets to meet needs and acquire food changed and concentrated demand in a new organisation of demand. The class of agents supplying food went through many processes of reorganisation and concentration, expanding the scale of their operations through a process of differentiation of inter-mediaries: primary producers, intermediary producers, distributors, market salesmen and organisers, credit agencies, retailers – and so on. Additionally, distribution channels changed and agricultural catchment areas expanded, historically the most revolutionary being the emergence of national canal and rail networks. International trade certainly brought many novel food-stuffs, apart from the sugar, tea and coffee so essential, it appears, to the coffee houses that became centres of the new commercial markets of the City of London. Tropical and Mediterranean fruits were channelled through Covent Garden, but these seem to be more a consequence of opening up and developing the organisation of trade, than of any food product innova-tion as such. Throughout this process, new classes of economic agent emerged and differentiated, with functions of selling, storing, transporting, wholesaling, retailing, brokering, and so forth separating out into spe-cialised, yet mutually dependent agents. How each of them was organised, as well as their relative economic power relations, was critical to the organisation of exchanges between them, the forms of competition, and the pricing institutions. The two key Polanyian instituted processes of distribu-tion and appropriation expanding the circulation of goods thus provide a powerful analytical framework for interpreting the successive ordering and changes of organisations of exchange. It seems almost possible to view this history without reference to food innovation as such, and just to focus on organisation of exchange.

Is there a counterpart Schumpeterian interpretation? There are three strands to a possible answer to this question. Firstly, of course, there was a transformation of agricultural production, not only with the wool trade, but, from the seventeenth and eighteenth century, a major revolution in agricultural production without which the expansion of towns and levels of urbanisation would have been impossible. Even within the narrower domain of foodstuffs flowing through Covent Garden, from the sixteenth century there were early innovations of glasshouse production, and cer-tainly improvements in fruit quality with new hybridisations, and improv-ing techniques in grafting (Webber, 1972). Although Henry VIII was supposed to have preferred the sweet potato as a New World introduction, Zuckerman (1999) has pointed to the significant but slow process of inno-vation that resulted from the introduction of the potato, which eventually, of course, transformed the staple diet of rural and urban populations through the introduction of an entirely new carbohydrate source. The Irish potato monocultural tragedy apart, it should be emphasised that for Western Europe as a whole the nineteenth century was the first to be free of regular, widespread and frequently decimating famines. These are just a few exam-ples of innovations in both production processes and novel products that can be properly seen as intra-market innovation. Secondly, there are the indirect but interdependent innovation processes that were also critical to the development of food markets: most obviously, innovations in the transport and distribution technologies, but also the expansion and development of urban trades, such as clock-making that had an impact on so much of the organisation of urban productive life (Landes, 1983). What a Polanyian account might take for granted, the expansion of towns or the extension and acceleration of distribution are themselves at least in part the outcome of properly Schumpeterian innovation. Thirdly, however, there is the process of new market formation for manufactured foods, the revolution in food processing and preservation, that effectively transformed the nature of the food we eat, and both displaced dependency on fresh food supply or more traditional methods of food preservation (salting, drying, pickling, curing, etc.), whilst at the same time revolutionising the ease of distribution of food, by making foodstuffs less restricted in time and space. If supermarkets eventually bypassed wholesale fresh food markets, manufactured foods had done so nearly a century beforehand, notably with the introduction of canning. Taking these three strands together, a Schumpeterian reading of market transformation from within, given also the interdependency between different markets, seems not only powerful, but necessary.

Beyond the Schumpeter–Polanyi encounter

These two explanatory accounts, each with their own plausibility, run in parallel rather than talk to each other. Neither seems in a position to fully address the questions asked by the other: a concern with product or process innovation seem quite inadequate to address the nature of change involved in the reconfigurations of the organisation of exchange, and, likewise, the organisation of exchange seems to have little to say about what is exchanged, let alone processes of innovation in production. The problem for a Schumpeterian account is that markets as organisation of intermediary distribution and exchange, subject to their own processes of order and change, appear much more than a selection environment for processes of innovation. The problem for a Polanyian account, most visible in *The Great Transformation*, but also in the restriction of economic processes to those of distribution and appropriation, is that production processes and products are almost absent as a potential source of change, as if *what* is distributed and appropriated is of little account. That is why, for him, capitalism is defined by a revolution in markets, not a revolution in production.

The fruitfulness of the encounter, however, is that it stimulates the question of what the nature of *interaction* might be, or what the dynamic processes of order and change there are, *between* intra-market and inter-market creation and destruction on the one hand, and changes in the organisation of intermediation and exchange on the other. The long history of Covent Garden is clearly only a very partial cut at a very complex reality of food provisioning, demonstrating, however, the historic transformations of the organisation of intermediation, one dimension only of the 'circular flow' or the integrative functions of markets, between the organisation of production and the changing structures of consumption. One of the key aspects of these changes in the organisation of intermediation, also in evidence from Braudel's and Skinner's historical accounts, concerns the changing articulation between exchange processes and distribution processes, on top of the changes within each of them. Skinner's unique and detailed study of modes of transition from traditional periodic markets to a modernisation and commercialisation of agriculture resulting in the destruction of periodic markets, 'true modernisation', was driven first by the industrialisation of towns including factory cloth manufacture from local cotton, but second, and critically, by the modernisation of transport, especially that of roads, rail and steam river navigation (Skinner, 1965: 195–228). One striking consequence of this was also the transformation of pricing institutions and associated weights and measures, once peculiar almost to each local market and with buyer–seller price negotiation,[22] then replaced by generalised regional continuous supplier-fixed pricing. This constituted a thoroughgoing commercialisation of both trading activities and agricultural production. In turn, there were consequential changes in the vertical layering of markets, including the exchange and credit markets supervening above consumer end-markets. Furthermore, as we have seen, the historical separation of intermediary wholesaling markets and consumer end-markets also involved a reconfiguration of the relations between distribution and exchange, as a consequence of the creation of separate phases of distribution on the one hand and a serial organisation of successive exchanges, on the other.

So a first cut at the answer to the post-encounter question is that there are clearly dynamic interactions between changes in distribution processes and changes in the nature of exchanges, and vice versa. The digitisation of information (sound, vision, data of all kinds) is just one recent historical case of where modes of distribution have transformed modes of exchange, and even challenged the tradability of certain products, because of the changed linkage between distribution and appropriation that resulted from the unlimited replicability of digitised information. During this transition, previously accepted boundaries between public and private provision and the scope of market processes have been radically revised and have brought forth new modes of regulation. Innovations of technique resulted in innovations of the organisation of exchange, which in turn have deeply influenced the incentives to and organisation of the associated innovation processes. In short, Schumpeterian innovations in distribution processes, and even in the qualitative characteristics of the objects traded, can fundamentally affect the conditions and modalities of property exchange.

This in turn can be broadened out to consider each phase and level of the 'circular flow' in terms of its organisation upstream and downstream, not only the succession of exchanges or the phases of distribution, but of the relations between economic agents, the mutual dependencies and asymmetries of power, involved from primary production through to consumption. In this chapter, we have primarily focused upstream, starting from the point of final exchange. The relation of producer to consumer, we have seen, was fundamentally transformed from the 'hand-to-hand, eye-to-eye' trading, with the differentiation of multiple phases of intermediation, and each new method of intermediation was an innovation in market organisation and function. The structure of these relationships of intermediation are, in this light, not so much an external selection environment for novel innovations, but the framing internal conditions under which innovation is undertaken, with different modes of innovation occurring under different conditions of intermediation, including, as we have seen different pricing institutions. It is clear, for example, that retailers do not normally innovate the new products that they trade in. But it is equally clear that manufacturers innovate in entirely different ways depending on the organisation of the retailer–manufacturer trading relationships – and indeed the organisation of retailer–consumer trading relationships. The Schumpeterian viewpoint is a view of innovation within one particular mode of innovation, and within a particular structured relationship of intermediation between producers and consumers. From Braudel, moreover, and his important contribution in analysing the 'layering' of markets, we can take the exchange process itself, and its institutional arrangements, as a significant domain of constant historical innovation. The emergence of financial institutions and instruments, the new classes of economic agent associated with them, results in changes in the ways that price fluctuations may occur, the activity of signalling becoming even a distinct division of labour within the exchange process. The institution of the arbitrageurs in financial markets, specialists in the process of trading in price discrepancies in order to minimise price spread (MacKenzie, 2003), along with innovation of their financial instruments, demonstrate how exchange is always an organised process, over time, and in space. How it is organised matters. Here again, therefore, we can see these innovations as both innovations in services (Schumpeterian) and transformations exchange processes (Polanyian).

The conditions of intermediation, the Polanyian focus, are themselves continuously subject to transformation, through innovations in distribution, innovations in the medium of exchange, and innovations in different institutions of appropriation. Some of these are 'hard' technologies, others soft organisational innovations, innovations in social technologies to repeat the Nelson and Sampat (2001) term, or innovations in the rules of exchange. A can of beans or a bottle of ketchup can primarily be seen as new product innovation – even revolutionary ones in terms of consumption – but they can equally be seen as collaterally contributing to a revolution in distribution, retailing, and eventually exchange process and pricing in consumer end markets.

So, although there are dynamic interactions between intra-market innovation and transformations in the organisation of intermediation and exchange, and indeed it is important to redress the limitations of an exclusively Schumpeterian or Polanyian perspective and explore these interactions as a field of empirical and theoretical investigation, it is also clear that one does not reduce to the other. There is an asymmetry and interdependence between these dimensions of order and change. Markets as organisations are not created (or destroyed) by innovating products alone, and the organisation of exchange and intermediation does not produce new products or services alone. But the interplay and interpenetration *between* the two dimensions of order and change are critical for understanding the dynamics of change *within* each of them.

This leads us to conjecture that each particular type of innovation in the sphere of production leads to complementary innovations in the organisation of the market and that the two spheres effectively co-evolve as each innovation finds its niche in the economic order. Indeed, markets are highly specific and instituted ways of organising flows of information and the consummation of exchange, and the specifics of the intermediation function are reflected in and reflect the process of innovation. Thus, in the automobile revolution, for example, the search for market demand and its consolidation led to major innovations in consumer finance stimulated in part by automotive producers without which the extension of the market would not have been possible and ongoing innovation would have been curtailed. Similarly, the growth of advertising by the auto industry can be seen as an attempt to regularise the certainty of demand in the face of ongoing innovation in product and process. Another example can be seen in the case of the evolution of retailing, the rise of the supermarket and the changes this induced in the innovative activities of processed food manufacturers. Indeed, if any principle enables us to link the very different concerns of Schumpeter and Polanyi it is that the process of innovation qua extension and refinement of the division of labour is conditioned by the extent of the market. Each stimulates the other, the characteristic that directs us towards the restless nature of capitalism in which, taking the system as a whole, innovations in one direction induce innovations elsewhere in the system in both technique and organisation. This is, of course, an open-ended process of the growth and utilisation of knowledge, a process that is not predictable in its longer-term contours but which continually transforms economic and social relations from within.

The fact that very different answers to the question 'What is a market?' have evolved is thus premised on the diversity in the conditions and kinds of production that follow upon innovation. The wholesale/retail example is one special case in which the establishment of a market order is the role of specialised intermediaries, who in modern conditions have been replaced by the supermarkets, who set prices, put goods on display and hold inventories against fluctuations in demand. More generally in a market system, it is suppliers that set prices and hold stocks[23] and it is the organisational arrangements in relation to exchange that determine their freedom to so do. These organisational arrangements do not appear by magic. To organise exchange and the process of exchange over time and space absorbs real resources and the emergence of new divisions of labour. The very same incentives to innovate in terms of production also lead to innovations in market arrangements as we see in the dynamics of the supermarket sector. Markets are not abstract spaces but concrete arrangements for carrying out specific functions of economic transformation over time and space. They are in reality a form of production of exchange services. This is one important reason why the firm–market dichotomy is so misleading: neither is independent of the other nor could they be; a point brought home by the fact that many important markets, such as the London Stock Exchange, are in fact firms, organised in that case to facilitate the trading and valuation of paper assets. When the 'market' is a 'firm' this brings home how difficult the dichotomy is. Equally relevant is the fact that not all forms of exchange are intermediated through markets. Health care is one important example where, in the UK for example, health care systems are operated in the main through public, not-for-profit institutions, and the matching of need to treatment is intermediated by a complex of professional actors ranging from the general practitioner to the consultant clinician. Since this system shapes how medical need is related to an economic demand for medical services that can be translated into an equivalent supply, it is not difficult to see that it has marked effects on the conduct of innovation within hospitals, the medical research system and the industry supplying new drugs, diagnostics and devices. Similarly, in the USA the emergence of the HMO system was a response to the concerns of a medical insurance industry faced with a cost explosion.

From this discussion, it appears that we can identify three types or levels of dynamic interaction between intra-market innovation and market-organisational change:

- First there are the 'collateral' impacts of novel products or processes on processes of intermediation, distribution and exchange.
- Second, there are the innovations in distribution and the organisation of exchange properly speaking, the activities of the economic agents involved in them, and indeed the emergence and differentiation of new classes of economic agent within each of these domains. These entail new relations of mutual dependency and asymmetries of power.
- Third, the emergence of new regularities, and new power relations in the processes of intermediation and exchange, constitute new framing conditions under which innovation of products and services may occur. This involves new instituted processes of innovation.

These three dynamics are interrelated, but, as argued above, irreducible to each other. Moreover, between the first and the third, there is clearly also a feedback, not in the sense of a closed circuit, but an open spiral. Innovation in product and process does not start from where it started before, on the one hand, and new processes and organisation of intermediation, distribution and exchange have emerged, on the other. This is the fundamental underlying principle: there are no static conditions of order (as in equilibrium), and change is irreversible; successive 'orders' can never equate or be commensurable with the ones they replace. That is history.

The deeper consequence of this argument is that there is no prospect of understanding the market economy as a closed steady or stationary, or even semi-stationary state. This is not a benchmark that can provide a basis for the analysis of capitalism. For, like all economic systems, capitalism is simultaneously knowledge based and developing; it cannot be stationary because no meaning can be attached to knowledge being stationary in capitalism. Indeed, its chief characteristic lies in its knowledge-generating and -adopting attributes; it is restless because knowledge is restless. This is why we have privileged the concept of transformation instead of the more familiar notion of transition. In the latter a movement is made between two states that leaves those states unchanged and so the move is in principle reversible. In the former the very process of movement alters the initial and succeeding states so that the change is irreversible. This is the advantage point we reach from the combination of Schumpeter and Polanyi, a market system in which change is premised on order but the material and organisational and instituted basis of that order is evolving from within. This is the lesson we draw from the case of retailing in the UK.

What matters in this account are not markets solely as loci of exchange and its correlates but of markets as loci of economic experimentation and the development of new knowledge. This experimental and adaptive capacity can only lead to change if markets are open systems capable of being invaded by 'mutant' activities; if they permit structural change, growth and decline such that developing economies always have a widespread edge of modernity. Schumpeter draws attention to the enterprise contours of this process, Polanyi situates it in a wider penumbra of instituted forces, and the point is that what takes place within the market and what frames the market co-evolve. Innovation matters in respect of both.

Notes

1 See Nelson (2002) for detailed discussion. Nelson and Sampat (2001) have coined the label 'social technologies' to capture the non-technological dimensions of the provisioning of goods and services.
2 On the relation between enterprise and organisational and strategic leadership see Metcalfe, 2004; Witt, 1998.
3 This is the theme consistently explored by George Shackle (1972) and Brian Loasby (1999).
4 'It was this innovation which gave rise to a specific civilization' (Polanyi, 1957a: 3).

5 'the utopian endeavour of economic liberalism to set up a self-regulating market system. Such a thesis seems to invest that system with almost mythical powers' (Polanyi, 1957a: 29–30).

6 'For as long as that system is not established, economic liberals must and will unhesitatingly call for the intervention of the state in order to establish it, and once established, in order to maintain it' (Polanyi, 1957a: 149).

7 'Such an institution [as the self-regulating market] could not exist for any length of time without annihilating the human and natural substance of society; it would have physically destroyed man and transformed his surroundings into a wilderness' (Polanyi, 1957a: 3).

8 'Social history in the nineteenth century was thus the result of a double movement: the extension of the market organisation in respect to genuine commodities was accompanied by its restriction in respect to fictitious ones . . . A network of measures and policies was integrated into powerful institutions designed to check the action of the market relative to labour, land, and money' (Polanyi, 1957a: 76).

9 'The concept of a self-regulating market was utopian, and its progress was stopped by the realistic self-protection of society' (Polanyi, 1957a: 141). In short, the idea of the double movement demonstrates that the self-protection of society is a 'spontaneous reaction' (Polanyi, 1957a: 149).

10 'The movements refer to changes in location, or in appropriation, or both . . . Material elements may alter their position either by changing place or by changing 'hands'. . . Between them, these two kinds of movements may be said to *exhaust the possibilities* [our emphasis] comprised in economic process as a natural and social phenomenon' (Polanyi, 1957b: 248).

11 'Exchange in order to serve as a form of integration requires the support of a system of price-making markets' (Polanyi, 1957b: 254). It is interesting to compare this with Skinner's account of markets in Ch'ing dynasty China, where he argued that the market was the primary integrative societal institution, as against either the productive unit of the village, or the political institutions of the administrative state: 'marketing had a significance for social integration in traditional China which at once paralleled and surpassed – which both reinforced and complemented – that of administration' (Skinner, 1964: 31); and 'Insofar as the Chinese peasant can be said to live in a self-contained world, that world is not the village but the standard market community' (Skinner, 1964: 32).

12 'Any of the patterns [of integration] may predominate, reflect the movements through which land, labour, and the production and distribution of food are merged into the economy . . . Other patterns may obtain alongside the dominant one in the various sectors of the economy and at varying levels of organisation' (Polanyi, 1968: 307).

13 *The Great Transformation* is replete with examples of trading and markets in pre-nineteenth-century Europe, stretching back to the fifteenth century, and indeed it is clear that Polanyi saw the self-regulating market *system* as emerging into dominance out of this historical backdrop.

14 'Above the markets, the shops, and the travelling pedlars, rose a mighty superstructure of exchange in the hands of extremely skilled operators' (Braudel, 1979: 81).

15 This is most sharply expressed as follows, where Braudel also constructs a non-market layer below, and an anti-market layer above, the various layers of

markets: 'I would argue that a third sector should be added to the pre-industrial model – the lowest stratum of the non-economy, the soil into which capitalism thrusts its roots but which it can never really penetrate. This lowest layer remains an enormous one. Above it, comes the favoured terrain of the market economy, with its many horizontal communications between the different markets: here a degree of automotive coordination usually links supply, demand and prices. Then alongside, or rather above this layer, comes the zone of the anti-market, where the great predators roam and the law of the jungle operates. This – to day as in the past, before and after the industrial revolution – is the real home of capitalism' (Braudel, 1979: 229–30).

16 Following Chamberlin's argument in Chamberlin, 1966.
17 'The laws of the market no longer apply to huge firms which can influence demand by their very effective advertising, and which can fix prices arbitrarily' (Braudel, 1979: 229).
18 Opium was calculated to be 'the world's most valuable single commodity trade of the nineteenth century' (Trocki, 1998: 94).
19 For a more detailed account see Harvey et al., 2002.
20 The sources for this section are secondary for historical material, and primary interviews and contemporary accounts for the recent history: Allen, 1998; Runciman Committee, 1957; Webber, 1969; Webber, 1972.
21 'London probably had the first true market gardeners – men who grew produce entirely for sale to the public' (Webber, 1969: 26).
22 Itinerant traders going between these markets had to carry ready-reckoners with them to convert the unit weights and measures.
23 This is typically so in markets for differentiated or branded goods. Wholesale intermediaries who set a spread of buying and selling prices, in part to cover costs of holding stocks, come into their own in cases of homogeneous or readily describable commodities such as steel or cotton. See the Conclusion to Metcalfe and Warde (2002).

References

Allen, C. 1998. *Transplanting The Garden: The Story of the Relocation of Covent Garden Market*. Covent Garden Market Authority. London.

Braudel, F. 1979. *The Wheels of Commerce: Vol II Civilisation and Capitalism*. Fontana Press. London.

Chamberlin, E. H. 1966 (1933). *The Theory of Monopolistic Competition: A Re-orientation of the Theory of Value*. Harvard University Press. Cambridge, MA.

Everitt, A. 1985. 'The market town', in Thirsk, J. (ed.), *The Agrarian History of England and Wales, Vol V, 1640–1750*. Cambridge University Press. Cambridge.

Harvey, M. 2002. 'Markets, supermarkets and the macro-social shaping of demand: an instituted economic process approach', in McMeekin, A., Green, K., Tomlinson, M., and Walsh, V (eds), *Innovation By Demand: An Interdisciplinary Approach to the Study of Demand and Its Role in Innovation*. Manchester University Press. Manchester.

Harvey, M. and Randles, S. 2003. 'Market exchanges and "instituted economic process": an analytical perspective', *Revue d'Economie Industrielle*, 101 (December), 11–30.

Harvey, M., Quilley, S. and Beynon, H. 2002. *Exploring The Tomato: Transformations in Nature, Economy and Society*. Edward Elgar. Cheltenham.

Kirzner, I. 1973. *Competition and Entrepreneurship*. Chicago University Press. Chicago, IL.

Landes, D. S. 1983. *Revolution in Time: Clocks and the Making of the Modern World*. Harvard University Press. Cambridge, MA.

Loasby, B. 1999. *Knowledge, Institutions and Evolution in Economics*. Routledge. London.

Loasby, B. 2003. 'Connecting principles, new combinations, and routines: reflections inspired by Schumpeter and Smith', in Metcalfe, S. and Cantner, U. (eds), *Change, Transformation, and Development*. Springer. Heidelberg: 169–82.

MacKenzie, D. 2003. 'Long-Term Capital Management and the sociology of arbitrage', *Economy and Society*, 32(3), 249–380.

Metcalfe, J. S. 2004. 'The entrepreneur and the style of modern economics', *Journal of Evolutionary Economics*, 14, 157–76.

Metcalfe, J. S. and Ramlogan, R. 2005. 'Limits to the economy of knowledge and knowledge of the economy', *Futures*, 37, 7, 655–74.

Metcalfe, S. and Warde, A. 2002. *Market Relations and the Competitive Process*. Manchester University Press. Manchester.

Nelson, R. R. 2002. 'On the complexities and limits of market organisation' in Metcalfe, J. S. and Warde, A. (eds), *Market Relations and the Competitive Process*. Manchester University Press. Manchester.

Nelson, R. R. and Sampat, B. N. 2001. 'Making sense of institutions as a factor shaping economic performance', *Journal of Economic Behaviour and Organisation*, 37, 31–54.

Polanyi, K. 1957a (1944). *The Great Transformation: The Political and Economic Origins of our Time*. Beacon Press. Boston, MA.

Polanyi, K. 1957b. 'The economy as instituted process' in Polanyi, K., Arensberg, C. M. and Pearson, H. W. (eds), *Trade and Market in the Early Empires*. The Free Press. New York.

Polanyi, K. 1960. *On the Comparative Treatment of Economic Institutions in Antiquity with Illustrations from Athens, Mycenae, and Alalakh*. University of Chicago Press. Reprinted in Dalton G. (ed.) (1968) *Primitive, Archaic, and Modern Economies. Essays of Karl Polanyi*. Anchor Books. New York.

Polanyi, K. 1966. *Dahomey and the Slave Trade*. University of Washington Press. Seattle, WA.

Robinson, J. 1979. *Collected Economic Papers*, Volume Five. Blackwell. Oxford.

Runciman Committee. 1957. *Report of the Committee on Horticultural Marketing*. HMSO, Parliamentary Papers. Cmnd 61.

Schumpeter, J. 1934 (1911). *The Theory of Economic Development*. Galaxy Books. Oxford.

Shackle, G. L. S. 1972. *Epistemics and Economics*. Cambridge University Press. Cambridge.

Skinner, G. W. 1964. 'Marketing and social structure in rural China part I', *The Journal of Asian Studies*, 24(1), 3–43; Part II, *The Journal of Asian Studies* (1965) 24(2), 195–228; Part III, *The Journal of Asian Studies* (1965) 24(3), 363–99.

Trocki, C. A. 1998. *Opium, Empire and the Global Political Economy. A study of the Asian Opium Trade, 1750–1950*. Routledge. London.

Webber, R. 1969. *Covent Garden: Mud Salad Market*. Dent. London.

Webber, R. 1972. *Market Gardening: The History of Commercial Flower, Fruit and Vegetable Growing*. David and Charles. Newton Abbot.

Witt, U. 1998. 'Imagination and leadership – the neglected dimension of an evolutionary theory of the firm', *Journal of Economic Behaviour and Organisation*, 35, 161–77.

Witt, U. 2003. *The Evolving Economy*. Edward Elgar. Cheltenham.

Zuckerman, L. 1999. *The Potato*. Macmillan. London.

5

The organisation of exchanges on the venture capital market. Empirical evidence and theoretical issues

Dorothée Rivaud-Danset and Emmanuelle Dubocage

Introduction

Economists consider that the relationships between venture capitalists and entrepreneurs raise questions of corporate governance which can be solved by the agency theory. Agency theory focuses on potential conflicts between managers and share owners, conflicts being triggered by diverging utility functions. The standard literature clearly acknowledges that problems due to conflicting interests between free persons, who have no authority over one another and are engaged in a joint activity, can be overcome by means of incentive contracts.

Sociological investigations of the US venture capital market reveal how the social networks in this community diffuse information and sustain exchanges. Sociologists show how rules have emerged within the specific context of Silicon Valley and shaped a business local community, after the Second World War.

This chapter follows a socio-economic approach: on the one hand, it shares the approach of sociological investigations of exchange, which reveal how institutions and networks shape transaction patterns among economic actors; on the other hand, it aims at answering basic questions which are in the realm of economic theory of organisations and market: What is the root cause of transaction difficulties? Or, in other words, is the conflict of interest between venture suppliers and entrepreneurs the main source of conflict? What is necessary for the meeting of demand and supply? How is price determined? How do these very specific groups of economic agents succeed in coordinating with each other, in spite of the high level of uncertainty which characterises the quality of venture-backed start-ups?

According to Akerlof's seminal paper, the venture capital market should not exist. Like in the second-hand car market, no price could coordinate venture capital suppliers and seekers; in other words, neither party could agree to exchange when quality is uncertain and price is determined by aggregated forces acting in an invisible way (Akerlof, 1970). In order to explain this puzzle, it is necessary to study practices which stabilise behaviours, support exchanges and institute an emerging market. However, such a study is unusual for economists, as they favour an abstract approach. An empirical approach has many consequences: of course it introduces complexity, but it also highlights key elements in the organisation of exchanges, which would be missed in terms of aggregated supply and demand function. For instance, the role of the network acting as intermediary actors is ignored by an abstract approach, as this latter assumes that demand and supply are ready made. On the contrary, we consider that both supply-side and demand-side are not determined *ex ante*, out of the exchange process.

The empirical observations reported in this chapter rely on first-hand sources for European countries and on the socio-economic literature for Silicon Valley, this second-hand source providing very interesting evidence (box 5.1).

This chapter starts with an outline critique of the dominant model of venture capital market, the agency theory. It argues that the misalignment of goals and the key role played by the contract are not decisive to an understanding of the instituted arrangements in this market, the root cause of transaction difficulties being the highly uncertain context in which participants are involved (section 1).

In order to study new and changing venture-capital practices, two issues have been selected: how the demand-side is designed, according to venture-capital norms (section 2) and how the corporate value and the share prices are determined (section 3). Finally, this chapter attempts to answer the question: what can we learn from this empirical research in regard to the dynamics of an emerging market? (section 4).

1. What is the root cause of transaction difficulties?

To discuss the explanatory power of the standard economic framework, it is necessary, firstly, to distinguish between two kinds of relationships:

1. the relationships between venture capital and upstream investors; and
2. the relationships between venture capital and entrepreneurs.

Box 5.1 Presentation of the empirical material

The empirical material utilised in this chapter consists of:

1. fifteen semi-structured interviews, in France, in each case lasting at least one hour, with the managers of start-ups, promoters of new projects, consultants, venture capitalists and managers of public funds; and
2. a questionnaire drawn up by Dubocage and sent to 188 venture-capital firms registered in the European Venture Capital Association (EVCA) directory. Answer rate is 20%. Various topics are covered, such as selection costs and stock ownership plans.

The limited explanatory power of the agency theory

Venture capital is a financial intermediary even if capital is supplied through equity instead of loan. It stands between investors and entrepreneurs. Since the 1980s, the literature on financial intermediaries has focused on the asymmetries of information between lenders and borrowers as the key concept to explain the nature of the transaction. It is well known that problems due to asymmetries of information can be overcome by means of adequate screening and monitoring, reputation or commitment. This provides an interesting framework which seems to fit well with the study of the relationship between venture capitalists and entrepreneurs. However, since the 1980s, because of the overwhelming influence of the agency theory (Gompers and Lerner, 2000), problems raised by asymmetries of information have often been seen as subjective problems which generate subjective conflicts, due to divergent goals.

In the strong version, the agency theory posits the hypothesis that the agent holds private information about the environment, or the quality of his project, or his future behaviour (the effort he is going to invest, his capabilities, in other words his qualities for implementing the mandate), or his actual behaviour (i.e. the effort he has actually put in). Asymmetries of information are only subjective, due to a lack of cooperation from the agent.

According to the weak version of the agency theory, managers and share owners may conflict because of diverging utility functions. The standard literature clearly acknowledges that problems due to conflicting interests between managers and share owners can be overcome by means of incentive contracts.

This framework of analysis appears to be good enough to understand the nature of the relationships between investors and venture capitalists (Figure 5.1). The nature of the relationships is contractual, and the contract explicitly provides an incentive to venture capitalists to behave in the investors' interest, as they would receive a percentage – typically, 20% – of the capital gain, in addition to annual management fees (Rabeharisoa, 1998).

Of course, between venture capitalists and entrepreneurs, the formal contract matters. The 'stock ownership plan' certainly helps to reduce conflicts; the means by which conflicts may be resolved are stipulated when the parties want to put an end to the relationship. However, the contractual approach is too limited. The analytic framework provided by the agency theory does not grasp the main aspects of the relationships between venture capitalists and entrepreneurs. Several arguments support this view.

The venture capitalist and the manager of the start-up share the same (or at least compatible) objectives: the creation of the firm's value. The venture capitalist and the start-up manager are both owners of the same start-up. Investment by the staff and at least by the entrepreneur is a necessary condition to initiate a consensual relationship. As a consequence, according to the textbooks, suppliers of venture capital and entrepreneurs are expected to have the same ultimate goal: maximisation of the firm's value. According

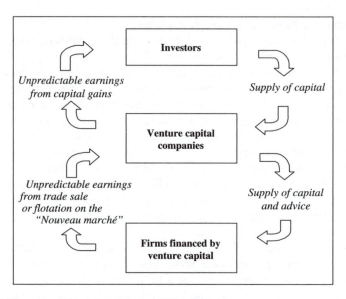

Figure 5.1 The protagonist of the venture capital market

to a less dogmatic view, we admit that action goals are not unique and each person has his or her own individual action goals, which can fit together from the beginning, or can become compatible.

The hypothesis of conflict over the choice of project to be implemented is no longer appropriate. This choice of project to be implemented is at the very foundation of the relations between the lead venture capitalist and the start-up manager: they have agreed on this subject; if they have evaluated the probability of the project's success, they share the same evaluation. The hypothesis of conflict over the ending of the relation cannot be exaggerated. Start-up managers know from the beginning that venture investment is finite, the main exits for the venture capitalists being either an IPO (initial public offering in the financial market) or an acquisition by a large firm. They share this financial view. If not, either they would not meet venture capitalists or their demand would be rejected immediately. In other words, those who do not share this convention are out of the venture-capital market.

The hypothesis of asymmetry of information is ill-suited to the relation between the venture capitalist and the start-up manager. Indeed, uncertainty is not due to an imperfect exchange of information, insofar as no economic agent has perfect and total information, the start-up future being strongly undetermined. Of course, they do not have access to the same information and do not draw perfectly similar conclusions from their observation. Because of their expertise in the management of start-up-type businesses, venture capitalists will have a more general view than start-up managers, who will be more focused on the particular case of their own business. Yet the key argument is: neither of the parties in the financing relationship has a decisive advantage; neither is 'better-placed' than the other. The entrepreneur does not possess decisive private information, insofar as he or she does not know with certitude which project will be realised: the project will evolve and neither of the two parties knows much more about the nature of this evolution. This situation does not give any significant advantage.

Of course, start-up managers do possess private information concerning their own qualities, but this advantage is not decisive, for the following reasons:

1. It is in their own interest to do everything in their power to contribute to the success of the business;
2. Researchers who wish to embark on the adventure of start-up management do not know what sort of entrepreneur they will be; and
3. The judgement of the venture capitalist on the quality of the manager is a decisive condition for his or her commitment to the business and, in certain cases, the venture capitalist can decide to nominate another executive as the manager of the start-up.

A very different perspective

Finally, these hypotheses and set of analytic tools are not very helpful for understanding of the venture-capital market. A critical analysis of agency theory leads us to interpret the practices involved from a very different perspective. Entrepreneurs and venture capitalists are better depicted as having complementary information and knowledge. Actually, a typical venture capitalist has a double competency: financial and scientific. Venture capitalists can be depicted as 'hands-on' financial intermediaries: they supply services as a manager would do, hiring members of staff for instance, and their scientific competency means that their representation on the boards of the firm cannot be viewed as a control mechanism: their competencies are used not only to screen demand and monitor managers' behaviour but also to participate in the start-up management. Non-financial and non-monetary aspects of venture capital are critical to its success (Gompers and Lerner, 2000: 127).

To sum up, it is assumed in this chapter that 'subjective conflicts', due to divergent utility functions between venture capital and entrepreneurs, are not the root cause of transaction difficulties. The set of hypotheses put forward by the agency theory orientates the analysis of the relationship between venture capitalists and entrepreneurs in a direction which does not allow it to be taken into account that the key difficulties of the transaction are raised by

1. the high possibility that the innovative project may fail; and
2. the common difficulties in anticipating correctly the future of the start-up, as the eventuality of failure cannot be estimated using empirical probabilities.

Even if it is assumed that both parties share the same ultimate goal (e.g. the maximisation of the start-up value over a span of five years) and are willing to cooperate and communicate relevant information, the innovative project is still uncertain and investment in such a project remains highly risky. Information is highly incomplete for both parties and nobody can evaluate correctly the probability of failure of the project. Each participant knows that the innovative project is very likely to be redirected in the course of its implementation, as new opportunities will appear.

Participants in the venture-capital market act in a highly uncertain context. Uncertainty is generated both by external factors and by the behaviour of the main actors. Five sources of uncertainty can be distinguished:

1. Science and technology: uncertainty is caused by innovative activity, the feasibility of the project is not certain, the expected scientific discovery is unpredictable, and so on.
2. The market: if the goods or the service supplied by the start-up are new, as it is often the case, avenues for products are virtual and the market may react in an unexpected way.
3. Competition among start-ups: many start-ups are involved in a highly competitive field, although new, which can be depicted as a race where the winner takes all.
4. Human behaviour: working in a team in an unstable context is challenging.
5. Financial needs: although financial needs are planned, the time needed to become profitable and the amount to be invested during the course of the relationship are likely to be dramatically affected by unexpected events.

For these reasons, start-up performances and investment profitability are hard to predict. Being able to formulate good predictions requires a lot of experience.

2. The building of demand-side

As a starting point of our investigation of exchanges, we admit that supply and demand are not given. Hence, understanding how venture capitalists actually meet 'the demand' is seen as critical to our analysis. This investigation leads us to analyse how the demand-side is shaped according to venture capital rules of games.

How venture capital suppliers meet entrepreneurs and the role of networks

As previously said, a typical venture capitalist has a double competency, financial and scientific. Learning by doing is vital to acquire such competencies; difficulties faced by new teams in countries with a poor tradition in that field testify to the role of practical experience. Building a network and updating it are part of this informal way to improve venture capitalists' competencies. Through networks of experts, they contact actors who have the appropriate knowledge and can judge the quality of the investee and, hence, the value of corporate shares they receive when offering equity funds.

Networks make easier coordination between venture capital suppliers and seekers. They play an important role at the initial stage of the exchange; indeed, as venture capitalists invest in new technology-based firms, they participate to the process of start-up creation. Venture capitalists are not passively waiting for customers and, in order to avoid missing a future success story, they may search for the right person able to become an entrepreneur. In such cases, networks will provide contacts.

Venture capitalists deal with networks which include public and private organisations, financial and non-financial firms as well as individual members (see Figure 5.2). Links with universities, research centres and incubators provide venture capitalists with the capacity to intervene at the birth of the start-up and, even, to create demand. Previous entrepreneurs funded by venture capital can introduce a new one. In Silicon Valley, law firms use their links in the local business community to put innovators in touch with venture capitalists, their main function being the pre-selection of demand. 'Prominent attorneys can provide the contacts and recommendations that ease entrance into the venture capital market' (Suchman, 2000: 80). This practice is less developed in Europe, consultants being the most frequent intermediary. Actually, results of Dubocage's survey[1] in 2000 indicate that 35% of surveyed venture-capital firms seek consultants' help to get in touch with entrepreneurs.

The financial network includes not only state and other non-profitable agencies specialised in the financing of innovation but also other venture capital firms. Of the European venture-capital firms surveyed, 65% were members of a venture-capital network and 27.5% use such a network to contact entrepreneurs. Relationships between venture capital firms are orientated in three directions:

1. informal cooperation, with non-monetary exchange of files and information;
2. formal partnership, called syndication, in the same project; and
3. competition.

Cooperation can lead to partnership: for instance, a venture capitalist with enough expertise sends a file to another one who will be the leader of the operation. Cooperation can also lead to competition, as the industry grows up; in Silicon Valley, the change from a very small business community based on cooperation in the 1950s to a competitive industry in the 1990s has been underscored (Kenney, 2000). Relationships can be market and non-market, monetary and non-monetary ones, non-monetary exchanges of information being by far the most important mode; according to Ferrary (2001), 90% of the information gathered by an average venture capitalist in Silicon Valley is free. Empirical evidence indicates that reciprocity, if any,

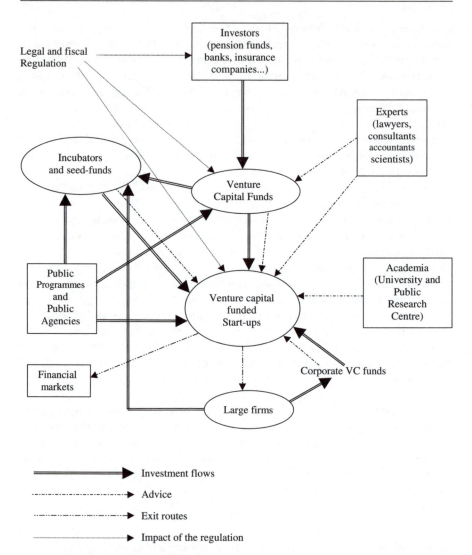

Figure 5.2 The venture capital market as a network

has to be analysed within networks and not within bilateral relationships. In order to analyse this kind of exchanges within groups of agents, academics refer to Mauss's theory of 'don contre don' (Ferrary, 2001).

Network effects on the process of exchanges are various. As a whole, they contribute to create a local business community where interpersonal trust relationships develop jointly with intensive competition. They contribute to the building of the supply-side and demand-side quality insofar as actors put them to work (see Box 5.2). In the following paragraphs we

---

Box 5.2 The role played by the network according to a venture capitalist

Here is an account by Regis MacKenna of the role played by the network:

The network of supporting infrastructure in Silicon Valley is the most sophisticated outside Wall Street. The catalyst for that network is the venture capital community, which has evolved to become a strategic planner, management consultant, and corporate watchdog. The network is put to work for new companies and many members of the network have been well honed on dozens of start-ups . . . In fact, one of the reasons . . . many companies do succeed is because the network goes to work to help companies survive: they help them find new customers, they help them do refinancing, the help them find new managers if necessary, they help them merge with other companies to be successful.

Source: Kenney, 2001: 101.

---

show how networks contribute to improvements in the quality of the demand-side and to the matching of supply and demand.

How the demand-side is shaped according to venture-capital rules

In order to govern exchanges, instituted practices have emerged. They can be considered, in a first step, as constitutive and conventional rules. Constitutive rules according to Searle's taxonomy define the behaviour principles or the rules of the game which characterise the exchange process (Searle, 1995); such rules are also conventional, they provide principles of behaviour which are taken for granted and help people who know them to coordinate, reducing uncertainty about participants' future behaviour (Lewis, 1969).

Instituted practices shape the demand-side from the first step. Remember that demand comes from innovators seeking resources to fund innovative projects with high growth potential. Typically, a project is the outcome of a knowledge-production process developed in research centres, which may belong to universities or to large firms. In order to become the seed of a new firm attracting venture capital, it has to be shaped according to venture rules.

First, files sent in an anonymous way are very likely to be rejected. Although demand is atomistic, it is not anonymous and, from the beginning, relationships are not at arms' length. The identity of the venture-capital seeker matters. Innovators must have a qualification, a track record and personal contacts. They may call for specialised intermediaries who provide contacts that ease entrance into the market. These intermediaries can be scientists or lawyers, the latter group being quite important in California. The role of informal networks and benchmarks such as diplomas is crucial (see box 5.3). Networks support strategies of reputation building, which mitigate the corporate quality uncertainty. Indeed, the venture capitalists' most important criterion is the quality of the innovator–entrepreneur and his or her team.

Box 5.3 The role of the network form the demand-side

Companies compete intensely, but simultaneously learn about changing markets and technologies through informal communications, collaborative projects, and common ties to research associations and universities. (Castilla et al., 2001: 223)

Larson's (1992) and Nohria's (1992) research on the development of successful start-up companies stresses how social networks with other firms are a means for quick access to resources and know-how that cannot be produced internally (Castilla et al., 2001: 223).

Castilla et al. show that engineers in Silicon Valley are organised through networks regardless of firms where they work. Saxenian (1994) affirms that: 'The region's engineers developed loyalty to each other and to advancing technology, rather than individual firms or even industries' (Saxenian, 1994: 28 in Castilla et al., 2001: 220). This unique culture, this large network and high turnover in engineers are correlated. This flexibility can become a positive factor for start-ups as far as competencies are concerned.

A second important function of the network is the diffusion of standard devices, which facilitate the matching of supply and demand. These devices have an effective impact on the organisation of exchanges and the constitution of the market. Non-financial intermediaries participate in the setting of conventional rules, which constitute the market. Lawyers provide advice, which structures demand. They orientate entrepreneurs towards selected venture-capital firms, and, for that purpose, introduce typologies of clients according to industrial sectors and financial needs. By introducing classifications which would be analysed as 'investissement de forme' by the French conventionalist approach (Salais and Thévenot, 1986), informal norms become formal rules governing the exchange process.

A third specific feature of this process contributes to rules spreading. At different times in his or her life, an individual can be either a start-up manager, or a venture capitalist, or a research centre director. This capacity to hold distinct jobs over time, which is part of the network, facilitates coordination insofar as it contributes to the spreading of conventional rules of action and to mutual understanding.

Although established by the supply-side and spread by the networks of intermediaries, the rules of the game create a consensus and are seen by both parties as conventional rules. This is shown by the following evidence:

- Among the rules, writing a business plan is a *sine qua non* for entering the market; the substance must be unique or at least original, as the venture-capital function is the financing of radical innovation, but the application has to follow standard models. The business plan is more than a classic tool of selection. Indeed, the meetings with the venture capitalist, which help the innovator to write this document, give the two parties an opportunity of testing the viability of a long-term and trust relationship. Moreover, the development of accumulated bodies of information shared by both parties reduces uncertainty.

- Some criteria of entrance in the venture-capital market are universal. Projects which do not fit the following criteria will immediately be rejected. As previously mentioned, the quality of the entrepreneurial team is a key criterion to enter the market. In many sectors, a 'good' team includes scientists with a high level of skills. The scientific quality of the team is evaluated through various indicators, like the *curriculum vitae* of the staff (scientific publications and so forth) (Darby et al., 1999). The so-called star scientist system, which prevails particularly in biotechnology companies, illustrates the role of quality signals and their evolution towards the rules of the game. Legal barriers protecting innovation are a *sine qua non* in several sectors. Interviews indicate that patents and other property rights which protect innovation are a criterion which makes consensus among these groups of actors. A probable competitive advantage coming from technology is often required, the start-up being expected to become the leader in its niche market or to be able to destabilise the commercial environment because of its technological advantage. A marketable output with high growth potential is also required. The ultimate criterion is rather unexpected: the innovative project(s) has or have to be costly. Indeed, the size of the investment has to be large – 1 million euro is often quoted as being the minimum – without upper limit. As unitary fixed co-ordination costs, which include the screening and mentoring of the start-up, are high, small investments cannot be profitable.
- These indicators have emerged in Silicon Valley and are internationally admitted, but their importance is not the same from one sector to the other. In biotechnology, as the life of investment is longer and the technological risk is high, scientific norms are more selective than in other industries, while in information technology, notably in the telecommunication equipment industry, technological barriers are required.

The shaping of demand by the venture capital market rules continues as long as venture capital has an interest in the start-up. Staged investment is becoming a well-established procedure. Investments decided by venture capital are allocated in a sequential way, step by step. At each step, new funds are allocated only if milestones, roughly defined in the contract, have been reached by the start-up. This procedure is efficient in a highly uncertain context as a way to reduce investors' risk. As a consequence, entrepreneurs adapt the corporate strategy to send quality signals. For instance, in the biotechnology sector, entrepreneurs are pushed to publish, obtain a patent and contract with pharmaceutical firms, as these actions provide standard devices which are supposed to facilitate the corporate quality assessment.

The need for signals and instituted practices is supposed to increase in proportion to increases in uncertainty. Biotechnology, which is by far the most risky industry, bears out this relation. However, signals of quality, even if they are costly to send, may be a vehicle for wrong information and some signals used by venture-capital suppliers to discriminate among seekers are particularly doubtful. For instance, during the so-called 'Internet bubble', it was admitted that quality was signalled by the amount of research and development (R&D) expenses.

Benchmarks have to be interpreted in context. It is possible to discriminate between venture capitalists based on their capacity to interpret signals sent by entrepreneurs (Dubocage, 2003). The distance between signals and genuine corporate quality is great, and difficulties met by venture capitalists in reducing the gap contribute to the ups and downs of supply.

The instituted practices, which govern the organisation of exchanges and its dynamics, cannot be seen as independent from legal, and *in fine* political, factors (Tordjman, 2001). The functioning of the venture-capital market cannot be considered as self-ruling. Legal rules contribute to define the nature of participants, the role of legal and political factors being particularly strong when public policy-makers want to impulse an activity. Venture capitalists at the emerging stage in the USA, in the 1950s, faced constraints to raise capital among institutional investors, due to corporate regulation. The Limited Partnership structure, which governs the relations between venture capitalists and upstream investors, was set up in the USA to reduce investors' risk, and the venture-capital industry strongly benefited from this new institutional context, which has been reproduced overseas in a large number of countries. Other elements which typify the functioning of venture-capital exchanges in Silicon Valley have also been copied by other countries, the specialised financial market being the most conspicuous. Hence, the disadvantage of European countries in comparison with the USA provided the rationale for European public authorities to take steps during the 1990s to modify the institutional context in order to support the supply and the demand of financing to innovative firms (Dubocage and Rivaud-Danset, 2004).

As a whole, most of the institutions, ranging from public regulation to professional practices, which govern the exchange process were driven by venture capitalists. The selection criteria, the business plan, and signals are designed by the supply-side. These benchmarks testify for the power asymmetry in favour of venture capital. In other words, the organisation of exchanges illustrates the power of finance over the entrepreneur. However, the two groups of actors are also mutually dependent (see section 3, on page 123).

Venture capital, being typically a knowledge-intensive industry, is characterised by a highly sophisticated division of labour, with new intermediaries acting in a network. On the venture-capital market, typically a highly risky financial activity, relationships are stabilised by institutions; they emerged at the end of the twentieth century and have become international, although inspired by the local procedures in Silicon Valley. Economists who refer to the agency theory ignore these key elements of the coordination; if

Table 5.1 The organisation of exchanges approach versus the standard approach

Issues and analytical framework	Agency and information theory	The organisation of exchanges
Main obstacles to coordination	Conflicting interests between VCist* and entrepreneur	Uncertainty due to an innovative activity
Allocation of information	Asymmetry of information favouring the entrepreneur	Information and competencies are complementary
Power distribution	The entrepreneur, being the agent, has a power of decision the VCist has not	VCist has an asymmetrical power over entrepreneur in a context of mutual dependency
Key actors	Entrepreneur and VCist	Entrepreneur and VCist are embedded in networks acting as intermediaries
The cement of the relationship	The contract designed by the VCist to control the entrepreneur	A set of institutions which helps actors to mitigate uncertainty

*venture capitalist

not, they analyse them from the corporate governance's point of view. Table 5.1 summarises the main differences between the organisation of exchanges approach and the classical one. Although the relationship between venture capitalists and entrepreneurs is effectively contractual, the notion of contract does not grasp what maintains the relationships between entrepreneurs and venture suppliers.

3. How prices are actually determined?

The price determination process can be seen as a synthesis of the nature of relationships among actors: the process can be anonymous or not, centralised or decentralised, the supply and demand powers can be balanced or unbalanced, and so on. On the venture-capital market, what is exchanged is ownership rights, in the form of shares of the start-up equity. The corporate price and, as a consequence, the share price depend on anticipated cash flows. Highly technology-based start-ups having a very limited amount of tangible assets compared to their potential cash flow; investment is highly risky. It is a pure case where pricing is totally determined by expectations. When venture capitalists decide to invest in a given start-up, its price is not given by the market, each transaction being unique and leading to a unique price. The corporate valuation is neither the consequence of the meeting of aggregated supply and demand, nor the consequence of a price-maker mechanism. In other words, venture capitalists are neither price-takers nor price-makers. This evidence does not lead to exclude interactions between agents but interactions have to be analysed in another framework. In this study, we consider that actors' embeddedness in networks and in a business community is part of the pricing process.

Effective procedure and theoretical modes of corporate pricing

The procedure which determines the price of shares is complex and original. The price of these shares is the result of an agreement between the managers of the start-up and venture capitalists. Parameters which are at the core of the price-fixation mechanism and influence the final decision are three-fold:

- financial needs (N), i.e. capital supplied by venture capitalists;
- percentage of shares required by both parties (α being the percentage required by venture capitalists and 1-α the percentage required by the entrepreneurial team); and
- pre-money valuation (V), i.e. the start-up valuation before the entrance of VC.

The post-money valuation (V') is the valuation reached after the venture entrance, so $V' = V + N$. It is assumed that financial needs are fixed, hence two cases can be distinguished:

- in the first case, financial needs and the percentage of shares owned are fixed *a priori* in a contractual bargaining and the post-money valuation is deducted ($V' = N/\alpha$); and
- in the second case, financial needs and the pre-money valuation are fixed *a priori*. The percentage of shares owned by each part is deducted ($\alpha = N/V'$). Hence, it is necessary to explain how the pre-money valuation is conducted.

For a better understanding of corporate pricing, let us recall that two alternative modes of assessment can be distinguished. The first is the fundamental valuation, which is an individual exercise; the second is the Keynesian conventional valuation, and mimetic behaviour. According to this approach, in an efficient market, it is assumed that investors value the firm by concentrating on its capacity to generate earnings in the future and by taking into account all the relevant information which influences this capacity. This valuation is subjective insofar as it depends on personal anticipations, but not inter-subjective, anticipations being orientated towards the firm's potential, independently of the opinion of other investors. However, this hypothesis makes little sense in the case of a highly technology-based young firm. Indeed, generally speaking, future earnings are anticipated on the basis of observed earnings in the past years, but most of the start-ups are not profitable when venture capitalists supply capital. As a consequence, this framework, which may explain how a group of investors decide in a financial market, has a very limited explanatory power in our case.

According to Keynes's approach to valuation and mimetic behaviour, investors aim to discover the average opinion of the participants as a way to anticipate the market price, independently of the fundamental value. This sophisticated mimetic valuation approach has been developed to analyse exchanges of liquid securities in open financial markets, which is not at all the case for the venture-capital market: this market is not orientated towards liquidity, capital shares being kept for a few years. Certainly, less sophisticated mimetic behaviour, with agents copying their neighbours, as modelled by Bikhchandani et al. (1992), can be observed among venture capitalists. Trivial mimetic valuation helps us to understand the behaviour of the newcomers, who lack competencies and try to imitate their seniors, but it does not explain how price is determined by the group of competent venture investors.

In our view, venture capitalists are better depicted as financial intermediaries who have competencies and formulate a judgement on the corporate potential. This judgement is not the 'average' judgement of the market, each transaction being unique and involving directly a limited number of participants. Nevertheless, the exercise of judgement is not personal; assessment is not done by an isolated agent, out of the influences of others. It can be described as the conclusion of an inquiry which involves not only the entrepreneur but also other intermediaries, and which uses conventional benchmarks. Each venture capitalist tries to anticipate the potential of the firm as it is assumed by the fundamental valuation approach, but he or she does not anticipate alone. Venture capitalists are neither the omniscient isolated agents of the first approach nor the short-termist agents who anticipate the behaviour of the group, according to Keynes's view, nor the poorly informed agents who mimic other agents' behaviour, assuming that these latter are better informed.

A matter of judgement and bargaining within a community

Pre-money valuation is a matter of judgement and bargaining. The pre-money valuation takes into account the contribution of the founders of the firm (the demand-side), this contribution being financial and non-financial. The valuation of the non-financial contribution is not the result of 'mechanical criteria' and is deeply linked with the issue of intangible asset valuation. These assets can be taken into account in the corporate accounting (patents, R&D expenses . . .) or not (human capital, innovative ideas . . .). The valuation can be shaped by using comparison with others firms (quoted or not) regarded as similar because of their activity. However, such a comparison has a limited value, as the valuation of similar enterprises encounters the same difficulties, both being young and belonging to a new industry.

Bargaining does not mean that the price is determined like goods in a bazaar, where sellers guess buyers' reserve price. Certainly, each party aims to maximise future gains, and price is influenced by the respective power of each party, but both also wish to create conditions of a long-term relationship based on interpersonal trust. Moreover, they belong to a business community, with its professional rules. An unfair valuation would handicap the relationship from the beginning. Under-valuation would reduce the percentage of shares owned by entrepreneurs, leading, in some cases, to an unwanted allocation of shares, as venture capitalists want to be minority shareholders. Over-valuation, which would favour the entrepreneur, could affect the capacity to collect additional funds from venture firms at the next stages. Over-valuation could have a more diffuse negative effect on the reputation of venture capitalists, as it affects their capacities to realise capital gains by selling their shares. Being financial intermediaries, they may have to explain to institutional investors their own method of assessing investees in their portfolios. Illegitimate valuations may entail the exit of a venture-capital firm and even a generalised crises of venture-capital exchanges in a community.

Fairness is another important dimension in the price determination process. This process ends when both parties agree on the price and it opens the formal long-term relationship between the parties. As previously said, each party has to be trustworthy; if not, both will not be able to deal with the various unexpected contingencies they will face during a long-term relationship. In this kind of relationship, trust is grounded on the respect of each party's interest, whatever the importance of the respect of social norms of the community. Fairness in price determination is often neglected by economists. It has no place in an abstract approach, while in a real market, asymmetry of power being often the case, it is tempting to exclude the notion of fair price. Although the organisation of exchanges is driven by venture suppliers, asymmetry of power goes along with mutual dependency; the entrepreneur team and the financial one are engaged in a joint activity which relies on an intense exchange of information, with venture capitalists providing non-financial services. This view emphasises the role of trust and, as a consequence, raises the question of fairness. According to Rawls's definition: 'The question of fairness arises when free persons, who have no authority over one another, are engaging in a joint activity and amongst themselves setting or acknowledging the rules which define it and which determine the respective shares in its benefits and its burdens. A practice will strike the parties as fair if none feels that, by participating in it, they or any of the others are taken advantage of, or are forced to give in to claims which they do not regard as legitimate' (Rawls, 1958: 178).

A legitimate valuation, in the venture-capital market, refers to two dimensions: the capacity of explaining the method and the feeling of fairness. To sum up, pre-money valuation is a matter of judgement and bargaining. Following Knight (1921), we estimate that start-up pricing is a matter of judgement because of the uniqueness of the start-up, which generates radical uncertainty. Bargaining between venture suppliers and entrepreneurs, who belong to a community with its economic and social norms, is necessary to reach a fair price. A mutual feeling of fairness is required, both parties being in a long-term and committed relationship.

4. The dynamics of exchanges in an emerging market

What can we learn from this empirical research on the venture-capital organisation of exchanges as regard the dynamics of an emerging market? Answers to this question concern firstly the nature of the exchanged product and the identity of the participants, then the price issue, and lastly the capacity of rules and instituted practices to evolve.

The identities of the exchanged product and of the participants are subject to changes

Observers of the real commodity market recognise that the nature of the commodity matters (Harvey and Randles, 2002). On the venture-capital market, ownership and property rights are exchanged. More accurately, capital shares of young technology-based firms with growth potential are exchanged against equity invested by venture capitalists. Such a definition indicates how the identity of the exchanged product and the identity of venture-capital seekers are jointly defined. The nature of exchanged asset and the identity of the participants of exchanges result from a social process of construction, involving legal rules, and economic and social norms. In a real market, these basic components of exchanges are not naturally given, and as a consequence they are subject to changes. This evolving process can be illustrated by two observations.

The nature of the exchanged product emerged in the USA after the Second World War and has been subject to changes in that country as well as abroad. For instance, in continental Europe, in the 1980s, many people involved in venture capital would not have agreed on the definition given in the previous paragraph, because they were not conscious of the need to select only firms with high growth potential in order to cover the high coordination costs.

The identity of supply- and demand-side actors and the number of classes of participants are not given. Division of labour has been increasing, with the entrance of new specialised intermediaries acting as information and reputation brokers. In Silicon Valley, the increased division of labour is boosted by private forces. However, in some other countries, this process of extended specialisation is also supported by public programs, in order to reduce the innovation gap with the USA and to stimulate the emergence of venture capital. Preparing a business plan pushes entrepreneurs to develop their managerial capacities and to call for other competencies, stimulating new jobs. In some countries, the development of new intermediaries epitomises free enterprise, while in other countries makers of public policy play an active role. The border between private and public dynamic forces is also subject to changes, particularly in an emerging market.

In this process of increased specialisation, the role of competencies is determinant. A high level of recognised competency is the *sine qua non* condition if one is to perform efficiently and keep a good reputation; in other words, it is a necessity to remain on the market. The role of competencies is also a determinant as regards price dynamics, as suggested below.

The price dynamics
On the venture-capital market, each transaction leads to a unique price, so the representative agent hypothesis, which is associated with aggregated forces giving rise to equilibrium, is not realistic. According to evolutionary economics, when the axiom of the representative agent disappears, aggregation of micro-behaviours does not engender equilibrium but complex dynamics. For instance, it is well established that mimetic behaviour produces bubbles. This view has been applied to financial markets, but not to venture capital. In Orléan's model, designed to analyse bubble formations on financial markets, price volatility depends on behavioural variables, like personal trust in one's personal information versus trust in information coming from the market. Dubocage (2003) refers to Orléan's theoretical model (1990) in order to explain venture-capital price determination. She suggests discriminating venture suppliers according to their degree of competency. Competent venture capitalists will trust in their information while newcomers will tend to rely on the market and to replicate the average behaviour.

The tendency to adopt a mimetic behaviour when uncertainty is high, although contagion produces bubbles, is intensified within financial actors. Applied financial models of valuation, based on the fundamentalist approach, invite financial experts to set equivalency between new innovative firms, characterised by the lack of accounting data, and firms listed on financial markets operating in the same sector of activity. When specific information is missing, it is admitted that the financial market sends good information. The validity of these professional practices is highly dubitable when it is applied to young not-profitable firms. However, academics support such practices, although they generate contagion.

Theoretical models and empirical observations lead to predictions that price dynamics are more unstable and market crashes more likely if the rate of newcomers is high, which is, of course, the case on emerging domestic markets. This proposal orientates towards the need for market regulation.

Rules and instituted economic processes
Empirical observation of venture capital, in terms of instituted economic process, calls attention to instituted practices. Exchanges within local business communities are governed by international norms, legal or customary, which define the quality of the exchanged product and the quality

of participants. These norms can be qualified as constitutive and conventional rules (see section 2, on page 116). Discussing these words and their analysis framework is a step towards a better understanding of the exchange dynamics.

Instituted practices among venture capitalists can be defined as constitutive rules, as opposed by Searle (1995) to normative rules. Constitutive rules are like rules of the game: they define how to play and are analysed as constraints for actors. According to Searle, they bring novelty, as they introduce new practices. Newcomers will have to learn instituted practices, like new players learn the rules of a new game. However, this comparison should not be developed too far. Instituted practices are also conventional. They are resources for people who want to interact in uncertainty, conventions being analysed like focal points, which help people to coordinate. According to this approach, economic actors are not like players who can choose between playing and breaking the rules of the game. Unlike rules of the game, instituted practices are not abstract, cannot be defined out of the context or out of the way they are implemented, and are subject to contingencies. Instituted practices, which contribute to the government of the exchanges, are answers to empirical problems faced by market participants. Many of them can be analysed as answers to economic constraints, which mitigate uncertainty. For instance, co-investment (i.e. where the venture capitalist invests only if the entrepreneur invests), gradual investment and syndication (see section 2 on page 116) are not arbitrarily chosen practices; they belong to risk management, and have emerged and been instituted because they help venture capitalists to deal with uncertainty. Hence practice influences constitutive rules, leaves room for interpretation and leads to changes. These constitutive rules emerge as answers to actual problems. In the case of venture capital, instituted practices help parties in collecting information and in mitigating risk, using practices, like syndication, which are inspired by other financial jobs or, like the business plan, which have inspired bankers.

This view strongly departs from North's approach. According to North (1990), institutions can be defined as rules of the game and are seen as constraints for actors; they are not supposed to improve with time and they handicap the possibilities of change. Hence, these efficient constraints on an emerging market would become inefficient constraints when the market has been established. Moreover, instituted practices which govern exchanges differ from the evolutionary routines. Institutions which organise exchanges and, broadly speaking, social and economic relationships are more than routines, rules of thumb or mere behaviour regularities. According to evolutionary economics, routines contribute to governing relations inside an organisation, and their evolving process can be depicted as a random process of selection of the best practices, as suggested by Winter's metaphor of the library, where the book's selection is partly intentional and partly hazardous (Winter, 1987).

We consider that instituted practices, learning by doing and regulation co-evolve. Unintentional consequences, which have to be corrected, stimulate changes. When unwanted consequences of instituted practices negatively affect group(s) of agents, public issues emerge as well as pressures to introduce or change the regulation. This point can be illustrated as following.

Venture capital is a long-term relationship, which is closed ended; the corporate shares will finally be liquidated. There are two main successful exits, the financial market and the merger and acquisitions market. The financial market, according to the National Venture Capital Association is 'the most glamorous and heralded type of exit. In recent years, technology IPOs have been in the limelight during the IPO boom of the last six years' (www.nvca.org. 2003). In the USA, the changing of regulations on NASDAQ (Coriat and Weinstein, 2002) and, in Europe, the development of specialised share markets, like EASDAQ, have been crucial steps in the economic institution of venture-capital activity. However, at the beginning of the 2000s, due to the Internet market crash, the number of venture-backed IPOs became very limited. This bust has had a negative effect on venture capital's capacity to raise funds among institutional investors. This handicap testifies for the need of market regulation to protect against the IPO of non-profitable firms. More constraining regulations would reduce the ups and downs which characterise specialised financial markets and, as a consequence, the venture-capital dynamics.

Conclusion

This chapter aims to explain how the organisation of exchanges, through the reduction of uncertainty, stabilises the venture-capital market. The displacement from market to exchanges highlights key elements to understand how supply meets demand. The identity of the latter is analysed as a joint construction, the quality of the demand-side being shaped according to instituted practices designed by the supply-side. Instituted practices which often belong to risk management are considered by both parties as a necessity to act jointly in an uncertain environment. Within this framework of analysis, the role of intermediaries is brought to the forefront; networks offer a way to provide contacts, exchange information and build reputations. The two parties are embedded in networks which have no clear boundaries, and which involve public and private actors, and market and non-market exchanges of information and knowledge. We consider that the role of instituted practices and of networks is to mitigate uncertainty through the development of trust relations and of accumulated bodies of information.

This framework of analysis is a good guide to understanding how the price is determined and, as a consequence, investment is decided. The two main views (i.e. the fundamentalist and the mimetic approaches), are not satisfying, the first one being normative and the second one inspired by myopic behaviour in the financial market. The typical venture capitalist is competent, embedded in a business community, long termist – the pricing includes the terms in which venture investment will be liquidated – and has to take into account the entrepreneur's own interest. Corporate quality valuation is highly subjective as a consequence of the lack of accounting data and of standard benchmarks. The price is an attribute unique to each deal; the 'fair' price is depicted as the outcome of an exercise of judgement and of bargaining conducted by the venture capitalist in accordance with the rules of business community, which takes into account the entrepreneur's motives.

The method used to analyse exchanges leads to consider that the organisation of exchanges is not defined once for all. The nature of the exchanged asset, the identity of participants and the institutions which stabilise the market are not given abstractly, out of the exchange process, so they are not given once for all. The definition of a venture capital market is 'naturally' subject to changes.

Note

1 For more information on the methodology of this survey, see box 5.1.

References

Akerlof, G. 1970. 'The market for "lemons": quality uncertainty and the market mechanism', *Quarterly Journal of Economic*, 84, 488–500.

Bikhchandani, S., Hirshleifer, D. and Welch, I. 1992. 'A theory of fads, fashion, custom, and cultural change as informational cascades', *Journal of Political Economy*, 100, 992–1026.

Castilla, E., Hwang, H., Granovetter, E. and Granovetter, M. 2001. 'Social networks in the Valley', in Lee, C. M., Miller, W., Hancock, M., and Rowen, H. (eds), *The Silicon Valley Edge: A Habitat for Innovation and Entrepreneurship*, Stanford University Press. Stanford, CA.

Coriat, B. and Weinstein, O. 2002. 'Organizations, firms and institution in the generation of innovation', *Research Policy*, 31, 233–45.

Darby, M., Liu, Q. and Zucker, L. 1999. 'Stakes and starts: the effect of intellectual human capital on the level and variability of high-tech firms' market values', *NBER Working Paper*, No. 7201.

Dubocage, E. 2003. *Le capital-risque: un mode de financement dans un contexte d'incertitude*, University of Paris XIII, thesis.

Dubocage, E. and Rivaud-Danset, D. 2004. 'The development of venture capital in Europe and the role of public policy', in The Development of *Capital Markets and the their Governance*, Tokyo Club Papers, No. 16, 69–113.

Ferrary, M. 2001. 'Pour une théorie de l'échange dans les réseaux sociaux, Un essai sur le don dans les réseaux industriels de la Silicon Valley', *Cahiers internationaux de sociologie*, 111, 261–90.

Gompers, P. and Lerner, J. 2000. *The Venture Capital Cycle*. The MIT Press. Cambridge, MA.

Harvey, M. and Randles, S. 2002. 'Market, the organisation of exchanges and "instituted econnomic process" – an analytical perspective', *Revue d'économie industrielle*, 120, 11–30.

Kenney, M. (ed.) 2000. *Understanding Silicon Valley*. Stanford Business. Stanford, CA.

Knight, F. 1921. *Risk, Profit and Uncertainty*. Houghton Mifflin. Boston.

Larson, A. 1992. 'Network dyads in entrepreneurial settings: a study of the governance of exchange processes', *Administrative Science Quarterly*, 37, 76–104.

Lewis, D. 1969. *Convention, A Philosophical Study*. Cambridge University Press. Cambridge.

Nohria, N. 1992. 'Information and search in the creation of new business ventures: the case of the 128 Venture Group', in N. Nohria and R. Eccles (eds), *Network and Organizations: Structure, Form and Action*. Harvard Business School Press. Boston, MA.

North, D. 1990. *Institutions, Institutional Change and Economic Performance*. Cambridge University Press. Cambridge.

Orléan, A., 1990. 'Le rôle des influences interpersonnelles dans la détermination des cours boursiers', *Revue Economique*, 41, 839–68.

Rabeharisoa, V. 1998. 'Le rôle du capital-risque dans le développement des petites entreprises innovantes', *Annales des Mines*, February, doc. mimeo.

Rawls, J. 1958. 'Justice as fairness', *Philosophical Review*, 67, 169–94.

Salais, R. and Thévenot, L. 1986. *Le travail, marchés, règles, conventions*. INSEE-Economica. Paris.

Saxenian, A. 1994. *Regional Advantage: Culture and Competition in Silicon Valley and Route 128*. Harvard University Press. Cambridge, MA.

Searle, J. R. 1995. *The Construction of Social Reality*. New York Free Press. New York.

Suchman, M. 2000. 'Dealmakers and counselors: law firms as intermediaries in the development of Silicon Valley', in M. Kenney (ed.), *Understanding Silicon Valley*, Stanford Business. Stanford, CA.

Tordjman, H. 2001. *How to Study Markets? An Institutionalist Point of View*. Seminar CEPN-CRIC, November, doc. mimeo.

Winter, S. G. 1987. 'Natural selection and evolution', in J. Eatwell, M. Milgate and P. Newman (eds), *The New Palgrave: A Dictionary of Economics*, vol. 3. Macmillan. London: 614–17.

6

The failure of the French New Market and the dynamics of rules

Valérie Revest

Introduction

Stimulated by strong European political will, the French New Market (FNM) was created in 1996 to improve the financing of growing French companies.[1] Because of its success, the NASDAQ (National Association of Securities Dealers Automated Quotations System), which specialised in high-tech industries, was chosen as a model for the organisation of exchanges in the FNM. After its creation, the FNM successively expanded and declined. In 2000, the FNM benefited from the boom in internet values, recording 52 introductions. During the following years, the decline that had affected the NASDAQ, the bursting of the so-called 'Internet bubble', reached the European markets. The FNM was particularly affected, recording only a dozen introductions in 2002. At the same time, it suffered the collapse of its index, which fell by approximately 45%. Since 2003, the FNM has not recorded any introductions.

We assume that the difficulties encountered by the FNM cannot be imputed solely to the financial internet bubble in March 2000. Even before this event, the FNM had never fulfilled the expectations of the French market authorities: the creation of a dynamic market connecting investors with French innovative firms in need of funds. This market was expected subsequently to become a reference in Europe. Yet the FNM has never exhibited a high degree of liquidity, the production of liquidity services often being regarded as the key function of a stock exchange.[2] Furthermore, even before 2000, the FNM never attained the importance of the Neuer Markt, the German growing firms market created one year later. The number of quoted firms between 1997 and 2001 illustrates the success of the Neuer Markt.[3] This segment numbered 11 firms in 1997, 129 at the end of 2000 and 340 firms in 2001. The FNM comprised around 100 firms at the end of 1999 and 164 firms in 2001. The FNM has failed to assert itself as the technological market of the Paris Stock Exchange.

In this chapter, the issue of the failure of the FNM is explored in the light of the dynamics of rules.[4] According to us, the dynamics of rules and the contents of the changes shed light on how a market functions, and also attest as to whether it flourishes or encounters difficulties. Using organisation theory – and more specifically March et al.'s (2002) approach – we study the dynamics of rules governing exchange on the FNM between 1996 and 2004, in order to appreciate the main factors involved in the FNM failure.

On the basis of an institutional approach, we make the hypothesis that rules are at the core of the market concept. So, the performance of a market is attached to the consistency of the set of rules that govern exchanges and the way rules change. First of all, it appears necessary to specify the connections between exchange rules and financial market performance. This involves taking into account the double dimension of the FNM as an institution and as an organisation (Revest, 2001a). While organisations represent 'groups of individuals bound by some common purpose to achieve objectives', institutions provide the framework necessary for organisations to function and develop (North, 1991: 5). In relation to its double dimension, the FNM has to be competitive (organisational dimension) and to ensure the best possible exchange conditions for growing firms and for investors (institutional dimension). Consequently, as rules change with time, the FNM performance depends on the coherence between institutional changes and organisational changes.

The first part of this chapter is dedicated to the conditions of the emergence of the FNM. In the second part, the link between financial market performance and exchange rules is examined. The failure of the FNM is explained in the last part, through the analysis of the dynamics of rules between 1996 and 2004.

The conditions of the emergence of the French New Market

At the end of the 1980s, several European Economic Community studies underlined the need to create European markets dedicated to growing firms.[5] For France, as for other European countries, the creation of a market raised the question of the choice of model for the organisation of exchanges.

The need for markets dedicated to growing European firms

As a rule, growing firms have no accounting or financial history and often present a lack of profit.[6] In addition, innovative growing firms present a high degree of uncertainty (Dubocage and Rivaud-Danset, 2002).[7] These characteristics induce two main consequences for the sources of financing. Firstly, in order to start up, innovative firms have to turn to venture capital financing. Secondly, young innovative growing firms do not fulfil the conditions necessary to be quoted on a traditional financial market segment.[8]

In 1996, the creation of the FNM satisfied the requirements of two classes of participants: professional venture capitalists and emerging firms. At the end of the 1980s and the beginning of the 1990s, venture-capital firms expressed regret at the lack of exit opportunities for their funds. 'Venture capital firms invested without knowing if there would be a way out for their investment. Then, the idea arose of creating markets where professional venture capitalists could gradually withdraw their funds and allocate them to new investments' (*Les Echos*, 5 October 1994).

From 1993 to 1995, several studies argued that growing firms needed more significant funds than those offered by the traditional financing system of venture capital firms and banks. In a memorandum of October 1993, the European Community stressed the need to facilitate the access of growing firms to long-term capital markets. One study conducted by the EEC in 1994, the European Business Survey, revealed that a quarter of the firms questioned cited the lack of financing as an obstacle to their development. Yet, according to Rivaud-Danset, although 'the lack of financial resources is an important obstacle to innovative activity among continental European firms, it is not the most important' (2002: 10). The economic risks of the project have to be taken into account.

Among the obstacles quoted, the European Community report sheds light on:

1. the lack of skills and information both in management and finance for a great number of firms;
2. the limits to bank funding;
3. the lack of exit for the venture-capital firms; and
4. the lack in the European Community of financial markets that could enable the funding of small firms, compared to the American financial markets (Commission des Communautés Européennes, 1995).

According to Graham Bannock & Partners' report (1994), the main European financial markets were not specialised in quoting small firms. In 1994, the ten biggest firms represented 23% of the whole capitalisation of the market in London, 25% in Paris and 74% in Amsterdam.

The aim of the expansion of secondary markets in some countries was to permit small firms to raise funds more easily, with less expensive terms of registration and information than those of the main markets (the 'first market' in France). However, it was not sufficient for the funding of very small firms: '56% of European firms with more than 500 wage-earners raise funds through financial markets. This percentage decreases to 2.2% for European firms with fewer than 500 wage-earners. Moreover, the crash of stock exchanges in 1987 induced the collapse of secondary European markets' (Perrin, 1997: 783). This collapse stimulated the strength of attraction of the NASDAQ for small and medium firms. The development of the NASDAQ market was also partly stimulated by the lack of interest of the New York Stock Exchange (NYSE) in small and medium firms (McCormick et al., 1998). In 1994, around 10% of the new quoted firms were European (Bannock, 1994). 'The flotation of the German Qiagen at NASDAQ in 1996 was a signal to reform the German finance community' (Peukert, 2003: 223).

The NASDAQ model

In 1995, The European Community feared that small and medium growing European firms would leave Europe to join the NASDAQ market. 'Once the firms are quoted on the NASDAQ, without doubt they will choose to expand in the United States, in order to issue new shares' (Commission des Communautés Européennes, 1995).

Following a study on the opportunities of creating a European Market for growing firms, the NASDAQ structure appeared to be the most appropriate (Commission des Communautés Européennes, 1995). According to a San Francisco research organisation, 20% of Initial Public Offerings (IPOs) on the NASDAQ concern high technology firms, compared to only 10% for the main European markets (Commission des Communautés Européennes, 1995). For several European countries and the European Community, the NASDAQ represented the best structure to satisfy the needs of small and medium growing European firms.

The NASDAQ was created in 1971 in order electronically to disseminate quotes of professional securities dealers for stocks not listed on exchanges in the over-the-counter (OTC) market. Prior to NASDAQ, quotes were disseminated by means of paper copy, newspapers, and a number of private electronic systems. Thus, the NASDAQ is in essence a telecommunications network linking thousands of geographically dispersed market participants, and there is no central trading floor like those used by the securities exchanges. According to the process of price setting on the NASDAQ, called a 'quote-driven market', market makers have to post continuous, two-sided quotes (i.e. bid and ask) which consist of a price and a size, to generate investors' orders. They have to post prices before orders are submitted. The alternative organisation to a 'quote-driven market' is an 'order-driven market', where the prices are determined by the confrontation between the orders of the buyers and sellers. In this latter case, therefore, orders are submitted first and only then are trading prices determined.

On the NASDAQ, the quotes displayed by the market makers must be 'firm'. This means that if any NASDAQ member presents an order to a market maker, the market maker is obliged to trade at terms no worse than its quotes. Failure to do so constitutes 'backing away', which can be subject to regulatory sanction.[9]

At the end of 1995, 5122 firms were quoted on the NASDAQ, with a total capitalisation of one thousand billion dollars.[10] The NASDAQ market prospered for several reasons. It was characterised by a high degree of liquidity. The conditions of entry on the market remained flexible. NASDAQ required one million dollars turnover for the NMS (normal market size), instead of 2.5 million for the NYSE. Moreover, according to Orsi (2001), the NASDAQ entry conditions have changed over time in order to promote technological growing firms. These changes followed two directions. Firstly, the quantitative criteria were relaxed. Secondly, qualitative criteria linked essentially to corporate governance concerns were strengthened. Concretely, two kinds of firms could enter into the NASDAQ:

1. firms making profit but with a low level of assets; and
2. firms exhibiting a high level of assets but without profit.

For example, firms without profit could be quoted on the NASDAQ if their capital was above eight million dollars. Relating to the 'qualitative listing requirements', the emphasis lies on three principles: information transparency, independent audit committee and direct shareholder representation.

Furthermore, as many high technology firms were quoted on the NASDAQ, specialised knowledge about high technology emerged and expanded in the financial community. For all these reasons, the NASDAQ was viewed as a model by the EEC for the financing of growing firms.

The identity of the FNM

If the choice of the organisation of exchange in the FNM is based largely on the NASDAQ model, the FNM has nevertheless developed its own inner organisational characteristics. The Roger and Faure report (February 1995) which built the foundations of the FNM stressed the fact that this market should have a proper identity, and, in particular, that it should be independent of the other French markets. According to the authors of the report, the specificity of this market should appear as early as the admission process. 'The market firm should support an active policy for prospecting and admitting firms, in order to confer to the FNM a strong identity' (1995: 26).

The identity of the FNM appears firstly in the setting up of a consultative committee with industrial and scientific skills. According to Roger and Faure's report, the aim of this committee was 'to catalyse trust and progressively build a "market culture"' (1995: 26). The second specificity of the FNM was the introduction of one unique ITM (*introducteur teneur de marché* (market maker)) per value. On the NASDAQ at this time, one could find around 12 market makers per share, and around 40 market makers for the large values.

Two main reasons can explain this fact. Firstly, market making introduced a new skill into France. The Bourse de Paris has always been characterised by an 'order driven' market. Market making is more typical of the markets of English-speaking countries, such as the NASDAQ and the London Stock Exchange. Consequently, the Bourse de Paris lacked experience in market making. Secondly, the members of the Bourse de Paris wished to establish a close link between the market maker and the firm quoted. The market makers were to be more involved with the firms quoted than they were on the NASDAQ. According to the Roger and Faure report, the role of the market makers was to help and support new firms, to provide market making and to promote these firms to the investors. Meetings between market makers and firms were regularly organised, in order to improve the knowledge of the market maker about the firms they followed. A market maker on the FNM testifies that his behaviour was quite different from that of the NASDAQ market makers: 'We are concerned about the firms we quote. That's different to the NASDAQ where the market makers regard firms as pawns in the game'.[11] The combination of an order-driven market and a price-driven market also represents a significant specificity of the FNM. The investors can choose either to call a market maker or to send their orders to the order book.

In summary, an examination of the construction of the FNM reveals two major phenomena. Firstly, the creation of the FNM was stimulated by the obstacles to financing encountered by small and medium European firms. Secondly, the organisation of exchanges on the FNM is the product of the influence of NASDAQ, of the characteristics of growing values and of the weight of the history of the Paris Stock Exchange.

An institutional approach to financial market performance

Before studying the main factors involved in the failure of the FNM, it is necessary to specify what we mean by 'financial market performance'. In which circumstances do we say that a financial market is successful or not? In order to answer to this question we rely on the analysis of the rules that govern the exchanges.[12]

Rules and market performance

Two main approaches explore the issue of exchange rules and market per-formance in the field of financial markets. Microstructure theory, in eco-nomics, breaks with traditional finance theory and focuses on the market exchange mechanisms. This theory studies the way that specific exchange mechanisms affects price formation mechanisms: 'underlying the study of market microstructure is a more basic curiosity: the desire to know how prices are formed in the economy' (O'Hara, 1995: 1). Microstructure studies explore the influence of the system of quotation and of exchange rules on the price mechanism and on certain market properties (Schwartz, 1991). According to this approach, market performance improves with a high degree of liquidity, low transaction costs, low volatility, high informa-tion transparency and a fair price discovery system. However, Schwartz (1995) admits that analytical research has never clearly demonstrated the superiority of a specific market structure (such as the order-driven system or quote-driven system) in relation to the set of performance criteria men-tioned above. Each market structure presents advantages and disadvan-tages, depending notably on actors' strategies.

Although microstructure theory only examines exchange mechanisms, which can be defined as a set of formal rules supporting the exchanges, O'Hara acknowledges that informal rules also matter: 'Whatever the setting, however, there are rules either explicit or implicit that govern the trading mechanism, and it is these rules that result in the formation and evolution of market prices' (1995: 7). In general, formal rules comprise 'written rules' such as constitutions, regulations, laws, contracts, and so on, and informal rules consist of social practices (conventions, customs, etc.).

Some sociological studies have emphasised the role of both formal and informal rules in financial markets. Abolafia (1984, 1996) describes financial markets as socially constructed institutions in which the behaviour of traders is suspended in a web of customs, norms and structures of control. From a different perspective, one can also mention the works of Baker (1984), who sheds light on the informal social rules that govern exchanges. 'One widely-reported control mechanism involves the use of what may be called the "first rule". The first person to orally respond to an offer is formally entitled to the entire volume offered at the offered price' (Baker, 1984: 120). Conducting an ethnographic investigation into the MATIF – Marché A Terme d'Instruments Financiers[13] – before 1988, Hassoun (2000) also reveals repeated informal rules, which are opposed to formal rules and yet positively contribute to the way the MATIF works. The author mentions, for example, the negotiators' practice of helping other negotiators facing personal or professional obstacles, by exchanging intensively with them. In a paper on the origins of financial derivative exchanges at the Chicago Board Options Exchange, Mackenzie and Millo (2003) point out that trading options were not initially thought of as part of an official exchange, yet they subsequently became an official exchange. If those different studies do not focus on the notion of performance or quality, they all underline the way formal and/or informal rules shape real markets.

An intermediate approach is envisaged, including at the same time the notion of financial market performance/quality and the analysis of the way rules permit a financial market to function. Adopting a Polanyian (1957) 'perspective', we advocate the point of view that the different ways of organising exchange (circulation of information, price mechanisms, etc.) shape markets, in their nature and the way they function and change. From this perspective, a market can be viewed as a physical or virtual structure of repeated exchanges governed by formal and informal rules. The rules being at the core of the market concept, the way a market works is linked to the degree of consistency of the set of rules supporting the exchanges.[14] Furthermore, the way these rules change and the contents of the changes explain, to a certain extent, a market's performance.

In the case of the FNM, in order to shed light on the dynamics of rules, only formal exchange rules are considered. These formal rules are created by the market authorities; they govern the way exchanges are concluded. Generally, the market authorities are represented by the market itself and by an independent regulatory organisation. In 1996, the COB[15] (Commission des Opérations Boursières) was the independent public organisation, of which the primary missions were to maintain the integrity of the French securities markets and to protect investors. The COB required public companies to disclose meaningful financial and other information to the public. It had the power to sanction individuals and companies that were breaking the securities laws; typical infractions include insider trading, accounting fraud, and providing false or misleading information about securities and the companies issuing them.

How can we judge that the different sets of exchange rules in a market – and the way they change – are consistent? One answer relies on the specific nature of the market studied. The set of rules and the dynamics of rules should respect the specific nature of the market. If all markets share the objective of enabling exchanges to take place, through formal and informal rules, they differ according to the characteristics of the actors, the nature of the good exchanged, the exchange organisation and the means of regulation.

The double nature of the FNM: organisation and institution

Organised financial markets such as the FNM can be defined as organisations and institutions, based on North's (1991) distinction. '*Organizations* are created with purposive intent in consequence of the opportunity set resulting from the existing set of constraints (*institutional* ones as well as the traditional ones of economic theory' (North, 1991: 5).[16] North made a bright analogy between organisations and institutions and a competitive team sport. The institutions are analogous to the rules of the game in a competitive team sport and the organisations represent the players: 'the purpose of the rules is to define the way the game is played. But the objective of the team within that set of rules is to win the game' (1991: 4–5). So as Ménard (1995) observed, there is a 'symbiotic relation between institutions and the consequent organisation'.

As an organisation, the FNM has to attract orders and make a profit. Financial markets fund regulatory and surveillance functions through income activities: quotations (registration fee for the quote), negotiations (transaction commissions and software renting), services (subscription for information circulation, clearing fees) and other products. For a long time, financial markets were non profit-making organisations. Following the deregulation waves of the 1980s, financial markets moved from being not-for-profit organisations to profit-making organisations. In Europe, the first changes appeared at the end of the 1980s with the growth of the Seaq International, a London Stock Exchange market dedicated to foreign values. As the Seaq International attracted many firms, Continental Europe modernised its structures and functioning rules in order to become more competitive. The financial markets were then confronted with the following changes: the introduction of competition, technical changes, capital opening and profit objectives. The evolution of the competitive context led financial markets to seek alliances with other markets. 'Financial markets appear to be at a decisive stage in their evolution, where phenomena of maturity and overcapacity, combined with major technological changes, are leading them to seek industrial cooperation agreements to ensure their competitiveness and obtain a measure of security for the future' (Andisel Choppin, 2001: 63).

The procedures that permit a regulated financial market to make profits are embedded in a specific institutional framework.[17] From an institutional viewpoint, the principal function of financial markets is to ensure the best possible exchange conditions: transparency, equity between agents and good-quality information. According to Champarnaud (2000: 21), 'from a juridical point of view, the "market firm" is certainly a commercial firm, but it is also responsible for a public interest and for the way the market functions'. Regulating a financial market means not only producing rules, but also ensuring that the system experiences harmonious and stable development. The two main objectives of financial regulation remain the security of transactions and the protection of investors. For instance, the markets authorities have to verify that intermediaries have the necessary skills and ethical behaviour. They also have to control the information supplied by the issuers and the performance of the negotiation systems.

If the FNM possesses characteristics of both an institution and an organisation, the notion of rules is fundamental because it is common to institutional and organisational fields'[18] (Chavance, 2001). Rules enable better understanding of the connections between organisation and institution. On the one hand, explicit institutional and organisational rules operate in the same way and share a wide common objective: the coordination of individual actions. On the other hand, institutional rules differ from organisational rules essentially in terms of the motivations at the origin of the rules. In the specific case of a financial regulated market, the organisational rules are essentially inspired by profit objectives and institutional rules by security and quality objectives. So, institutional and organisational motives stimulated the market authorities' decisions to create and/or change some rules.[19] According to this viewpoint, the performance of a financial market such as the FNM depends on the consistency between organisational and institutional motives at the origins of the rules.

In certain circumstances, the coexistence of what we have referred to as institutional and organisational motives may generate conflicts of interest. This was the case for the NASDAQ in the mid-1990s. During this period, the regulatory authority of the market, the NASD, motivated partly by competition with the NYSE, supported collusive practices on the part of the market makers (Revest, 2001c). In the case of the FNM have institutional rules and organisational rules opposed each other at any moment? What were the consequences for the global functioning of the FNM and for its performance?

From the dynamics of rules to the failure of the FNM

In this section, we study the relation between the dynamic of rules in the FNM during the period 1996–2004 and the difficulties encountered by this market. Relying on the approach of March et al., we show that the rule changes were not always consistent with the double nature of the FNM, as an institution and an organisation.

The dynamics of rules: a tool for the analysis of the FNM's failure

Despite its youth, the FNM underwent various rule changes between 1996 and 2002. These changes affected several dimensions of the market's functioning, such as the obligations of shareowner leaders, the obligations of the ITM or the quotation mechanisms. The legal organisation of the FNM has also changed several times since this market emerged. In 1996, the FNM was a regulated market managed by a market firm: La Société du Nouveau Marché (SNM). In 1999, the SNM was taken over by the Société des Bourses Françaises (SBF). The latter then disappeared in 2000, with the birth of Euronext. Regulated financial markets were created in 1993 by the European Investment Services Directive (ISD) in order to facilitate the emergence of efficient, integrated and orderly EU financial markets. Those markets dedicated to financial instruments function in a regular way and have firm entry, organisation and negotiation conditions.[20] Moreover, regulated financial markets obtain the status of 'market firm'. This means that, like other traditional organisations, they seek to make profits. They compete with each other not only for the order flows, but also for the other activities of their production line, such as the negotiation mechanism, the clearing room, and so on.

According to Reynaud (2002: 2), even if many economists recognise that rules are a coordination tool, very little research exists to explain how they actually make exchange possible or how they change. A major contribution to the question of the way rules change has been written by March et al. (2002), who offer a framework for the analysis of the dynamics of written rules in an organisation.

In order to examine the dynamic of formal rules in the FNM between 1996 and 2004, we rely on the approach of March et al. (2002). The authors analyse the dynamics of written rules in a specific organisation: Stanford University. March et al. carried out a quantitative analysis of the historical patterns and statistical properties of the formation and changing of rules in Stanford University between 1891 and 1987. The results of the quantitative analysis reveal certain regularities in the dynamics of rules: 'rule histories have regularities that might not be obvious either from focusing on increases in organisational size or complexity, or from assuming an efficient historical match between rules and their environments, or from the usual telling of detailed contextual stories about rule adoption' (2002: 161). Beyond the results of the quantitative analysis, the force of March et al.'s analysis lies in their explanation of the dynamics of rules.

Their approach concentrates on three dimensions.[21] Firstly, rules evolve over time in response to new problems. Frequently, problems originate from outside the organisation. These external problems often relate to historical concerns. 'When a rule is created, changed or eliminated, it records a reaction to external or internal pressures on the organization' (March et al., 2002: 2). Secondly, according to the authors, rules are inter-related within an organization. The adaptation of rules may be local, but rules are not autonomous. Within a set of rules, a change in one rule will probably affect the others. 'These ecological connections matter and we need to treat the development of organizational rules as a co-evolutionary process within a population of interconnected rules' (2002: 57). Thirdly, rules both record history and reflect learning within the organisation. 'As organizations accumulate experience with particular sets of procedures and problems, they develop competencies that reduce the need for new procedures' (2002: 57).

As the approach of March et al. is essentially descriptive we need to incorporate the notion of financial market failure. If the way rules change reflect financial market performance, the main factors involved in the dynamics of rules have to be connected to the performance – or quality – of the FNM. This leads us to the following proposition: the strain of the environment, the ecology of rules and the learning process should respect the specific nature of the market studied. In the case of the FNM, these three dimensions should take into account in their process the equilibrium between institutional and organisational motives. Consequently, the dynamics of rules should incorporate, at the same time, the necessity for the FNM to be competitive and to guarantee the best exchange conditions for the different actors.

Examining the dynamics of exchange rules between 1996 and 2004 reveals: a consequent strain of the competitive environment; a deficiency of the organisational learning relating to market making; and a lack of respect of the ecology of rules.

The influential strain of the external environment: the role of competition

According to March et al. (2002), the environment is the major source of problems confronting the organisation. Some authors, such as Scott (1981) and Granovetter (1985), refer to the embeddedness of organisations in their social, political and cultural context. Consequently, the strain of the environment on the organisation leads to changes in the written rules. However, although the link between rule change and the external environment is widely acknowledged, the way the environment influences organisations is still under debate.

One approach emphasises the role of the institutional environment in shaping the internal operations in organisations (DiMaggio and Powell, 1983; Sutton et al., 1994). From this point of view, the rate of rule formation and rule change grows with increases in the importance of external factors. An alternative view considers the propensity for organisations to substitute external regulations for organisational regulations. The propensity to create and/or to change rules thus declines with the increased adoption of external rules (March and Olsen, 1995). March et al. recognise that the relation between the strain of the environment on one side and the reaction of the organisation on the other remains ambiguous. 'These various arguments make it quite unclear what kind of relation we should expect between external pressures and organizational response' (2002: 60). According to us, these two approaches are not inconsistent; one can imagine that, over the course of time and according to specific economic and social conditions, environmental pressure might induce new rules or contribute to the production of fewer rules. Whatever the direction of the effects, the external environment affects rules in organisations.

Over recent years, international financial markets have been characterised by increasing competition. This competition leads to merger. In Europe, the first wave of mergers started with growing values markets. Through the Euro-NM, a network of certain European financial markets, the FNM rapidly found itself competing with another European market dedicated to growing values: the EASDAQ (European Association of Securities Dealers Automated Quotations). Both Euro-NM and EASDAQ failed to become attractive enough to growing European firms (Revest, 2001b). With increased competition, mergers expanded to a European and international level. In 2000, the merger of the Paris Stock Exchange and the stock exchanges of Amsterdam and Brussels resulted in Euronext, a unique platform of exchanges. The German Stock Exchange and the London Stock Exchange also tried to merge, but their project, called iX – International Exchange – failed because of a hostile takeover attempt by the Stockholm market firm OM Grupen. At the worldwide level, one can mention the project of the NYSE called Global Equity Market, involving nine stock exchanges, including Euronext. The NASDAQ is also attempting to conclude alliances with markets dedicated to growing values. Recently, the NASDAQ Japan emerged and the EASDAQ changed into the NASDAQ Europe. Concurrently, another competition is growing between financial markets and ATS (alternative trading systems). These are electronic systems for the transmission and automatic execution of stock market orders. They include Instinet, Tradepoint, Archipelago, Attain, Brut and Island. They represent unregulated financial markets. ATS initiated by large agencies of financial information, broker firms and investment banks make lower transactions costs possible and remove the need for an intermediary.

This context of increasing competition, which expressed the strain of the environment, resulted in several rule changes in the FNM. We shall examine two of these changes. Firstly, in 1998, the FNM moved from a call auction mechanism to a continuous auction mechanism. Secondly, during the same year, the period of lock-up was reduced from three years to one year.

In a call auction, orders accumulate up until a specific moment, at which time they are executed. In a continuous auction, orders are matched continuously throughout the day. Continuous auctions are more suitable for dynamic stocks that are bought and sold very often and that involve large volumes being exchanged. Call auctions, on the contrary, are more suitable for less active stocks. The subject of introducing a continuous quotation on the FNM was first discussed during the meeting of the Board of Directors on 27 November 1997. Mr Leblanc, director of the FNM, presented a study of the liquidity of the FNM for the third quarter. On the basis of this study, the possibility of quoting certain shares continuously was examined. The criteria used were those employed by the SBF in the 'first' and 'second' markets. According to Mr Leblanc, eight out of fifteen shares could be quoted continuously. However, the opinion of the other members of the Board of Directors differed, because of the problems of fragmentation, reputation and the opinion of the intermediaries. They thought that the FNM was not dynamic enough to move towards a continuous auction system. However, approximately one year later, Mr Leblanc observed that the Neuer Markt was about to set up a continuous system of quotation. This information finally convinced the members of the board of directors to adopt a continuous system of quotation on the FNM. Nevertheless, this system remains expensive because orders have to be matched continuously. In addition, market making in the case of a small number of exchanged stocks increases the risk borne by the market makers. Finally, a continuous auction system with non-active stocks may produce a negative image of the market and have a negative impact on its reputation.

The second example of the influence of the external environment concerns the lock-up period.[22] This rule, issued by the COB, refers to the shareholders leaders' obligation to keep a minimum percentage of shares from the time of introduction until the expiry of a minimum period. In 1993, this period was three years on the FNM. The objective of the 'lock-up' is to avoid a too rapid selling-out of the shares. This rule discourages a short-term view, and obliges the shareholder leaders to think about the firm's wealth in a medium-term perspective. In December 1998, the market authorities decided to reduce the lock-up period from three years to one year, because numerous shareholders' leaders found this obligation too constraining. In addition, the other European markets for growing values chose a shorter period of preservation.

In these two cases, changes were solely explained by the strain of competition. Firstly, at the end of 1997, the FNM did not display enough liquidity to be quoted continuously. Secondly, the initial lock-up period – three years – achieved appropriately its purpose: to encourage a medium-term perspective for the investors.

The deficiency of organisational learning: the case of market making

In general, according to organisational theory, the age of the rules positively affects the persistence of an organisational structure. One of the mechanisms described by March et al. (2002) is the rise of abilities linked to the rules: 'Improvements in rules and enhanced abilities to use them reduce incentives for revision' (2002: 73). Rules are the technologies of organizational life (Levinthal and March, 1993). They become stabilized through competency traps as other technologies do (Arthur, 1989). A first group of abilities comprises increased skills at operating within existing rules – that is, organisational learning. 'Organisations become better at doing the things they do' (March et al., 2002: 73). Organisation members accumulate competence in interpreting rules, developing exceptions to rules, and understanding the boundaries and flexibility of rules. Another process refers to the accumulation of competence in changing rules. Part of the competence gained from experience is the ability to recognise the side benefits of engaging in rule change. Decision makers learn how to recognise problems in rules, how to mobilise attention on those problems, and how to prepare changes.

For the activity of market making, however, organisational learning and accumulation of ability in changing rules appear to be insufficient. Introduced as part of the NASDAQ model, market making is specific to the FNM; it does not exist in the other French segments. The Paris Stock Exchange had always been order-driven until the creation of the FNM. Both the intermediaries and the investors lacked experience in market making. 'The FNM, as the younger Paris segment market, was a victim of the historical practices and customs of the Paris Stock Exchange' (Perwald, 2002: 275). Several factors explain the failure of market making on the FNM. In a statistical study on market making carried out in 1999, French ITM expressed a negative opinion about the double quotation system on the FNM comprising both an order-driven market and market making (Revest, 2001b: 198). An investigation by Ernst and Young in collaboration with the Agence Nationale de Valorisation de la Recherche (ANVAR) and the SNM revealed a negative appraisal of market making from the 28 FNM-quoted firms. These firms complained that ITM acted too prudently and they regretted the lack of real market making. The limits of French market making have been emphasised during periods of high volatility. During these periods, ITM did not post prices and consequently could not buy or sell anything. 'Because of the lack of punishment, nothing was done to improve the ITMs' respecting of obligations' (Perwald, 2002: 270).

Nowadays, in reality the function of market maker has almost disappeared in France. Market makers act more to stimulate the market (as 'puffers') than actually to carry out market making. Investors who like to negotiate blocks of shares call the ITM, and then bargain via posted prices. This fact illustrates the inability of the FNM to apply the law concerning market making and to recognise the necessity of engaging in rule change. The intermediaries were unable to perform market making and the market authority (the COB) was unable to resolve this difficulty.

The lack of respect of the ecology of rules

The last dimension relates to the fact that the dynamics of rules are linked to their ecological structure. In other words, rules are not autonomous.

More precisely, they are inter-related. 'Rules are linked to other rules in functional and procedural ecologies that place any particular rule in close proximity to some other rules and more distant from others' (March et al., 2002: 64). 'Rules are bound together and separate from each other by barriers within an ecology of written rules' (2002: 2). The analysis of the FNM's dynamics of rules between 1996 and 2004 show that those changes have not always respected the ecology of the rules.

The first example concerns the choice taken by the COB and the market firm (Société du Nouveau Marché) to authorise some technological firms to be quoted on the first market, although their characteristics should have led them to the FNM. The lack of competence linked to market making. This was the case for CompleTel[23] and Liberty Surf[24] being authorised by the COB (French Stock Exchange regulatory body). Other firms such as Wanadoo and Orange made the same choice.[25] The image projected by the FNM did not suit these firms and has driven them to apply for entry onto the *first market* instead of the FNM.[26] In order to understand why some technological firms ask to be quoted on the first market, it is important underline that the FNM admitted non-technological firms, such as Saveurs de France, Joliez Regol and Proxidis.[27] This decision resulted in the heterogeneity of the share-list (Perwald, 2002). Compared to other markets, the FNM share list did not appear completely rational. The Neuer Markt, on the contrary, only admitted small and medium innovative firms.

To a certain extent, the COB decision allowing some technological firms to be quoted on the first market had a negative consequence on the FNM image. Firms that join the FNM or the second market wish also to be quoted in the French first market. As a contrast, firms that enter the NASDAQ wish to remain in the NASDAQ. At the end of 2000, 20% of French technological firms were quoted in the first market, 26% in the second market and 54% in the FNM (Euronext).

A second example relates to exceptions to the conditions of entry onto the FNM that have been granted. The most frequently authorised dispensation concerns the obligation to spread to the public at least 20% of the firm's capital. This was the case for Selftrade and Netgem. The argument for dispensation initiated in other regulated markets. On the French first market, for example, dispensation for spreading at least 25% of shares to the public was frequently granted. This was the case for Alsthom and Rhodia, for example.

The third example is that the exceptions to the conditions of entry lead the FNM during the internet bubble to admit unreliable firms characterised, for instance, by unviable projects, unskilled managers or a deficient demand. For instance, La Tête Dans Les Nuages, a chain of video gaming rooms, presented implausible forecasts. The investors of Belvedere, a trader in strong alcohol, discovered a dispute about the ownership of the brand name. Guyanor, a gold prospector in Guyana, was not successful enough. After the introduction of these firms, investors often observed the collapse of quoted prices. The methods of assessment, relying notably on potential earnings (for instance the number of visitors per web page for Internet firms) have been strongly criticised (Zadjenweber, 2000). The FNM has failed in its institutional duty to protect its investors (Dubocage and Revest, 2004).

The examples mentioned above raise the issue of the credibility of the FNM during the related period. In such circumstances, how can investors be confident in the market authorities? Champarnaud (2000) warns against the intensification of competition: 'It could lead the regulators to yield to temptation to favour the development of financial activities in their jurisdiction, reducing the degree of protection of investors and regulatory supervision'.

Conclusion

The FNM was created in order to fund French and European small and medium growing firms, but it was never recognised as a successful market, even before the Internet bubble. In this chapter, the performance of the FNM has been studied in the light of the dynamics of rules. The way that formal rules changed in the FNM between 1996 and 2004 testifies to the difficulties encountered by this market. It has disclosed relevant elements about the factors involved in the failure of this market.

The performance of the FNM is viewed as connected to a fragile equilibrium between organisational and institutional motives. Both organisations and institutions generate rules, but these rules are governed by different motivations in each case. On the one hand, regulated financial markets must secure investors and maintain fairness and transparency. On the other hand, they must make profits and compete with other financial markets.

The analysis of the FNM's dynamics of rules between 1996 and 2004 testifies a lack of consistency and relevance in the new rules, given the double dimension of the FNM, as an institution and an organisation. The coexistence of different institutional and organisational motives have undermined the functioning and the development of the FNM. The study of the dynamics of rules reveal more precisely a consequent strain of the competition, a deficiency of organisational learning related to market making and a lack of respect of the rules' ecology.

We observe that several rules changed because of the increasingly competitive environment. On the one hand, this specific environment increases the rate of change and undermines the global stability of the market organisation. On the other hand, these environment-induced changes were not totally consistent with the characteristics of the FNM – that is, its history and capabilities. The lack of respect of the ecology of the rules through the exception effect, for instance, has weakened the identity of the FNM as a market for technological values. The fact that some technological firms obtain dispensations to be quoted on the first market has made it difficult for the FNM to build a strong identity. The case of market making reveals an example of deficient organisational learning of rules changes. Organisation members should accumulate ability in interpreting rules, developing exceptions to rules, and understanding the boundaries and flexibility of rules. However, the rules on market making were not applied in the way they should have been.

What have we learnt from the FNM case study?

Firstly, this case study raises an important issue: how can we determine if a financial market works 'well'? In other words, what criteria can we use to evaluate the quality of the functioning of such a market? For instance, the failure of the FNM reveals two components. Firstly, this market failed to stimulate exchanges and so to ease the encounter between investors and firms. The FNM has never been characterised by a high degree of liquidity and activity. Secondly, the failure of the FNM is also an institutional failure: during the internet bubble, the FNM accepted firms that were too unreliable to be quoted on a financial market. Therefore, the FNM failed as an institution responsible for the security of its investors. The FNM's behaviour had a negative effect on its own credibility. Consequently, it is important to take into account not only the criteria employed by the microstructure theory – liquidity, transaction costs, transparency, etc. – and the usual criteria for firms – turnover, profitability, etc. – but also criteria linked to the consistency and relevance of institutional and organisational choices within a financial market.

Secondly, this case study testifies to the difficulties encountered in building a financial market and making it change in an appropriate way. The initial organisation of exchange on the FNM was based simultaneously on an existing successful model – the NASDAQ – and on the local history of the Paris Stock Exchange. The French market authorities knew that duplicating a market organisation not only required reproduction of the same set of rules, but that it was also necessary to take into account the history of the place and the experience of the actors. However, the market authorities were faced with a highly complex task in building a financial market. This requires a process which must take into account an extremely difficult coordination of the following elements:

1. the local history of the exchanges;
2. the identity and the skills of the different actors: firms, intermediaries and investors; and
3. the institutional framework.

In June 2004, after the failure of the Next Economy to stimulate growing innovative firms, Euronext Paris announced the end of the FNM experiment. In January 2005, a major reform in the quotation system brought about the end of the French market segments: the first market, the second market and the FNM. They were replaced by a single official list (Eurolist by Euronext), where securities were classified by alphabetical order and their capitalisation indicated. Simultaneously, a new unregulated market, Alternext, was created in order to finance small and medium firms. Euronext's reform represented a dramatic change for growing firms. With the reform, the organisation of exchange became more homogeneous and the specificity of the growing firms disappeared from the list. Several of these firms, which could not be quoted on the official list, were directed toward the unregulated market – Alternext. However, one may wonder whether this new organisational model will be able to stimulate the financing of French growing firms and whether it will enable the tension to be reduced between institutional and organisational motives.

Notes

1 According to the criteria of the Paris Stock Exchange, firms admitted onto the FNM are characterised by a growth in turnover which must exceed 30% per year and by forecast growth (Société du Nouveau Marché, 1996).
2 Liquidity distinguishes markets where it is possible to buy or sell shares rapidly at sensible prices under bearable costs (Biais et al., 1997: 3).
3 The Neuer Markt, which was successful towards the end of the 1990s, finally disappeared in 2002. See Burghof and Hunger, 2004.
4 Solely rules that are recorded in written form (formal rules) are envisaged, even if unwritten rules (informal rules) – such as social norms, standard practice, tacit understanding and rules of thumb – are also important in understanding how an organisation or a market works.
5 Posner (2005) shows that the primary causes behind the creation of Europe's new stock markets lie in the political skill motivations of supranational European Union bureaucrats.
6 Growing firms can be split into two groups: innovative growing firms and non-innovative growing firms.
7 According to the authors, innovative firms are characterised by different kind of uncertainty from technological uncertainty, market related uncertainty, and so on.
8 Until now, the Paris stock exchange has been divided into three segments: the first market, the second market and the New Market. Firms with high capitalisation and turnover are quoted on the first market, firms with medium capitalisation and turnover are quoted on the second market, and growing firms with low capitalisation and turnover are quoted on the NM.
9 The years 1994 to 1996 were characterised by substantial controversy regarding the fairness of the NASDAQ market. Christie and Shultz (1994) revealed a 'tacit collusion' between NASDAQ market makers. This controversy culminated in major reforms to NASD governance and NASDAQ trading rules (Revest, 2001c).
10 The NASDAQ has experienced remarkable growth and today represents a serious competitive alternative to the dominant equity exchange in the USA, the New York Stock Exchange (NYSE).
11 Interview with an ITM, 2001.

12 Our analysis differs from the economic concept of 'market failure', which refers to situations where markets fail to efficiently provide or allocated goods and services. See, for instance, Arrow, 1962; Bator, 1958.

13 This French market is dedicated to derivative financial instruments.

14 An alternative approach is based on the analysis of the organisation of economic exchange, instead of studying markets (Harvey and Randles, 2002). This approach makes it possible to analyse the variety and dynamics of exchange processes, without making the usual presumption of a well-defined market.

15 In order to strengthen the power of the French public authorities, the COB and the CMF (Conseil des Marchés Financiers) merged in 2003 into the AMF (Autorité des Marchés Financiers).

16 Based on the link between 'organisation' and 'institution', Kichou and Rizopoulos (2001) suggest distinguishing between two classes of organisations: organisations that 'consume' rules and organisations that 'diffuse' rules. Institutional innovation is then perceived as the result of the interaction between these two classes of organisations.

17 In a different way, Favereau (1989) defines the financial markets as 'market organisations'. Financial markets have the characteristics both of a market (the role of prices) and of an organisation (the role of rules).

18 The field of organisations is marked by a prolific literature about rules in organisations. See, for example, Dosi et al., 1997; Grossman and Hart, 1986; Holmström, 1979. Organisational theory made a major contribution (Cyert and March, 1963; March and Simon, 1958).

19 The concrete decision process is certainly more complex than the dichotomy between institutional motives and organisational motives, yet this distinction illustrates one important dimension of the market authorities' process of decision.

20 According to the ISD, the term 'non-regulated' markets, on the other hand, refers to OTC markets. In these markets, there is no regulation or control, however transactions are organised.

21 Technological progress has also continuously contributed to rule changes on the FNM. On the influence of technology on market functioning, see Muniesa, 2000.

22 This rule concerns young firms.

23 CompleTel is an alternative operator of urban fibre-optic networks for businesses and the public sector as well as for telecommunications operators and Internet access in France.

24 In 2001, Liberty Surf was bought by Tiscali, which asked to be quoted on the FNM.

25 At this period, Wanadoo provided Internet access in Europe.

26 The capitalisation of these firms enabled them to be quoted on the first market.

27 Saveurs de France designs and manufactures frozen specialties and industrial pastry products, Joliez Regol is an insurance broker and Proxidis a hairdressing chain.

References

Abolafia, M. 1984. 'Structured anarchy: formal organization in the commodities futures markets', in Adler, A. and Adler, P. (eds), *The Social Dynamics of Financial Markets*. JAI Press. Greenwich, CT: 129–50.

Abolafia, M. 1996. *Making Markets: Opportunism and Restraint on Wall Street*. Harvard University Press. Cambridge, MA.

Andisel, Choppin J. 2001. 'Coopérations industrielles et positionnement concurrentiel: application aux marchés financiers organisés', *Revue d'Economie Industrielle*, 95, 61–82.

Arrow, K. 1962. 'Economic welfare and the allocation of ressources for innovation', in Nelson ed., *The Rate and Direction of Inventive Activity*. Princeton University Press. Princeton, NJ.

Arthur, W. 1989. 'Competing technologies, increasing returns, and lock-in by historical events', *Economic Journal*, 99, 116–31.

Baker, W. 1984. 'Floor trading and crowd dynamic', in Adler, A. and Adler, P. (eds), *The Social Dynamics of Financial Markets*. JAI Press. Greenwich, CT: 107–28.

Bannock, Graham and Partners. 1994. 'The second tier markets for new technology based firms', *European Commission DG XIII-D4* (SPRINT). European Commission. Brussels and Luxembourg.

Bator, F. 1958. 'The anatomy of market failure', *Quarterly Journal of Economics*, 72, 351–79.

Biais, B., Davydoff, D. and Jacquillat, B. 1997. *Organisation et qualité des marchés financiers*. PUF, Finance. Paris.

Burghof, H. P. and Hunger, A. 2004. 'The Neuer Markt: an (overly) risky asset of Germany's financial system', in Giudici, G. and Rosenbook, P. (eds), *The Rise and Fall of Europe's New Stock Markets*. Elsevier, Advances in Financial Economics, vol. 10, 295–329.

Champarnaud, F. 2000. 'Régulation et développement des places financières', *Revue d'Economie Financière*, special edition: *Quelles places financières pour demain?*, 57, 95–107.

Chavance, B. 2001. 'Organisations, institutions, systèmes: types et niveaux de règles', *Revue d'Economie Industrielle*, 97, 85–101.

Christie, W. and Schultz, P. 1994. 'Why do NASDAQ market makers avoid odd-eighth quotes?', *Journal of Finance*, 49, 1813–40.

Commission des Communautés Européennes 1993. *COM (93), 528 Final*. Office des publications officielles des Communautés européennes, L-2985 Luxembourg.

Commission des Communautés Européennes 1995. *COM (95), 488 Final*. Office des publications officielles des Communautés européennes, L-2985 Luxembourg.

Cyert, R. and March, J. 1963. *A Behavioral Theory of the Firm*. Prentice Hall. Englewood Cliffs, NJ.

DiMaggio, P. and Powell, W. 1983. 'The iron cage revisited: institutional isomorphism and collective rationality in organizational fields', *American Sociological Review*, 48, 147–60.

Dosi, G., Marengo, L., Bassanini, L. and Valente, M. 1997. 'Les normes comme propriétés émergentes d'un apprentissage adaptatif', in Reynaud, B. (ed.), *Les limites de la rationalité, les figures du collectif*, Vol. 2. La Découverte. Paris: 45–64.

Dubocage, E. and Revest, V. 2004. 'La valorisation à l'introduction des start-ups sur le Nouveau Marché français: une approche conventionnaliste and institutionnaliste'. Paper presented at the workshop 'Mieux comprendre la valorisatin des titres sur les places financières: regards croisés des sciences sociales', 24 May, Lille.

Dubocage, E. and Rivaud-Danset, D. 2002. 'L'organisation des échanges sur le marché du capital risque', *Revue d'Economie Industrielle*, 101, 31–46.

Favereau, O. 1989. 'Organisation et marché', *Revue d'Economie Française*, 4(1), 65–95.

Granovetter, M. 1985. 'Economic action and social structure: the problem of embeddedness', *American Journal of Sociology*, 91(3), 481–510.

Grossman, S. and Hart, O. 1986. 'The costs and benefits of ownership: a theory of vertical and lateral integration', *Journal of Political Economy*, 94, 691–719.

Harvey, M. and Randles, S. 2002. 'Markets, the organisation of exchanges and "instituted economic process" – an analytical perspective', *Revue d'Economie Industrielle*, 101, 11–30.

Hassoun, J. P. 2000. 'Trois interactions hétérodoxes sur les marchés à la Criée du Matif. Rationalité locale et rationalité globale: une relation non contradictoire?', *Politix*, 'Marchés financiers', 13(52), 99–119.

Holmström, B. 1979. 'Moral hazard and observability', *Bell Journal of Economics*, 10, 74–91.

Kichou, L. and Rizopoulos, Y. 2001. 'L'innovation institutionnelle en tant que processus d'interactions organisationnelles', *Revue d'Economie Industrielle*, 97(4), 139–52.

Levinthal, D. and March, J. 1993. 'The myopa of learning', *Strategic Management Journal*, 14, 95–112.

Mackenzie, D. and Millo, Y. 2003. 'Constructing a market, performing theory: the historical sociology of a financial derivatives exchange', *American Journal of Sociology*, 109 (May), 107–45.

March, J. G. and Olsen, J. P. 1995. *Democratic Governance*. Free Press. New York.

March, J. G. and Simon, H. 1958. *Organizations*. Blackwell. Cambridge, MA.

March, J. G., Schulz, M. and Zhou, X. 2002. *The Dynamics of Rules: Change in Written Organizational Codes*. Stanford University Press. Stanford, CA.

McCormick, D., Selway, J. and Smith, J. 1998. 'The Nasdaq stock market: historical background and current operation'. NASD working paper 98-01, Nasdaq Department of Economic Research.

Ménard, C. 1995. 'Markets as institutions versus organizations as markets? Disentangling some fundamental concepts', *Journal of Economic Behavior and Organization*, 28, 161–82.

Muniesa, F. 2000. 'Un robot walrasien. Cotation électronique et justesse de la découverte des prix', *Politix*, 13(52), 121–54.

North, D. C. 1991. *Institutions, Institutional Change and Economic Performance*. Cambridge University Press. Cambridge.

O'Hara, M. 1995. *Market Microstructure Theory*. Blackwell Business. Cambridge, MA.

Orsi, F. 2001. *Droits de propriété intellectuelle et marchés financiers dans les nouvelles relations science/industrie: le cas de la recherche sur le génome humain, doctorat en Sciences Economiques*. PhD thesis, Université Aix-Marseille II.

Perrin, E. 1997. 'Marché financier de petites capitalisations', in Simon, Y. (dir.), *Encyclopédie des Marchés Financiers*. Economica. Paris, vol. 1, 779–801.

Perwald, K. 2002. *Le NM: un outil évolutif pour le financement des entreprises de croissance*. PhD thesis in private law, Paris 1.

Peukert, H. 2003. 'The German Neuer Markt as an adaptative institution', in Pelikan, P. and Wegner, G. (eds), *The Evolutionary Analysis of Economic Policy*. Edward Elgar. Cheltenham.

Polanyi, K. 1957. 'The economy as an instituted process', in Polanyi, K., Arensberg, C. and Pearson, H. (eds), *Trade and Market in the Early Empires*. The Free Press. New York.

Posner, E. 2005. 'Sources of institutional changes. The supranational origins of Europe's new Stock Markets', *World Politics*, 58(1), 1–40.

Revest, V. 2001a. 'Une réflexion sur la place des institutions au sein des théories de la microstructure', *Revue d'Economie Industrielle*, 96(3), 105–23.

Revest, V. 2001b. 'Le Nouveau Marché: la construction d'une identité', *Revue d'Economie Financière*, 61, 193–202.

Revest, V. 2001c. 'La nature sociale des marchés financiers: le cas du NASDAQ', *Histoire et Anthropologie*, 22(1), 109–22.

Reynaud, B. 2002. *Operating Rules in Organizations: Macroeconomic and Microeconomic Analysis*. Palgrave Macmillan. Basingstoke and New York.

Rivaud-Danset, D. 2002. 'Innovation and New Technologies: Corporate Finance and Financial Constraints'. Paper presented at the international conference: Financial systems, corporate investment in innovation and venture capital EU-DG research and the Institute for New Technologies of the United Nations University, Brussels, 7 and 8 November.

Roger, B. and Faure, P. 1995. *Rapport du groupe de travail 'Nouveau Marché'*, SBF, Bourse de Paris, February, pp. 1–44.

Schwartz, R. A. 1991. *Reshaping the Equity Markets: A Guide for the 1990s*. Harper Business. New York.

Schwartz, R. A. 1995. Interview in Mérieux A. and Marchand, C., *Les marchés financiers américains*. Revue d'Economie Financière. La Bibliothèque.

Scott, W. 1981. *Organisations: Rational, Natural and Open Systems*. Prentice Hall. Englewood Cliffs, NJ.

Société du Nouveau Marché. 1996. *Règles de fonctionnement du Nouveau Marché* (March–May).

Sutton, J., Dobbin, F., Meyer, J. and Scott, R. 1994. 'The legalization of the workplace', *American Journal of Sociology*, 99, 944–71.

Zadjenweber, D. 2000. *L'économie des extrêmes*. Flammarion. Paris.

7
Markets as systems of rules: the case of local household services in France

Patrick Haddad

Introduction

The extension of market exchange to new activities compels us to re-examine what a market is and to rethink the approaches of market analysis. The neo-classical paradigm showing under very restrictive hypothesis that supply and demand match through price coordination for the benefit of all cannot explain the reality of most market exchanges today. Institutional economics aim to introduce the social context in markets' analysis. They generally proceed by considering the market as a system of rules. Sharing this assumption, we develop here our approach by answering the following questions: what are the fundamental rules governing markets? What are their sources and the interaction between these rules? How do rules shape different markets and influence their evolution?

The empirical field that we study is local household services. Called 'services de proximité' in France and in French-speaking countries, these local household services share some common aspects in different European countries. According to the European Commission reports since 1992 (Commission des Communautés Européennes, 1993, 1995; European foundation for the improvement of living and working conditions, 2001), some specific characteristics of these services can be highlighted:

- a strong relational and social dimension;
- a labour intensity, explaining the dynamism and the potential in job creation;
- an immersion in the non-profit sector;
- a public economy dimension, explaining the implication of local and national governments;
- the diversity of exchange forms and, in particular, the existence of important informal exchanges.

A lot of services may match these characteristics and thus belong to this field. Here, we focus on local household services that are provided at the consumer's residence. Since the mid-1980s, in France, these services have fallen under specific legislation, which aims to support the movement of externalisation to the market of those services that used to be provided within the household. The three most important services concerned are child care, services to elderly people and housekeeping.

Different providers external to the household may sell these services. Some are individuals with no link to an organisation, whether they work under the legal status of a contract linking them to the household or not, and so provide marketable services in an informal (and illegal) way. Some providers are organisations, mostly non-profit and public organisations linked to local governments. These organisations started to operate in this sector after the Second World War, helping families in need. Since the mid-1980s and the public financial incentives, there has been a renewal in the creation of organisations providing these services, including firms since the mid-1990s. This renewal has been accompanied by a diversification of the services offered, with the provision of services such as small repairing and gardening, tutoring, door-to-door delivery, and so on. These last services can be considered as peripherals, so we will barely mention them, focusing on the three main services mentioned above.

In this chapter we will proceed with a theoretical discussion clarifying the definition of a market from an institutional point of view and showing how it differs from the neo-classical paradigm. We will then emphasise the fundamental rules determining the market, as well as their nature and their importance (section 1). Then, thanks to this clarification, we will be able to offer elements leading to a methodology of analysis allowing us to study local household services markets. What are the factors – the change in rules – that led to the extension of market exchange to these services? How does their provision form different markets? What are the main characteristics of these markets and the main structural differences between them? And, finally, how do markets evolve? (section 2).

1. Markets, institutions and rules

Orthodox and institutional economics approaches of the market

Mainstream neo-classical economics have not really framed a concept or a theory of the market. Walras (1954) describes a process where supply and demand match through price coordination. More recently, new micro-economics, the renewal of neo-classical and orthodox theories, have extended the paradigm and consider the market as a mechanism of property rights transfer.

A major characteristic of market exchanges is their spontaneous aspect. It makes the difference between coordination by the market, and allocation by redistribution inside an administrated system. Orthodox theories go further by considering that these spontaneous behaviours only meet, in a perfect market, financial constraints (of cost, price or income) necessary to the equilibrium process. The other constraints, the institutional ones, are seen as not relevant for economists, but only for sociologists and historians. This is the main difference with institutional economics. From an institutional point of view, the orthodox framework is limited in its understanding of individual behaviour and the organisation of exchanges that are, in reality, governed by rules.

For institutional approaches, since institutions are considered necessary conditions for the emergence, existence and reproduction of markets, their study is also part of the economist's analysis (Ménard, 1990). Sharing this idea, we find a large variety of definitions of institutions. But it seems that the idea generally accepted is to assimilate institutions to rules.

Institutions as systems of rules

In North's conception (1991: 97), 'Institutions consist of formal rules, informal constraints (norms of behavior, conventions and self-imposed codes of conduct) and the enforcement of both'. It is also the conception of Favereau (1995: 511), who defines an institution as 'any system of rules endowed with a certain coherence'.

More precise elements are given in Ménard's definition, which tries to summarise what institutions could be for economists: 'a set of socio-economic rules, settled in historical conditions, upon which individuals or groups of individuals have little control in the short or middle term. From an economic point of view, those rules aim at defining the conditions in which individual or collective choices of allocation and usage of resources will operate' (1990: 15).

One of the interesting aspects of this definition is to explicitly introduce the emergence of institutions. History is, with sociology (Ménard speaks of socio-economic rules), the other discipline that can help the economist understand the institutions' genesis as well as their evolution. The historical aspect hence introduced clarifies the link between the agents or their decisions, and the rules. The rules influence agents' behaviour, but the agents have very little influence on institutions in the short or middle term.

Following this, we can consider that an institution is a set of rules, formal and informal, that influences agents and groups of agents' behaviour. Formal rules are intentional, in contrast to informal ones, which are not necessarily so. Institutions are of variable importance. Some, such as laws and regulations, apply to a whole population. Others, such as social habits, thoughts or representations, can concern only some of the agents. In any case, rules have a certain degree of generality. Agents and groups of agents have little influence on institutions, and this influence only operates in the middle and the long term. This confers institutions a certain stability.

The market as a specific institution

Logically, institutional economics consider markets as governed by rules. For example, Boyer (1995) from the French school of regulation thinks that to be efficient a market needs a complete network of institutions. Here, the market, although presented as dependent upon institutions in order to be efficient, is not itself explicitly qualified as an institution.

For Hodgson, the market is a 'a set of social institutions in which a large number of commodity exchanges of a specific type regularly take place, and to some extent are facilitated by those institutions' (1988: 174).

There are at least two interesting points in this definition:

- the fact that there is a market (only) when there is a large number of exchanges;
- the assumption that, in a market, the commodities exchanged are of a specific type.

Aside from those considerations, qualifying the market as *a set of social institutions* does not help to make a distinction between the market itself, meaning the place, often virtual, where exchanges take place, and the other institutions, which establish the prerequisite conditions for the exchanges to occur. It would seem clearer to consider the market as *one specific institution*.

So, to summarise this institutional conception of the market, we can assume that a market is an institution, that is to say a congruent set of formal and informal rules. The market appears to be different from other institutions because it is a place where exchanges of commodities (goods or services) occur and generate a monetary compensation. These rules, and the way they change, explain the emergence, the functioning and the evolution of the market. So, to go a little further, we can focus on the sources of rules that govern markets.

The sources of rules governing markets

Let's assume that those rules have three sources:

- *Market exchange*. What we understand by that is the price coordination mechanism by which supply and demand match. This is, in a way, the constant rule, common to every market. According to the market, this rule can be more or less important. This will depend upon its balance with rules coming from other sources.
- *Institutions other than the market*. They can be formal, as public regulation, or informal, as social habits or representations. In any case, they produce rules that have an influence on the market. These institutions are different regarding the society, the time and the specificity of the commodity exchanged.
- *The organisations*. The organisational dimension of the market has been underlined (Favereau, 1989). Organisations produce internal rules to function and to coordinate its members (March and Simon, 1958). But as they participate in market exchange, organisations are open, and so they produce rules that go beyond a strictly internal frame. Organisations

with their rules contribute to shape the market. They can be supply organisations, such as firms, but also organisations of consumers, unions, and so on.

In return, the market has some influence on institutions and organisations. For example, the increase of inequities due to market exchange may have, as a consequence, the creation of institutions or organisations designed to correct these inequities.

As a conclusion to this discussion, we have obtained a few elements on which to base the study of market exchanges of local household services.

2. Studying the market: the case of local household services

An important characteristic of these services is their ability to mix different modes of exchange: market, non-market, formal and informal. In other words, not all local household services are exchanged through the market. Some of them are provided freely by reciprocity inside networks of families, friends and neighbours. Others are provided through the administrated system. However, market exchanges of these services have recently increased under the influence of societal evolutions and of policy incentives.

Three main societal evolutions explain the emergence of new needs or of the necessity of finding new ways of satisfying needs: the increasing number of women at work, the population getting older and the weakening of familial links. These evolutions have made households externalise services that used to be provided inside the family towards market exchanges. The increase of the general standard of living has made the externalisation financially possible for a more important proportion of households.

These market exchanges are of various forms according to the rules that influence them. We assume that these exchanges do form different markets. To justify this assumption, the first step of the analysis is to determine the boundaries between markets. We proceed by identifying systems of rules. Then, the key characteristics of the market may be underlined.

Delimiting markets by identifying coherent set of rules

The three main sources we have exposed must be helpful in delimiting systems of rules. The rules coming from market exchange are not the most relevant to distinguish different markets because they are present in all of them. The rules produced by institutions other than the market and by organisations can give the criteria necessary to establish an institutional typology of markets.

Informal and, at the same time, non-market services should not be taken into account in our typology, for, to be in a market, there should occur repeated exchanges with a financial compensation. Therefore, only informal services exchanges that have a monetary counterpart should be taken into consideration. The existence of monetary transactions defines whether there is a market or not. Then, the nature of the transaction, formal or informal, allows us to distinguish two different markets. This is the first criterion.

Another criterion of distinction between markets is the presence or absence of supply organisations. Organisations supplying local household services do have a real influence in the functioning of the market. They play particularly important roles in evaluating needs, organising labour and being an intermediary between the person providing the service and the person consuming the service. Within organisations, a distinction should be made according to their public or private aspect. Between public and private suppliers, there are differences such as their goals, their relation to the users or the consumers of the services, and their internal organisation.

Thus, our typology of markets relies on 'two plus one' criteria:

- the nature of the transaction: formal or informal;
- the type of supply: individuals (with no link to a supply organisation) or organisations;
- the status of the organisation (when there is one): public or private.

Four elementary markets

The conjunction of these criteria gives systems of fundamental rules governing markets. Proceeding this way, we have distinguished four markets.

A first market refers to a situation where a person (or a household) pays another person for executing certain tasks, without signing a contract or any other formal document. In this case, supply is only constituted by individuals not linked to an organisation. This market comes from the heritage of domestic staff and has grown with the evolution of informal institutions such as change in social representations and habits. Thus, it has been extended since the late 1970s to a greater part of the population. We call this market the *informal market*.

Inside the field of formal household services, some are directly provided by local governments or by non-profit organisations contracting with local governments. Developed under a state tutelage since the 1970s, these can be considered public services. This case is on the borderline of what should be considered as a market. On one hand, the users/consumers are paying for part of the service and there are repeated exchanges, but on the other hand public institutions produce strong non-market rules, such as the definition of the beneficiaries, government-financed programmes, or public control over supply organisations. With these two aspects, this market can be considered as an *administrated market*.

In the formal area, there are also services provided by a private supply, even if their development has relied on subsidies and other public regulations. According to the type of supply, two markets can be distinguished:

- A market where services are provided by individuals directly employed by the household using the service. This market is largely financed by

Table 7.1 Local household services markets typology

Type of supply	Organisation		Individuals
Type of transaction	Public	Private	
Formal	*Administrated market*	*Subsidised market of organisations*	*Subsidised market of individuals*
Informal			*Informal market*

public funds, via tax cuts. We call this market *subsidised market of individuals*.

- A market where services are provided by private organisations. These are, in a large majority of cases, non-profit organisations, even if a few firms are now also present and their number is increasing. But even when the service is provided by a firm, it benefits from subsidies, so there is no purely private exchange. Financed by public institutions through demand (subsidises to households) and, in a lesser way, through supply (subsidises to organisations), this is a *subsidised market of organisations*.

These four markets can be classified as in Table 7.1.

By hypothesis, the organisation of exchanges on these markets depends on the rules they are governed by. It is then logical that the functioning of two markets gets more similar with the increasing of the number of criteria that these markets share. Historically, the influence of rules has occurred from the older markets – the administrated market and the informal one – to the 'new' ones: the subsidised markets.

These four markets are socially constructed by different rules, coming from different institutions. Thus, they can not be analysed with the standard methods of mainstream economics. The methodology consists in identifying each market's essential regularities, by studying six fundamental dimensions that take particular forms in these services:

1. Commodities (here the services) exchanged. They may be services to elderly persons, child care, housekeeping and sometimes peripheral services. Depending on the market, some of these services are provided more than others.
2. Demand. This emerges mostly from wealthy households, but public policies via subsidies may open the access to the services to a greater proportion of households. Here, the demand is constituted not only by the person receiving the service but by the entire household: housekeeping obviously concerns the household, child care is a demand from the parents and services to elderly people may benefit a whole family. So, the household or sometimes the family is the purchasing agent, often supported by subsidies.

3. Supply. Services are provided by individuals that may be linked to a supply organisation or not. In most cases, they are women, and these are part-time jobs that constitute their main activity.
4. Competition. Depending on the market, there can be more or less competition. In general, competition is rather low because most organisations are from the public sector, in which case they benefit from monopoly positions, or from the non-profit sector, which does not have a culture of competition. Competition between workers is also weak, because these jobs are unattractive (badly paid, hard working conditions, very little social gratitude) and not so many people want to hold them despite the importance of the needs they satisfy and the high rate of unemployment in France.
5. Prices. These have functions such as indicating the value of the service, the wage of the worker and the subsidies given to the demand. Price formation plays an important role in coordination: it has to be high enough to cover the labour cost, but low enough to attract the household to the market. It is partly, or sometimes totally, fixed outside of the market by institutions (minimum wage, labour cost, subsidies, fixed prices in the administrated market). Part of the price is also determined in the relation between supply and demand.
6. Coordination mechanisms. We consider that the mechanisms have to align supply and demand and settle an agreement on the price and on the quality of the service. They may take various forms according to the market and, more precisely, according to the rules each market is governed by.

The quality of the supplied service is a particularly important issue in these activities. There are situations such as those described by information economics, *adverse selection* and *moral hazard*, which can classically be resolved by the settlement of mechanisms that efficiently signal quality on the market. But here, the problem is not as easily solved as the textbooks would suggest. Firstly, quality, before being signalled, needs to be defined. This process of definition, of finding a common ground regarding what is a good-quality service, is not easy, for it has to do with the actors' subjectivity. Secondly, trust is often required for the transaction to happen. The role of trust is not proper to these activities but, here, the fact that they occur at home and that they often concern vulnerable individuals – children and elderly people – gives a particularly strong importance to trust. Trying to take into account these considerations, we assume that quality has itself two dimensions: an objective one, founded on the skills or the experience of the worker, and a subjective one, founded on the trust and the reputation[1] of the worker and the organisation he or she belongs to, when there is one.

The informal market   The very nature of this market makes it very difficult to collect fully reliable information about it. Still, after some observations, we try to underline the main characteristics of this market.

The two main services provided here are housekeeping (including for elderly people) and child care. Sometimes these two kinds of services are linked and done by the same person. Assistance to elderly people is also provided here, but to a lesser extent because it is more often dealt with by public subsidies. Most housekeeping services last from three to four hours a week, while child-care services are more extensive: five to six hours a week. The average hourly price for these services is 7 € to 8 € for housekeeping and 5 € to 6 € for child care. Child care services are cheaper because hourly prices seem to be degressive with the number of hours provided.

Apart from the elderly people, demand is constituted by middle- and upper-class working households, including young ones that reproduce their parents' habits and use their family's network to find an employee. Concerning housekeeping, supply is mainly constituted by workers specialised in these services. Working half time or so, they need to work for several households. Most of them are immigrants, whether they come from a recent wave of immigration or an older one (as far as the 1960s). But most workers in child care are students, in general young women who do not plan to hold these jobs in the long term.

According to the local context, there is more or less competition between the workers. But the coordination between supply and demand relies more on a social network than on a process where a very well-informed consumer is able to choose between different suppliers competing on prices and quality.

The coordination mechanisms operate inside social networks. The price is established by a social convention that takes into account different possibilities for satisfying the needs: different workers, different markets and self-production. This conventional process tends to homogenise prices. Quality, regarded as the correspondence between the need and the service provided, is only observable after the provision of the service. The need to evaluate the quality *a priori* is fulfilled inside social networks by interpersonal recommendations. It is also within these networks, by 'word of mouth' or through advertisements in local shops that supply and demand enter in relation with each other.

With the establishment of fiscal incentives since the end of the 1980s, in order to create jobs in the formal economy, this informal market still exists but a part of it has swung to the subsidised markets.

The subsidised market of individuals   This market finds its origins in the employment of domestic staff. This kind of employment decreased after the Second World War and then, since the mid-1980s, has been re-developed by tax reductions: half of the amount paid to employ a person at home can be deducted from income taxes, and there is a reduction of social insurance contributions when the employer is an elderly person or a parent of a young child. This market is at the same time a services market and a labour market. A great part of its recent development comes from a shift to an expanding informal market. Thus, the characteristics of these two markets are very close. However, this subsidised market of individuals is also influenced by the public rules that apply to it and this makes it different from the previous market.

The main services provided here are housekeeping and the two services that benefit from more subsidies: assistance to elderly people and child care. For all services together, the average number of hours per week is 7.7.[2] But child care services, when they benefit from all subsidies, total an average of 16.5 hours a week. This shows that this market corresponds, better than the informal market, to greater needs, in terms of hours, expressed by households with children.

The hourly price before subsidy is, in general, the legal minimum wage plus social contribution – that is to say, around 12 € an hour. But with the subsidies via tax reductions, the real price paid can be much lower, down to 4 € an hour. For those who can benefit from all the subsidies – parents of young children, elderly people and households that pay income tax (50% of French households) – services are, here, often cheaper than they are in the informal market. These are the households from which the demand emerges. It is more or less the same demand as the informal market, but elderly people and parents of young children are more represented here as they get specific subsidies.

Supply mainly comprises workers specialised in these services, even for child care. They are often immigrants. As in the informal market, coordination is effected within social networks of families, friends and neighbours. As prices are quasi-fixed administratively (via labour costs and subsidies), interpersonal recommendations in these networks operate by helping supply and demand meet and settle an agreement on quality. Sometimes public or non-profit local institutions also play a role in coordination.

The subsidised market of organisations   The presence of organisations in this market introduces new rules and, thus, significant differences when compared to the previous market.

The main services provided here are housekeeping and assistance to elderly people that together represent 90% of the activity. Child-care services and tutoring are also provided here. While housekeeping services typically last from three to four hours a week, assistance to elderly people lasts longer (ten or so hours on average), and child care last half a dozen hours (but in some cases this can turn into full-time employment). The hourly price before subsidy is approximately 14.5 € on average. Income-tax reductions also apply to this market, which means that the price after subsidy is 7 € or so for the households that pay this tax.

Demand is primarily constituted by elderly people, then secondly by working households from the middle and upper classes. Supply is mainly constituted by non-profit organisations. Since the mid-1990s legislation has changed and extended tax reductions to the services provided by firms.

Since then, the number of firms has increased but they are often specialised in peripheral services: cleaning, tutoring and housekeeping, but very little child care or assistance to elderly people.

Depending on the area, there can be more or less competition. Theoretically, a number of organisations can provide services in several areas, but in reality organisations are based locally. The fact that they often are non-profit organisations is not a neutral factor with regard to competition, as non-profit organisations do not have a culture of competition (they rather produce rules that weaken competition). So, in general, one organisation is often associated with one territory (city or county), in a situation of quasi-monopoly.

Coordination mechanisms are diverse. On one hand, the presence of organisations creates formal mechanisms. They can use advertisements and commercial means and, more often, contract with public authorities to become known as providers of services of general interest. On the other hand, non-profit organisations emerge from local initiatives taken by citizens. This may create trust and a reputation conveyed by informal networks through interpersonal recommendations. Thus, supply and demand may enter in relation through these interpersonal recommendations, but also via institutional recommendations of public local authorities or institutions specifically designed to help this coordination by orientating demand to the supply organisation(s) corresponding to the need.

Part of the price is fixed by public institutions through labour cost, tax reduction and other subsidies. Market price is established by the meeting of supply and demand when there is enough competition. Often prices are fixed by the supply side on a conventional basis taking into account institutional constraints and opportunities (legally fixed labour costs and tax reductions) as well as the purchasing power of the potential demand.

The evaluation of quality is also carried out by a range of mechanisms. The objective dimension of quality, relying on skills and experience, is defined and signalled by the qualification of workers and public selection of organisations. Some organisations have a chart of ethics. Sometimes these charts are implemented by territorial associations of organisations, often in partnership with public authorities. The subjective dimension of quality, which relies on trust and reputation, is carried by personal recommendations. Trust is also created by mediation by public authorities or health-sector professionals. The social dimension of non-profit organisations, the fact that their goal is to provide services of general interest and to help people in need, can also help in creating trust.

The administrated market This 'market' has been developed to match the social needs of elderly people. It is mostly governed by legally defined administrative rules.

The only services provided here are housekeeping and assistance to elderly people. The hourly price before subsidy is around 14 €, but most services are financed by public funds, via local governments or the social security system. The price effectively paid in most cases is under 6 €. It is free for the poorest segment of the population. Most of the time, services are cheaper here than in the other markets, but this can not make the market grow because the amount of services provided to each household is administratively fixed after a medical evaluation of their needs (i.e. their difficulties n performing domestic tasks).

The supply is constituted either by public organisations or by non-profit organisations contracting with local governments. These organisations are almost all in a situation of *de jure* monopoly.

The coordination mechanisms are those of a public service administratively governed. Each citizen according to his or her social situation in terms of dependence and of resources has a right to get a certain amount of services at a certain price. To access these services, he or she has to apply to the local municipality. Coordination is not done via prices as they are administratively fixed. Quality in its objective dimension is evaluated by a public control over the organisations and the qualification of workers. In its subjective dimension, quality relies on the trust that local governments, as democratic institutions, can produce.

Boundaries between markets and evolution

The boundaries between markets are not hermetic. On the demand side, a household can switch from one market to another. For example, fiscal incentives have made the subsidised market of individuals cheaper than the informal market, and thus some households have left the latter for the former. The maximum amount of tax reduction is often revised. The higher this amount is, the bigger the volume of hours consumed on subsidised markets.

On the supply side, workers can move from one market to another. This is also the case with organisations, as some of them do operate both on the subsidised market of organisations and on the administrated market. But this is not the case of most organisations that operate on only one market.

It seems that these four markets are now well established and are going to last. Still, it is possible that a fifth market, made up of firms, will emerge. They are specialised in specific commodities: the ones with less relational aspects such as housekeeping or the ones that are more solvable (such as tutoring, but this is at the borderline of what we study). Today their volume of activity is still too small to consider that they form an entire market but tomorrow, if they find enough of a profit in these exchanges, their volume of activity may increase and form a whole market.

Coordination mechanisms appear to be the most important variables explaining the development and the dynamism of markets. Besides prices issues, quality, including in its subjective aspects, is a key factor for the existence and the development of the markets. Social networks that produce trust by recommendations explain the importance of the informal market as well as the importance of informal coordination mechanisms in other markets. But we now assume that a main condition for the development of formal markets, and in particular markets of organisation, is the emergence of a formal reference of quality common to every agent. This could be assured by real process of certification, instead of various initiatives that are too divided and not sufficiently recognised as reliable.

Public support is also crucial for the development of markets: public rules are powerful because they apply to a whole population. Thus, economical and social policies have a great influence upon quantitative and qualitative development. The stakes of public regulation can then be underlined, producing the regulating rules that facilitate the qualitative and quantitative development of formal exchange, without introducing too much of the rigidity that would constrain this development.

Conclusion

Local household services constitute an interesting object of analysis because their form of exchange is evolving. These exchanges used to be embedded in restrained familial networks. Under recent evolutions of demand, of supply and of public policies, their forms of exchanges are diversifying. They are becoming more formal and more marketable. The social context in which these exchanges are embedded is becoming more complex. It is influenced by a variety of rules: rules produced by market exchange, by public institutions, by representations and social habits, and rules by the organisations – public, private and non-profit organisations – providing the services.

The analysis of these forms of exchange shows a great diversity of rules that may influence markets. The study of local household markets with the concept of rules has underlined some empirical results as well as elements of methodology.

Markets can be identified by the coherence of the system of rules they are governed by. Rules also influence the functioning of markets and, in particular, their coordination mechanisms. Coordination mechanisms are very important characteristics of markets. They are various and concern price formation, quality definition and signalisation, and the entry in relation to supply and demand. In fact, they design almost all the variables that exist between supply and demand. With this conception, coordination mechanisms appear very different from one market to another, and thus explain for a large part the development and dynamism of markets.

The evolution of markets can be correlated to their coordination mechanisms and the efficiency of these mechanisms; that is to say, their ability to make supply and demand match. Only changes in rules can make coordination mechanisms evolve and become more or less efficient. Thus, changes in rules explain the emergence and the development of a market, or the regression of another.

Probably more in our specific field of analysis than in others, it seems that the rules coming from political institutions, as they are of general application, have a strong influence. This influence operates in particular on coordination mechanisms, as public policy rules participate in the formation of prices, through subsidies, and in the definition and signalisation of quality. Of course, changes in rules can not be reduced to political decisions. Yet public policies may have a profound impact on the evolution of the different markets.

Notes

1 Reputation may have an objective dimension but we consider here that it has a more important subjective dimension.
2 Data used here are taken from studies of the DARES, Direction de l'animation de la recherche, des etudes et des statistiques, a department of the French Ministry of Labour.

References

Boyer, R. 1995. 'Vers une théorie originale des institutions économiques', in Boyer, R. and Saillard, Y. (eds), *Théorie de la régulation, L'état des savoirs*. Editions La Découverte. Paris.

Commission des Communautés Européennes. 1993. *Livre blanc – croissance, compétitivité, emploi: les défis et les pistes pour entrer dans le XXIè siècle*. Office des Publications Officielles des Communautés Européennes. Bruxelles.

Commission des Communautés Européennes. 1995. *Les initiatives locales de développement et d'emplo*. Document de travail des services de la Commission. Paris.

European foundation for the improvement of living and working conditions. 2001. *Employment in Household Services*. Office of Official Publications of the European Community. Dublin.

Favereau, O. 1989. 'Marché interne, marché externe', *Revue Economique*, 8(40) (March).

Favereau, O. 1995. 'Conventions et régulation', in Boyer, R. and Saillard, Y. (eds), *Théorie de la régulation, L'état des savoirs*. Editions La Découverte. Paris.

Hodgson, G. M. 1988. *Economics and Institutions. A Manifesto for a Modern Institutional Economics*. Polity Press. Cambridge.

March, J. G. and Simon, H. A. 1958. *Organizations*. Blackwell Publishers. Cambridge, MA.

Ménard, C. 1990. *L'économie des organisations*. Editions La Découverte, Repères collection. Paris.

North, D. C. 1991. 'Institutions', *Journal of Economic Perspectives*, 5(1) (Winter), 97–112.

Walras, L. 1954 *Elements of Pure Economics*, trans. W. Jaffe. Irwin. Homewood, IL. (Originally published as *Eléments d'économie politique pure*, 1874.)

8

Making biological knowledge private and public: the multi-modality of capitalism

Andrew McMeekin and Mark Harvey

Turbulence in knowledge, turbulence in economy

Over the past few decades, there has been a much acclaimed revolution in biological science, most publicly visible in the completion of the human genome, but more deeply evident in terms of methods of experimentation, digitisation of data, and more complex theoretical accounts represented by systems biology (Cook-Deegan, 1994; Gilbert, 1991; Moody, 2004; Strohman, 1997; Zweiger, 2000). This epistemic upheaval has been accompanied by considerable controversy, even international diplomatic incidents, over the economic characteristics of the new knowledge, how it should be resourced, or whether it should be a private or public economic good. The period witnessed attempts to establish new forms of knowledge market: for example, for digitised biological data and their corresponding analytical software tools. There was a question of just how much of the new knowledge would become tradable goods, through various modes of private appropriation and market creation. Changes were made to US patent regulation, redefining what is appropriable and what is not (Eisenberg, 1989, 1991; Zuhn, 2001). Equally, new forms of public institution, dissemination, and production of knowledge emerged. At its outset, the Human Genome Project involved a transformation of public resourcing of research on a scale quite new to biology, provoking controversy within the biology community and instigating US Congressional Committee hearings.

In retrospect, it is often difficult to appreciate the magnitude of the issues at stake. The human genome race, for those participating in it, was much more than a question of whether a publicly financed, international collaboration would compete effectively and be first to complete the genome, against a private corporation (Celera), in part financed by the almost monopoly providers of key equipment, the high-throughput sequencers. The race raised the question of whether the human genome, or rather the access and use of knowledge of it, would be publicly available or be owned by a private corporation. It was as if the human biological heritage was up for grabs. During one of the most controversial early phases of this race, the US National Institute of Health filed claims to patents on 'keys' to genes, that promised to lock up 80–90% of the human genome under what was effectively a state monopoly licence (Harvey and McMeekin, 2007; Roberts, 1991a, b).[1]

Empirically, this epistemic and economic turbulence challenges many received assumptions concerning knowledge as an economic good, perhaps most of all any static conception of what constitutes the 'public' or 'private' character of knowledge. These appear as institutional characteristics that develop over time, and in relation to each other. As such this recent history provides rich material for re-thinking issues of what makes knowledge private and public.[2]

In addressing these issues, we are immediately confronted with a difficulty of terminology. The terms 'public' and 'private' are overburdened with multiple meanings, whether in natural spoken or technical economic language. The 'public' of public broadcasting or public property or public sector are commonly used, but a moment's reflection points to their very different meanings. Likewise, 'private' can carry meanings of secrecy, tacitness, exclusion and ownership, as well as being synonymous with 'marketised' or 'tradable'. It is often assumed, in particular, that if knowledge is 'out there', and not privately appropriated, that it is *ipso facto* public. The public is a kind of residual – that which has not been made private. Discussions of 'the commons' (Hardin, 1968; Heller, 1998; Heller and Eisenberg, 1998; Nelson, 2004), especially when applied to knowledge, have ill-served the development of a dynamic concept of the public, especially when counterposed by the notion of an anti-commons, seen as the worst of both worlds (David, 2001, 2004). Yet what is most conspicuous about recent developments in biological knowledge institutions is the appearance of new public forms, such as global biological databases or open source software, and their quite dramatic growth. We will argue that making knowledge public involves much more than simply putting knowledge out there, making it non-rivalrous in use. Rather, it involves complex processes of developing public control, standards and norms for the production, distribution and use of knowledge. As against much of the academic debate that has succeeded the 1980 Bayh–Dole Act[3] (Coriat and Orsi, 2002; Mowery et al., 2001), we believe the overwhelming historical evidence so far has been one of the emergent dominance of these new public knowledge institutions over potential commercial rivals. This is a primary example not of government intervention to address 'market failure', but of the failure of markets to compete effectively with the dynamics of creation and dissemination of public knowledge.

We clearly would confuse matters further if we were to attempt to abandon the terms public and private, and, constrained to work with them, we will attempt to place them in a theoretical framework within which a more highly specified and complex meaning is clearly set out. In Harvey and McMeekin (2007) we explored how the terms public and private were diversely used in five recent debates, each picking up on an important dimension, but with few attempts to bring coherence across them. The terms public and private are articulated in different ways within each of these perspectives:

- Types of knowledge. This dimension emphasises a different possible mapping of the terms public and private onto differentiable types of knowledge, such as, most simply, science and technology, and more sophisticatedly, Stoke's Pasteur's Quadrant (Hall, 2003; Mokyr, 2002; Nelson, 2004; Stokes, 1997).
- The notion of knowledge as a unique kind of public good by virtue of intrinsic properties, such as its supposed indivisibility, ease of replication, infinite expansibility or non-rivalry in use (Dasgupta and David, 1994; David, 2004; Foray, 2004).
- The resourcing and organisational institutions of knowledge (public science institutions, R&D laboratories, not-for-profit NGOs, etc.). Here, public means institutions resourced from public taxation as against those resourced from corporate profits (Machlup, 1962; Martin, 2003).
- The embodiment of knowledge, and the information–knowledge distinction, or tacit-codified distinction (Callon, 1994; Cowan et al., 2000; Johnson et al., 2002). Coded and tacit knowledge, information and knowledge, are mapped variously onto concepts of tradable and untradable, dissemination (market or public) and retention of knowledge.
- The property notion as applied to knowledge is a different meaning again, and has been most developed in relation to private property, although heavily biased towards formal intellectual property rights. But it has also been partially developed in relation to public property, although rarely exploring the latter in contrast to its various forms of public ownership rights manifest in public infrastructure, public education, public enterprises, rights over space, international rights, and so forth (Kaul and Mendoza, 2003).

Each of these five debates articulates concepts of 'public' and 'private' under particular perspectives that touch on and inform each other, but they all fall short of a coherent overall account. It might be thought that there is an easy alignment between fundamental science, public good, public resources, codified information and scientific commons, on the one side; and applied technologies, private goods, market financing, tacit knowledge, and private or anti-commons property, on the other. In this case, there would be a consistency across the dimensions of types of knowledge, economic good, modes of financing, knowledge embodiment, and property rights. The theoretical case for such consistency has not been made, and historical evidence is overwhelmingly against any such easy alignment.

Moreover, a static taxonomic impulse seems to characterise each debate, mostly in terms of antithetical (as opposed to complementary) dichotomies. It is striking how many of the dichotomies are based on assumptions of zero-sum games between alternatives. In each case, this impulse inhibits consideration of processes of differentiation within and between categories, but, more importantly, also of the dynamics of interaction between differentiated forms of economic or epistemic activity that might lead to a theory of complex growth (economic *and* epistemic).

Rather than repeat our discussion or condense a rich set of debates here, however, we think they serve well to highlight the complexity hidden behind the terms public and private, and the need to develop a framework within which different meanings are both made explicit and articulated with each other. Above all, however, we need to think of 'public' and 'private' outside descriptive adjectival alternatives, and in terms of ongoing historical processes of differentiation. We also believe that there is a multiplicity of different forms of public and private. The scientific public, for example, is quite different from the journalistic public, in terms of the norms and standards of how knowledge is produced, disseminated and 'consumed'. Likewise, there is a multiplicity of forms of private appropriation and private agents, from families that keep (or sell) their secrets to corporations that protect their knowledge base by firewalls. In this chapter, however, we are focusing only on the new forms of 'public' and 'private' that emerged with respect to biological knowledge in the late twentieth century.

Economies of knowledge and instituted economic process

The broad perspective adopted is an economic sociology one, so asking some different questions as well as returning to the issues alluded to above. In particular, the concept of 'instituted economic process', first adumbrated by Polanyi (1957), but extended and developed in various empirical domains, and here to 'economies of knowledge'. The core concept is one of economic processes, such as exchange and distribution, articulated together in such a way as to integrate human activities for a given historical phase and constituting various geographic scales. In this perspective, instituted economic processes are manifest in types of organisation (firms, universities, NGOs, etc.), formal and informal rights, behavioural norms and routines, and resource flows (capital appreciation, rents, taxes, grants, etc.).

The central proposition that we are advancing here is that historically ongoing differentiation and interdependency between public and private domains are the outcome of the changing articulations between processes of production, exchange, distribution, and use of knowledge. Let us unpack this bald statement in two steps.

In the first step, the processes of differentiation and interdependency can be presented in the schema in Figure 8.1.

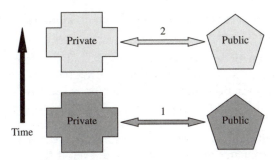

Figure 8.1 The differentiation and interdependency between public and private knowledge

Neither the public nor the private domain at Time 1 is the same at Time 2. Activities undertaken in one domain can split and be redistributed between domains as the boundaries between them are re-drawn over time. So what constitutes the two poles of interaction is continuously being transformed. Nonetheless, and in a societal division of labour of a higher order, activities in one domain are mutually dependent on activities in the other. This illustrates the first part of the proposition, namely that the differentiation between public and private, as well as the nature of their interdependency, changes over time as a dynamic process. Economies of scientific knowledge, the focus of this chapter, are exemplary of this characteristic of capitalist development. The growth of knowledge in capitalist economies is inconceivable without a combined dynamic of public and private domains of knowledge. At a fundamental level, it is a concept of a multi-modal economy, and a departure from the view of capitalism often characterised as a market economy. Market formation and destruction is only one side of a process, itself inexplicable without adding the other side of the dynamic, the growth of the public domain, in terms of resources, institutions, goods and activities. An exploration of this dynamic interdependency reveals that the societal division of labour between public and private domains is never one of static complementarity. Indeed, interdependency is persistently characterised by tension, competition and rivalry, including that over finite, if expanding, resources for sustaining activity in either domain. Our empirical examples will illustrate this well.

Taking the second step, we are proposing that each phase of differentiation and interdependency can be characterised by an economy of knowledge. An economy of knowledge involves the specific articulation between four processes, economic only by virtue of their inter-connection. One of our contentions is that different facets of public and private and public pertain to each of these processes, and that specifying them for each process and articulating them together gives a more integrated, if complex, account of what can be meant by 'public' and 'private' domains. Here we merely present the four processes. In the next section, we illustrate them with two empirical examples.

Each of the four processes entails different kinds of transformational activity. They are:

- Transformation of knowledge, its growth and development, conceptually, empirically and methodologically. Broadly these are processes of knowledge production, and how production is socially organised creates distinctive publics and private, open and closed, and groups of agents.
- Transformation of place, or processes of distribution. Here different dimensions of public and private divisions are created according to how knowledge circulates and is disseminated, even if they overlap and intersect with public and private producers of knowledge.
- Transformation of who holds rights over knowledge resources, or processes of appropriation. This involves processes of making knowledge public or private property, including rights of exchange, access, and use knowledge. Different modes of appropriation are clearly linked to resourcing of production, distribution and use.
- Transformations of knowledge through use. Once produced, disseminated or appropriated, there are many possibilities for different public and private uses of knowledge.

An economy of knowledge is constituted only in and through the articulation between all four processes, and it is through their articulation that the complex institution of public and private domains is achieved for any historical phase. We can illustrate this with an example, but with the strong health warning that in so doing we are freezing history at a particular time, in order to present a static picture of what turned out to be a highly unstable, and in the end unsustainable, configuration. The presentation is not given in evidence, but as a schematic illustration.

The height of the human genome race, towards the late 1990s, witnessed the emergence of new forms of both public and private institution around the production, dissemination, appropriation and use of nucleotide sequence data. Figure 8.2 represents these public and private domains.

The public domain (1) is constituted institutionally by the emergence of biological databases with sequence data of multiple organisms. These new institutions, notably Genbank, EMBLbank (Europe) and DDBJ (Japan) were the outcome of international agreements between states, and national financing on a large scale from taxation. Epistemically they were novel, insofar as they institutionalised a separation of data from experimentation and theory construction. To an extent, this separation was driven by the technologies of knowledge production, with high-throughput sequencers capable of producing vast quantities of genomic data. However, this mass data, so critical for comparative genomics, was a relatively new variety of knowledge, not slotting into any easy dichotomy of information versus knowledge. By the same token, the databases involved quite new publics of production, rules for data deposition, quality standards and protocols, as well as agreements with scientific journals to change the rules of publication

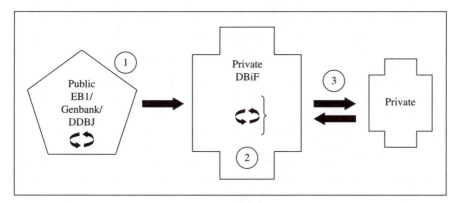

Figure 8.2 Interdependencies between genomic databases in the 1980s

for purposes of validation and replication of results. For example, an extraordinary and controversial agreement was reached by the scientific community involved in public science genome projects to deposit all new genomic sequences above a certain threshold of sequence length into the public databases within 24 hours – the so-called Bermuda Rules (Bentley, 1996; Marshall, 2001). Public control was exercised over the temporalities of distribution. Dissemination and access for the major databases was assured firstly by the World Wide Web, without the subscription typical of scientific journals. However, as we shall see, various software packages (both publicly and commercially available) were critical for making the data useable, whether by expert bioinformatic users, or by biologists, or by pharmaceutical companies, so effectively creating various 'publics' by dissemination. In all respects, these institutions entailed radically new norms and controls for constituting knowledge as 'public', regimens of inclusion and exclusion from the public domain, that distinguished them from earlier forms of public knowledge.

The private domain (2 and 3) is constituted on the one hand by newly emergent markets and firms, trading in biological and especially genomic data, and on the other hand by commercial users of that data, large pharmaceutical corporations. The new type of firm, represented by companies such as Celera and Incyte, imported and depended on data available from the public-domain institutions. But internally they worked on and developed data, adding their own sequence information, as well as providing enhanced additional information and enhanced ease of use. The dedicated bioinformatic companies (DBiF) thus appropriate, produce and use public knowledge to produce new private knowledge. This combination of co-produced public and firm-internal knowledge[4] is protected by technical secrecy (firewalls), the market being created by the qualitative difference between publicly and privately available data and its additional functionalities. Under licence, pharmaceutical firms subsequently purchase this knowledge to use it for purposes such as drug discovery, so creating a new private domain of use of knowledge. But they too frequently engage in fundamental, firm-internal, scientific activity developing their own bio-databases. Thus, there is both creation of new markets for knowledge, new knowledge-trading firms, and firms producing non-knowledge products (drugs) based both on traded knowledge and their own, non-traded, firm-internal knowledge.

This static example demonstrates the emergence of differentiated public and private domains around a new object of knowledge, the biological database, where private market formation is entirely dependent on the existence, and indeed growth, of public-domain knowledge and institutions. The growth of public-domain institutions is dependent not only on resources flowing from taxation, but also those from a wide range of commercially provided equipment and scientific instrumentation essential to their opera-tion. More broadly, the dedication of resources to the public institutions is dependent on public consent that such scientific endeavours provide benefits to human health, in part delivered by pharmaceutical companies. There is differentiation of activities and, in consequence, asymmetric interdepen-dency between these transitory public and private domains. Although only sketched in outline, this illustration highlights a complex articulation between processes and production, distribution, appropriation and use, underpinning a new configuration of public and private domains within an economy of knowledge.

The historical differentiation and interdependency between public and private domains of economies of knowledge

Especially in times of rapid and radical transformations of knowledge, such static configurations tend to be extremely unstable, and are 'instituted' for relatively short durations. Moreover, there is a risk in presenting the divi-sion between public and private as an outcome rather than an ongoing process. Two contrasting empirical cases are now given to demonstrate the main proposition concerning the multi-modal dynamic of making knowl-edge public and private. Both cases are given a formal treatment, stripped of most empirical detail.[5] The object of the exercise is to provide worked examples of historical processes of differentiation and interdependency. The contrast between the two cases, moreover, emphasises variety creation, and the absence of any single model of development. They are both historically significant cases, the one relating to the most widely used and important software package used in sequencing genomes, the GCG package, from the Genetics Computer Group at Wisconsin University; the other relating to a critical phase in the development of genomic knowledge, the gene hunt using Expressed Sequence Tags. In each case, we describe several phases, characterised by a particular configuration of economic processes, but then identify the frictions, tensions and competition that induce destabilisation and transition to a further phase.

The development of bioinformatic software

Phase 1   In the early 1980s, a new division of labour within the academic scientific community emerged with the development of bioinformatic tools for analysing the rapidly increasing digitised data from various sources: DNA, RNA and proteins. Initially, the software packages were co-produced by a community of expert producer-users, made possible by open-source software (Devereux et al., 1984; Sender, 2000). The public of co-production literally involved groups of scientists from various locations introducing modifications and improvements to the original software, in the course of its use for various empirical tasks. It should be noted that the public of co-production was rapidly internationalised, and in Europe the package was developed within the European Molecular Biology Laboratory, and had an E-version, EGCG, distributed independently. During this phase, there was cost recuperation on a not-for-profit basis, with all users paying a licence fee, although significantly at a different rate between academic and commercial users. The software was distributed on tapes that combined the analytical tools with copies of data taken from public sequence databases. So data were disseminated along with rights to use software. There were multiple uses of the software package, ranging from comparative genomics and development of evolutionary theory to drug target identification, thus a differentiation between communities of users.

Lasting a few years, this configuration was destabilised as a result of the reaction of a private sector firm, one of the pioneers of new knowledge markets that had spun out of Stanford University. Threatening to sue Wisconsin University for unfair trading by distribution of products subsidised by the public purse, the University was forced to abandon its Genetics Computer Group, and the GCG package.

Phase 2   From a number of alternatives, the decision was made to spin a company out, whilst retaining the main principles of operation of the previous configuration. The GCG package remained open-source, in an open trading model that enabled commercial as well as academic users to benefit from improvements introduced by its worldwide community of experts. Maintaining its two-tier Ramsey pricing of licensing, the company remained viable for several years. EGCG, however, also continued to operate in the public domain without hindrance. The one major change, arising in part from the development of the World Wide Web and in particular the direct access to genomic sequence data from public databases, was that the software package was detached from data dissemination and traded separately.

The trigger for change this time came from pressure of the capital markets and the need of the company to list on exchanges for expansion. As a small company, it was also a target for acquisition, but only if it changed its *modus operandi*.

Phase 3   In the developing commercial knowledge markets for biological software, GCG's main competitors were engaging in acquisitions and developments in order to create a 'one-stop-shop' for integrated suites of software. GCG therefore was threatened by marginalisation, and so took the critical step of black-boxing its source code.[6] Subsequently, it was indeed acquired in successive capital market acquisitions until the package was housed in the major global software suite company. The commercial vision behind this strategy was to become the Microsoft of biological knowledge markets. The effects of black-boxing for the economy of knowledge were manifold. Most notably, co-production by a dispersed group of expert users ceased, and from then on software development was firm-internal, and appropriation protected by technical secrecy. Driven by the commercial incentives to expand markets, a sharper divide was created between producer-users and producer-consumers. By developing its interface, the skill requirements of users were diminished to enable much wider use. Obviously, that also meant that expert-users, whose demand was for software that could be tailored to their own requirements, found GCG increasingly unattractive. However, it should be emphasised that the commercial package acquired its market value only by virtue of its use as a tool for mining and analysing public databases, a value enhanced with the growth of such databases. In this respect, although not unique, as a knowledge tool it is symbiotically dependent on the vitality of public knowledge, in contrast to instrumentation used for the direct exploration of natural phenomena.

Unlike the Microsoft success story, however, the black-boxing of the GCG package led to a new potential disturbance for this emergent knowledge market, partly as a consequence of its reduced functionality for expert users and the loss of the academic market, and partly because of a direct obstruction to its public domain offspring, EGCG.

Phase 4   Suddenly, the public domain, having enjoyed development and use of the major sequencing software, was faced with total dependency on commercial companies, and obstructed from developing self-customised functionalities. The response was to develop a public sector alternative, EMBOSS, once more with open-source software and all the advantages to development by multiple expert users that it bestowed (Rice at al., 2000). It was embedded in other public software suites, creating a fully parallel public domain equivalent to the commercial alternative. Of course, as with the original GCG package, but this time without any licensing or trading features, EMBOSS became available to multiple users, both by public and commercial users, whether for further knowledge development or for pharmaceutical or medical purposes. Unlike its predecessor, however, EMBOSS is protected by a General Public License developed and administered by the Free Software Foundation (Rice at al., 2000). As such, it creates a distinctive mode of public domain appropriation, preventing its adoption and development for subsequent commercial trading.

A significant aspect of this new development has been the key role of 'knowledge bearers', primarily the experts involved throughout the history of GCG, EGCG and EMBOSS. In effect, there is both a circulation of knowledge through dissemination and a circulation of experts between public and private domains that proved critical. The developers of EGCG were the creators of EMBOSS. Although we cannot develop the point here, much deeper analysis is required to understand the functioning of labour and capital markets and the tradability or circulation of the knowledge of knowledge bearers. Their knowledge is not 'black-boxable' or exchangeable in the often assumed manner, even if, under capitalist wage relations, its uses and outputs may be partially appropriated by the bearers' current employers, whether public or private. The circulation of experts thus often entails a layer of interdependency between public and private domains, hidden by the separation of the institutions that experts peripatetically inhabit.

And next? As there are no absolute beginnings or endings, it is clear that the present phase of a commercially successful, strategically important software package existing in parallel to a recently emerged, now fully distinct, public software package with equivalent functionalities may well prove as unstable as preceding phases. The market may be undermined by a strong public competitor. From our perspective, however, the importance of this worked example is to demonstrate a dynamic interaction, of tension, competition and rivalry, as well as of complementarities between public and private domains. There are now newly emergent and differentiated public and public domains, resulting from their different internal dynamics and demands, as well as their interdependencies. The users of the commercial package, their skills requirements and the purposes to which they put the software are certainly distinct from those of the public domain equivalent. How and whether these may be sustained by licensing, subscription and taxation remains an open question.

Keys to genes

Our second worked example involves knowledge of genes: would genes be bought and sold, or would they become public knowledge? In the early days of the progress towards whole genome sequencing, a scientific controversy arose when leading scientists such as Brenner (UK, Molecular Research Laboratory) and Venter (US, National Institute of Health), proposed a shortcut to identifying all human genes. The shortcut involved reverse engineering sequences of DNA from the RNA already expressed in human tissue. That way, only the protein-encoding exons would be sequenced and located, leaving 97% of the human genome aside, or for later. A technique was developed for identifying only those protein-encoding segments of DNA, using what are called 'expressed sequence tags' (ESTs). The promise – indeed, for some, scientific belief – was that up to 90% of human genes would be discovered, and, using high-throughput automated technologies, in a relatively short space of time. For others, ESTs would never achieve its promised goal, resting on both faulty science and questionable methodology. This was the object of knowledge that triggered a decade and a half long turbulence in economies of knowledge. Given its significance, the stakes for all concerned were high.

Phase 1   A publicly funded EST programme was launched by the National Institute of Health (NIH), led by Venter. After an initial publication in *Science* promising rapid progress to gene identification, the NIH filed claims for patents on an initial batch of patents, to be followed in quite rapid succession by further large batches of many thousands of keys to genes. As genes had already been patented, the NIH Office Technology Transfer considered it critical to patent ESTs (Adler, 1992), fearing either that failure to do so would preclude any future patenting of genes once keys to genes had been published, or that other nations' researchers or corporations would do so. As a consequence, the prospect was that at least potentially the NIH would become the holder of patents to a significant proportion of all human genes, to be licensed to the pharmaceutical industry.

The patent claim caused major controversy, threatening to break up international public science collaboration on human genome research, provoking counter-claims by the Medical Research Council for some of the same ESTs, and occasioning high level diplomatic traffic across the Atlantic (Anderson and Aldhous, 1991; Roberts, 1991b, 1992). The final element leading to the next phase, however, was the rejection of the first claims by the US Patent Office, on all grounds.

Phase 2   A second route to private appropriation opened up with Human Genome Sciences Inc (HGS) funding the not-for-profit Institute for Genomic Research (TIGR), under Venter with his whole ex-NIH team (Marshall, 1994). The furore had also resulted in public funding for further EST research effectively drying up, pushing Venter to leave the NIH. HGS had exclusive rights to commercialise ESTs, and soon afterwards SmithKline-Beecham (SKB) made the first ever significant investment in bioinformatic knowledge with a $125 million deal. The property rights were protected by technical secrecy (firewalls), and SKB had exclusive rights to all new keys to genes. Other companies rapidly followed suit (Zweiger, 2000). Any ESTs deposited on the public database by TIGR were subject to Reach Through Licence Agreements, effectively blocking their availability to public university-based scientists.

The appropriation of thousands of ESTs by several competing companies threatened the balkanisation of the human genome as well as its commercialisation. This inevitably led to a counter-reaction in the public domain, but also competitive fears within the biotechnology and pharmaceutical industry. Political change in the US administration led to the withdrawal of all NIH patent claims, reverting to a model of public knowledge for public funding for genomic data.

Phase 3 A new sub-division of Genbank, the main global public sequence data warehouse, was established for ESTs (dbEST) (Boguski et al., 1994) New protocols and procedures were being developed to deal with the pro-liferation of ESTs – the number of keys to genes was growing rapidly, and there was much uncertainty about how unique and reliable they were. A major intervention was then spearheaded by Merck, pioneering a public–private consortium, to generate and deposit many thousands of ESTs per week into dbEST. Whatever its motivation in relation to its pharmaceutical competitors, the key point of this intervention was the fact that growth of the public domain data could effectively undermine the commercialisation strategies of appropriation behind firewalls, so disrupting unchallenged market growth.

The commercialisation of ESTs was doubly undermined, however, not only by competition with new public domain, but, at least as significantly, also by the development of scientific knowledge especially within the now massive international public science programme for human DNA sequenc-ing. The race to rapidly sequence genes using ESTs, far from proving a shortcut, was producing too many keys relative to reasonable estimates of the number of genes. The keys were proving not to be unique, and there seemed to be no end to the number of keys that were being discovered (Zweiger, 2000).

Phase 4 The major commercial protagonists of EST databases withdrew from the gene hunt using ESTs, some switching to whole genome shotgun DNA sequencing, triggering the next race. Unigene was established as a new public database within dbEST, as a public resource of a non-redundant set of keys to genes, much reduced in number. Processes of validation and replication for reliability, as well as new public quality standards for EST data, supported this creation. The scientific – and hence commercial – value of ESTs was radically reduced from the original promise of a shortcut. Residually, however, ESTs as tools for gene identification continued to be subject to patent claims, and in response patent regulations especially on the utility criteria were progressively changed. ESTs became patentable only under a much restricted scope for claims, especially excluding the patent for a key to a gene from including the gene itself (Zuhn, 2001). Even as late as 2005, patent claims were being rejected on grounds similar to the rejection more than a decade earlier. But effectively, from the late 1990s, ESTs formed part of a new public domain resource, with its new protocols and norms as to what was recognised to be valid public data.

The trajectory of EST economies of knowledge swung quite dramatically from a prospect of a new private market and domain for the vast majority of human genes, to an almost exclusively public resource. This public resource, as is evident from the Merck intervention, was to be available without restriction to both public domain scientists, and all commercial users on a level playing field. Thus, in an apparently stable final configuration, the growth of knowledge created new institutions and resources and a new public–private interdependency.

Conclusion

With uniquely and globally significant series of events such as the two cases just described, it is always difficult to draw general conclusions. By their nature, they cannot be claimed to be representative. Self-evidently, it would also be possible to take a different empirical cut on these same events, although our focus on objects of knowledge around which economies of knowledge develop has an advantage of capturing the dynamic role of knowledge accumulation. The two cases demonstrate processes of differentiation and interdependency between public and private domains with emergent properties. Moreover, they strongly suggest a variety of processes with different outcomes. In this sense, when freezing an historical frame at a given point in time, 'public' and 'private' domains could be presented as broad umbrellas sheltering a complex interplay between many strands and dynamics resulting from the development of economies of knowledge. Changes in processes of knowledge production, distribution, appropriation and use result in multiple intersecting 'publics' and 'private' forms at any given point in time.

Against some accounts of recent developments, the approach developed here and the evidence of the cases suggest the need to recognise a much more dynamic aspect of public-domain formation, with new norms and institutions of knowledge. Interaction, competition, tension and rivalry between public and private domains, often triggered by developments in knowledge production, are critical for understanding processes of differentiation and asymmetries of interdependency. Markets for knowledge are formed in the context of the growth of public domain knowledge, and vice versa, if throughout historical transformations the very character of the differentiation between public and private creates an asymmetry of interdependency, in terms of new societal divisions of labour.

Finally, the multi-modality of economies of knowledge requires an understanding of dual or multiple and interacting dynamics between public and private domains, and this itself is a persistent source of instability. Although there may be periods of relative stability, there are apparently no permanently stable configurations – indeed, why should there be? Turbulence in knowledge can always provoke a reconfiguration of economies of knowledge, and the emergence of new complexes of private and public forms of knowledge. After all, the 'settlement' of the EST configuration only provided the platform for the next period of disruption, and the whole human genome race proper.

And, as a concluding note, we would like to insist that the character of new knowledge itself plays a role. Bioinformatics is a peculiarly multivalent form of knowledge, comprising both new knowledge and new forms of instrumentation. An EST is not only like a telescope on the genome, but also what is seen through the telescope, a connected fragment of the genome itself. Bio-databases are at once repositories of acquired knowledge, in a sense the outcome of the first period of the biological revolution, and the raw experimental material for further scientific progress. This creates a level of uncertainty relating to use, worth and identity of knowledge that contributes to the turbulence we have witnessed.

Notes

1 As the whole episode was of considerable significance, we use the empirical material schematically later in the chapter.
2 This chapter focuses on some key aspects addressed in our book *Public or Private Economies of Knowledge: Turbulence in the Biological Sciences* (Harvey and McMeekin, 2007). Case studies in Europe, the USA and Brazil of the development major databases, software, and theoretical paradigms, within publicly financed institutions and private corporations form its empirical basis.
3 The Bayh–Dole Act encouraged US universities to commercialise and patent the discoveries of their research scientists, and to obtain an additional income stream.
4 The firm-internal knowledge involves teams co-producing knowledge with internal validation procedures, as well as those borrowed from the public domain. But as is well known, many corporate scientists also submit papers to journals for public validation, so contributing to the growth of public domain knowledge.
5 For more detail see Harvey and McMeekin, 2007.
6 The black-boxing of software components involves making them technically unavailable for use, inspection or manipulation by outsiders.

References

Adler, R.D. 1992. 'Genome research: fulfilling the public's expectations for knowledge and commercialization', *Science*, 257, 908–14.
Anderson, C. and Aldhous, P. 1991. 'Secrecy and the bottom line', *Nature*, 354, 96.
Bentley, D. 1996 'Genomic sequence should be released immediately and freely in the public domain', *Science*, 274(5287), 533–4.
Boguski, M.S., Tolstoshev, C.M. and Bassett, D.E. 1994. 'Gene discovery in dbEST', *Science*, 265, 1993–4.
Callon, M. 1994. 'Is science a public good?', *Science, Technology and Human Values*, 19(4), 395–423.
Cook-Deegan, R. 1994. *The Gene Wars. Science, Politics and the Human Genome*. Norton. New York.
Coriat, B. and Orsi, F. 2002. 'Establishing a new intellectual property rights regime in the United States. Origins, content and problems', *Research Policy*, 31, 1491–507.

Cowan, R., David, P.A. and Foray, D. 2000. 'The explicit economics of knowledge codification and tacitness', *Industrial and Corporate Change*, 9(2), 211–53.

Dasgupta, P. and David, P.A. 1994. 'Toward a new economics of science', *Research Policy*, 23, 487–521.

David, P.A. 2001. 'Tragedy of the public knowledge "commons"? Global science, intellectual property and the digital technology boomerang.' MERIT. Maastricht. Available online at http://arno.unimaas.nl/show.cgi?fid=262 (accessed 10 November 2009).

David, P.A. 2004. 'Can "open science" be protected from the evolving regime of IPR protections?', *Journal of Institutional and Theoretical Economics*, 160(1), 9–34.

Devereux, J., Haeberli, P. and Smithies, O. 1984. 'A comprehensive set of sequence analysis programs for the VAX', *Nucleic Acids Research*, 12, 387–95.

Eisenberg, R.S. 1991. 'Genes, patents, and product development', *Science*, 257(5072), 903–8.

Eisenberg, R.S. 1989. 'Patents and the progress of science: exclusive rights and experimental use', *University of Chicago Law Review*, 56(3), 1017–86.

Eisenberg, R.S. and Nelson, R.R. 2002. 'Public vs. proprietary science: a fruitful tension?', *Daedalus*, 131(2), 89–101.

Foray, D. 2004. *The Economics of Knowledge*. MIT Press. Cambridge, MA.

Gilbert, W. 1991. 'Towards a paradigm shift in biology', *Nature*, 349, 99.

Hall, B. 2003. 'On copyright and patent protection for software and databases: a tale of two worlds', in Granstrand O. (ed.), *Economics, Law and Intellectual Property*. Kluwer. Boston, MA.

Hardin, G. 1968. 'The tragedy of the commons', *Science*, 162(3859), 1243–8.

Harvey, M. and McMeekin, A. 2007. *Public or Private Economies of Knowledge? Turbulence in the Biological Sciences*. Edward Elgar. Cheltenham.

Heller, M.A. 1998. 'The tragedy of the anticommons: property in the transition from Marx to markets', *Harvard Law Review*, 111(3), 621–88.

Heller, M.A. and Eisenberg, R.S. 1998. 'Can patents deter innovation? The anticommons in biomedical research', *Science*, 280(5364), 698–701.

Johnson, B., Lorenz, E. and Lundvall, B.-A. 2002. 'Why all this fuss about codified and tacit knowledge?', *Industrial and Corporate Change*, 11(2), 245–62.

Kaul, I. and Mendoza, R.U. 2003. 'Advancing the concept of public goods', in Kaul, I., Conceicao, P. Le Goulven, K., and Mendoza, R.U. (eds), *Providing Global Public Goods*. Oxford University Press. Oxford.

Machlup, F. 1962. *The Production and Distribution of Knowledge in the United States*. Princeton University Press. Princeton, NJ.

Marshall, E. 1994. 'A showdown over gene fragments', *Science*, 266, 5183, 208–10.

Marshall, E. 2001. 'Bermuda rules: community spirit with teeth', *Science*, 291(5507), 1192–3.

Martin, B.R. 2003. 'The changing social contract for science and the evolution of the university', in Geuna, A., Salter, A.J. and Steinmueller, W.E. (eds), *Science and Innovation. Rethinking the Rationales for Funding and Governance*. Edward Elgar. Cheltenham.

Mokyer, J. 2002. *The Gifts of Athena. Historical Origins of the Knowledge Economy*. Princeton University Press. Princeton, NJ.

Moody, G. 2004. *Digital Code of Life: How Bioinformatics is Revolutionizing Science, Medicine and Business*. Wiley. New York.

Mowery, D.C., Nelson, R.R., Sampat, B.N. and Ziedonis, A.A. 2001. 'The growth of patenting and licensing by US universities: an assessment of the effects of the Bayh–Dole act of 1980', *Research Policy*, 30(1), 99–119.

Nelson, R.R. 1989. 'What is private and what is public about technology?' *Science, Technology and Human Values*, 14(3), 229–41.

Polanyi, K. 1957. 'The economy as instituted process', in Polanyi, K., Arensberg, C.M. and Pearson, H.W. (eds), *Trade and Market in the Early Empires*. The Free Press. New York.

Rice, P., Longden, I. and Bleasby, A. 2000. 'EMBOSS: The European Molecular Biology Open Software Suite', *Trends in Genetics*, 16(6), 276–7.

Roberts, L. 1991a. 'Gambling on a shortcut to genome sequencing', *Science*, 252, 1618–19.

Roberts, L. 1991b. 'Genome patent fight erupts,' *Science*, 254(5029), 184–6.

Roberts, L. 1992. 'NIH gene patents, round two', *Science*, 255, 912–13.

Sender, A.J. 2000. 'Bioinformatics boom: gone bust', *Genome Technology*, 18, 36–42.

Stokes, D. 1997. *Pasteur's Quadrant: Basic Science and Technological Innovation*. Brookings. Washington, DC.

Strohman, R.C. 1997. 'The coming Kuhnian revolution in biology', *Nature Biotechnology*, 15, 194–200.

Zuhn, D.L. 2001. 'DNA patentability: shutting the door to the utility requirement', *Marshall Law Review*, 34, 973–99.

Zweiger, G. 2000. *Transducing the Genome. Information, Anarchy, and the Revolution in the biomedical Sciences*. McGraw Hill. New York.

Index